INTELLECTUALS AND (COUNTER-)POLITICS

DISLOCATIONS

General Editors: August Carbonella, *Memorial University of Newfoundland,* Don Kalb, *University of Utrecht & Central European University,* Linda Green, *University of Arizona*

The immense dislocations and suffering caused by neoliberal globalization, the retreat of the welfare state in the last decades of the twentieth century, and the heightened military imperialism at the turn of the twenty-first century have raised urgent questions about the temporal and spatial dimensions of power. Through stimulating critical perspectives and new and cross-disciplinary frameworks that reflect recent innovations in the social and human sciences, this series provides a forum for politically engaged and theoretically imaginative responses to these important issues of late modernity.

Intellectuals and (Counter-)Politics

Essays in Historical Realism

Gavin Smith

berghahn
NEW YORK · OXFORD
www.berghahnbooks.com

First published in 2014 by
Berghahn Books
www.berghahnbooks.com

Library of Congress Cataloging-in-Publication Data

Smith, Gavin A.
  Intellectuals and (counter-)politics: essays in historical realism / by Gavin
Smith.
    pages cm -- (Dislocations; volume 12)
  Includes bibliographical references and index.
  ISBN 978-1-78238-300-0 (hardback) -- ISBN 978-1-78533-347-7 (paperback) --
ISBN 978-1-78238-301-7 (ebook)
1. Intellectuals--Political activity. 2. Ethnology--Political aspects. 3.
Social movements. 4. Protest movements. I. Title.
  HM728.S65 2014
  303.48'4--dc23

                                                                2013042958

British Library Cataloguing in Publication Data
A catalogue record for this book is available from the British Library

ISBN 978-1-78238-300-0 (hardback)
ISBN 978-1-78533-347-7 (paperback)
ISBN 978-1-78238-301-7 (ebook)

CONTENTS

To

Winnie, Corin, Laura, David and Tim

'I think you like history, just as I did when I was your age, because it is about living people. And everything that is about people, as many people as possible, all the people in the world united among themselves in societies, working and struggling and bettering themselves must please you more than any other thing.'

–*Antonio Gramsci's last letter from prison, to his son Delio, written shortly before his death*
[I have changed his 'men' to 'people' – I feel sure he would not have minded.]

I am only too well aware of what might be termed the pre-scientific and pre-philosophical nature of these essays. In them, requirements are stated and a polemical position taken up; but their theoretical stance is neither rigorously grounded nor fully developed. My decision, despite this, to publish them together in book form is based on the belief that, at the present stage of Marxist discussion, they can fulfil a provisional function of critical stimulus.

–Sebastiano Timpanaro, 'Forward', *On Materialism*

It is hoped that those of my own and a younger generation can make the detour of Marxist theory a necessity, not only for radical academics but also for capitalism's many discontents in the wider world.

–Noel Castree, 'The Detour of Critical Theory'

ACKNOWLEDGEMENTS

The essays collected here form the loosely woven elements of a tentative and incomplete intellectual and political position, and were written for that purpose over the past couple of years. Nonetheless most of them are the result of practice runs in various forms – presentations at conferences, invited papers, contributions to workshops and so on – that have occurred over a much longer period. The research moreover that forms the basis for many of my arguments goes back to the beginning of my career as an anthropologist and in fact perhaps to earlier careers in sundry other occupations. Over the course of those years I have accumulated many debts in terms of what people have given me and in terms of what I have neglected to give others in my pursuit of goals too narrowly defined. It would be absurd to try to affix names to this accrual but I would like to express my awareness of the 'austerity' that people close to me may have suffered as a result of my placing too high a priority on my professional interests, especially those in my immediate and more extended family but also those friends I have had over many years across generations and across the distances that migration perforce produces, and with it the waxing and waning of intimate ties.

I have been especially fortunate in the countries where I have done my research because the warmth, good humour, and guidance of the people I have met in field sites have been matched by the colleagues and friends I have made in a wider setting. This has been the case in Peru and Spain, and were it not for these people's generosity and loyalty as friends and as disputants I would know but a tenth of what I do (if that). I have already thanked many of these people by name in previous books and so I won't repeat myself.

But two things especially need noting. The first is that this has largely been a one-way kind of thing: I had more reason to be exhaustively inquisitive about them than they had reason for their hospitality – not just the people in the fieldsites but also my wider sphere of friends and colleagues. And the other is that I have not experienced the kind of openness of mind and spirit, the constructiveness of interchange, and the sheer excitement of it all – often in the most difficult of conditions – in other countries where I have pursued various academic exchanges through my career. It goes without saying that I can speak only of my own experience, and I am sure my particular personality has much to do with it, but I have to say that the academies of the contemporary 'north' where I spent sabbatical time provided an almost perfect mirror image of the *esprit* I found in the places where I have done fieldwork, be it Peru or Spain or, more briefly, Mexico or Italy. I believe that the contrast of these experiences needs recording. It is after all the more informal and personal dimension of a power–knowledge imbalance that anthropologists are only too aware of.

Perhaps even to draw attention to this distinction between the *esprit* of the intellectual settings I have experienced in north and south shows the cynicism of age, but it is an observation that a younger person would find hard to record in public, and it is an important one, and so I say it. Of the vastly more generous people than myself, whose example in scholarship, integrity, political engagement and personal friendship I aim for but will never achieve, I wish to thank the late Eric Wolf and the late Eric Hobsbawm. Here too I have had the gift of friendships whose scales weighed so heavily in my favour.

I have been equally lucky with younger generations. The students and post-doctoral fellows I have worked with, of course in Toronto, but also in so many settings – Spain, Peru, Italy, Mexico – have been so open with the dilemmas and hesitations they were having only to discover that I was hesitating at that point too. As a result ours has really been a richly coloured balance between the stimulus I have had from their adventurousness and what I hope I have been able to give back in terms of the fruit of my own experience. It has been quite a long journey but more recently there are some people who have been especially generous in conversations with me. These include Marnie Bjornson, Claire Montgomery, Aaron Kapler and Lindsay Bell in Toronto. In Barcelona I have benefited from the really wonderful collective spirit of the students who Susana Narotzky has gathered around her, especially Gemma Anton, Jaime Palomera, Diana Sarkis and Irene Sabate. In Mexico I have likewise learned from the students at the Colegio de Michoacan, both those in Zamora and Angeles López and Nubia Cortés in Toronto. Andy Roth made most of that happen and I thank him for that, as well as much else besides. Shalini Randeria made it possible for me to meet some quite extraordinary young scholars in Switzerland at the Institut des hautes études internationals et du développement. I would like to thank them and especially Niklaus Miszak who helped me while there and taught me things about politics that I needed to know.

Among the many people who have helped me through their constructive engagement, their intellectual generosity and their companionship I want to single out a crucial band of suspects who have been especially responsible for this product (like it or not!). One particular accomplice who has been at the scene of the crime from the outset is Don Kalb who, like all heavy-duty cyclists, knows how to push you up the long climbs and then how to laugh with you through those joyous moments when the wind comes rushing through what little we have left of our hair. He started this whole enterprise and has held by me throughout. I have also been immensely fortunate in the friends who have engaged with me over it: Malcolm Blincow, Tania Li, Susana Narotzky and Winnie Lem have done this over the long haul and have earned my thanks and sympathy in equal measure. I have learned a huge amount too from conversations with Doug Holmes, Leslie Jermyn, Chris Krupa, Carlota McAllister, Katharine Rankin, Roger Rouse, Ignasi Terradas and the late Krystyna Sieciechowicz. I would also like to thank Gadi Algazi, Silvia Bofill, Nick Bradford, Victor Breton, Jesus Contreras, Jonathan Friedman, Harriet Friedmann, Andrés Guerrero, Enzo Mingione, Enrique Mayer and Gerald Sider.

Jaume Franquesa came into all this when I was a fair way up the hill and I am really grateful to him, firstly for allowing me to spend time with him during his fieldwork in La Fatarella in the Terra Alta of western Catalonia and for sharing so much with me, and secondly for introducing me to Marion Werner who joins so many of the geographers who, knowingly or not, have contributed to this endeavour. Especially among these latter I owe an immense and impossible-to-repay debt of love and of the spirit-of-the-fight to the inspirational Deb Cowen and to the irrepressible and irreplaceable Neil Smith.

In the last few years I have had the advantage of being among a group of young scholars at the University of Toronto whose work puts my own generation to shame both in its energy and daring and in its insights and edginess. These include those in my own department like Joshua Barker, Girish Daswani, Andrew Gilbert (now at McMaster), Andrea Muehlebach, Valentina Neopolitano, Todd Sanders, Shiho Satsuka and Jesook Song; geographers like Kanishka Goonawadena and Scott Prudhon; and historians like Ken Kawashima and Ritu Birla. It is through our informal conversations that the excitement of thought and action has been kept alive in me and in the workshops and seminars that they have organized and allowed me to be part of.

I especially want to acknowledge the importance to me over the past decade or more of three collectivities, all of which started in a relatively fragmented and informal manner but have now emerged as open-minded and highly constructive collective subjects. I need to single out Pauline Barber, Belinda Leach and Winnie Lem in thanking all those who have participated in what has come to be known as 'The Anthropological Political Economy Seminar' (APES); also Susana Narotzky, who has gathered around her in Barcelona an extraordinary group of graduate students and faculty who now constitute a collective body. I am particularly grateful to Susana and her colleagues for their spontaneous generosity in allowing me to join them. Finally I would like to thank the editorial collective of *Focaal – Journal of Global and Historical Anthropology*, among whom Luisa Steur stands out, for simultaneously widening my vision and keeping me on a well-directed path.

Winnie, I really don't know how to thank you with so cold an item as a bound set of black and white pages, but Corin has told me that material objects can carry obscured mysteries and so herein is some occluded kind of evidence of my love. Corin, Laura, David and Tim – we have together made one another even as each one of us has been cobbling together her or his self. I would like this book to convey the energy as well as the (com)passion that each of you in some particular and special way has provided for me.

I can release nobody from responsibility, but *la responsabilidad del receptor se vuelve más ligera por la inconsecuencia del regalo.*

I would like to acknowledge with gratitude the Social Sciences and Humanities Research Council of Canada and the Wenner Gren Foundation for their support in the course of various research trips and attendance at workshops and conferences. Likewise I express my thanks to the Ministerio de Economía y Competitividad de España for supporting my participation in the 2012–2015 project 'Addressing the Multiple Aspects of Sustainability: Policy Programmes and Livelihood Projects' (AMAS); and to the Agencia de la Gestión de Ayudas Universitarias i de Investigación (AGAUR) for making possible my presence at the University of Barcelona under the 2009 Ayuda de movilidad para profesores e investigadores visitants senior (PIV 2008). I am also grateful to the Department of Anthropology at the University of Toronto for making possible a number of short-term research trips under the small grants programme.

Gavin Smith
Toronto and Paris, June 2013

INTRODUCTION
Intellectuals, Historical Realism and Counter-politics

ℰ⁓

[[I]ntellectual formations have lost their bindingness, because they have detached themselves from any possible relationship to social praxis and become ... objects of purely mental apprehension. They become cultural commodities exhibited in a secular pantheon in which contradictory entities – works that would like to strike each other dead – are given space side-by-side in a false pacification: Kant and Nietzsche, Bismarck and Marx ... (Adorno 1998: 141. Quoted in Brennan 2006: 196)[1]

The title of this book takes some explaining – which I find annoying. I am not fond of titles that seem intentionally thought up to titillate through puzzlement. *War and Peace* didn't seem to me a misleading title for the novel, nor did *The Book of Laughter and Forgetting* for that matter. Looking back I suppose *Pensées Sauvages* was a bit politically incorrect, but you had to forgive the author; it did after all capture in a nicely playful way what he was talking about. A book entitled *Intellectuals and Politics* would seem fairly straightforward, but why the 'counter-politics'? Wouldn't 'politics' be enough? And what about 'historical realism'? Why not 'historical materialism' or 'philosophical realism'?

What I find disconcerting is that my intention has been to avoid being misleading: to be sure that the title is quite precise in saying what this book is about. And yet the result comes off as pretentious. The fact is that the term intellectual has a vaguely distasteful flavour of exclusivity about it (something I will return to shortly) and placing 'counter' in front of 'politics' does seem to follow the vogue for the negative prefix: like 'post' which itself seemed to many a form of pretention as in 'I'm not talking about modernism but I'm not prepared to say exactly what comes after'. Or, 'I am talking about post-Marxism but by use of this term rather than non- or anti- I want to make clear that I walk the high ground. We do not need to dissociate ourselves from Marx or write anti-communist manifestos; we need simply to bury those old bones and move on.' Statements like these emanate of course out of the politics of intellectuals and, combined with the fact that intellectuals themselves take such statements so seriously, do much to explain why the term 'intellectual' seems almost synonymous with pretention.

Having worried over using terms that might not be immediately enlightening, and as a result risked giving my book the air of pretentiousness I wanted to avoid, I still ended up with this title – so I want to use this Introduction to explain why. I will start with some thoughts on intellectuals, then explain what I mean by historical realism, and just touch on the issue of counter-politics near the end, since this last is best discussed in the Conclusion.

Many of us, whether supposedly intellectuals or not, find ourselves frustrated by a sense of helplessness; not necessarily passivity but rather a feeling that the effectiveness of what we do seems to have little impact. The ability to assess the limits of the possible and hence help to give collective action the leverage that would make it effective praxis appears to be elusive today. But there is nothing unique about this. There might indeed have been moments in history when collective will found an eventful crack in the edifice of an apparently immovable history – say with the coming of the French Revolution or, perhaps less dramatically, in the labour movement in the global North whose pressures made possible the welfare state, or peasant struggles in the South without which there would have been no land reforms not to mention actual changed structures of entire societies. But these moments arose out of prior periods when it was not clear who would be the agents of change or who precisely they should direct their energies against. As Hobsbawm long ago noted, 'successful revolutions are hardly ever planned in spite of the efforts to do so', adding that if the Left have some work to do on what the future society might be, 'that does not make it any the less desirable or necessary, or the case against the present one any less compelling' (Hobsbawm [1978] 1984: 287, 291).

So if today it is by no means obvious where the seeds of collective will are to be found or through what means some leverage might be achieved, this does not reduce the need for intellectual intervention – rather it impels us to ask what the nature of that intervention might be. For it is not automatically apparent what needs to be taken into account for a useful assessment of the conditions of possibility for the successful intervention of collective will. The global scale of today's social world? The environmental tipping point? The uneven placement of differing kinds of economic relations – from Export Production

Zones to Silicon Valley? The unchecked polarization of wealth and power? The remoteness of the state from our lives? These all seem to crowd in for attention. Nor is it possible to hold off one element with the hope that another can be studied in isolation. This alone surely must act as a challenge to people who do intellectual work. But just as societies have changed over the past half-century, so too have the nature and role of people making a profession of being intellectuals.

Intellectuals

In most of the courses, graduate and undergraduate, that I have taught over the past ten to fifteen years, I have devoted some time to a discussion of 'the intellectual': what kind of job that was, and how it positioned one vis-à-vis the people you were studying, or those you were teaching. I was especially interested in having a conversation about the books and articles they read as being peculiarly the products of intellectuals' labour: the way they thought, the way they presented what they thought, the relative value of these kinds of products versus perhaps less 'academic' ones, and so on. Most of the time, those with whom I spoke were polite but indifferent. The undergraduates tended not to think they were themselves such people, or even that they were at least partly such people while still students. Most of them didn't think of the university as putting them among such people – among teachers possibly, but not among 'intellectuals'. Some thought questions about intellectuals were really only interesting to me in so far as perhaps, in a somewhat hubristic way, I thought I was one. And this latter idea – that it was self-flattering to identify oneself as an intellectual – both said something about what intellectuals are taken to be and also got in the way of the kind of dialogue I wanted to have. It spoke of social distinction and of essential difference.

The dialogue I wanted to have, naively as it turned out, was based on the premise that in the context of the university we were all for the moment 'intellectuals', spending time put aside for us to reflect critically on issues for which there was little time otherwise in a busy (or leisurely in some cases) day. And I wanted to discuss with people how that kind of practice might be the same or different from other kinds of practices in a given day or week; how for example it compared with the practice of a cabinet maker, beginning her day's work, fitting up a router and assessing the material she left unfinished the day before. I wanted to ask, as well, if reflections on this issue of the cabinet maker would have some effect on cabinet makers, cabinetry and perhaps broader questions of skill and work. In other words whether there was some relationship, positive of negative, between the kind of work being done by the 'intellectuals' in the classroom and the builders outside.

As will become obvious in what follows, perhaps one of my many mistakes was employing the generic word 'intellectual' to refer to a broad range of people who are not often boxed up in the same wrapping. Had I spoken only of 'social anthropologists' and 'the people they study', or of 'scientists' or 'philosophers,' perhaps even of 'artists', the conversation would have been clearer, easier.[2] But that is precisely what I did not want to do then, nor what I want to do now. Although I will perforce return to it, I want to take anthropologists away from their treatment as a special case. The question I am interested in is what kind of political leverage social analysts in general have. Were they to want to be part of collective praxis, what part would they play? Is there a distinct role for people called 'intellectuals', or were my student interlocutors onto something: that intellectual is just a fancy word for a job like any other?

If so, the impetus that had taken me out of my day job in my late twenties as an investment analyst and back into graduate school was mistaken. I had thought the move would increase the contribution I could make to a political project, and even my choice of anthropology was based on its association with working at the grass-roots level, making it an especially direct form of engagement (Smith 2011). In the reflections that follow however I want to avoid restricting the purview of the argument to those who Charlie Hale (2006a) calls 'activist researchers'. Instead I want to think in terms of the *leverage* most forms of progressive intellectual work can have on a largely intractable social reality.[3] The chapters that follow have all been framed in this way. I have tried to make quite clear in each case *why* I think the issue being discussed needs to be discussed; or put another way, how my purpose-at-hand has led me to a question and then shaped the way I have addressed that question. As with other kinds of work, so with intellectual work: the horizons of knowledge relevant to them are a result of their purpose-at-hand in the pursuit of a task.

Gramsci of course is especially associated with a kind of Left politics that insists on addressing precisely what role intellectuals might play in enhancing and giving direction to the praxis of 'common people'.[4] And yet for Gramsci, intellectual work was not to be confined exclusively to people with that ascription. Jokingly Gramsci remarked that 'because it can happen that everyone at some time fries a couple of eggs or sews up a tear in a jacket, we do not necessarily say that everyone is a cook or a tailor' (Gramsci 1971: 9), and the same applies to intellectual work. It is a kind of reflective activity that goes along with practical work: everybody does it all the time, at some times more and at some times less; it's 'the spontaneous philosophy which is proper to everybody' (ibid.: 323).

Evidently, for Gramsci the different modes of attention do matter. There *is* something about the distinction between practical work and a kind of activity of reflecting which is critical intellectual work. And this is my starting point. The issue has to do with the forms of attention associated with particular kinds of task, what Schutz (1971) called the different 'purposes-at-hand' as we shift from one kind of task to another. Carpenters don't only need to know about cabinet making, they also need to know where to place their fingers on the router. This practical knowledge, or knowledge of practice, is the difference between having five fingers and losing one. A sure way to find the router carving away at your finger, and not at the emerging shaped recess in the wood, is to start reflecting on the nature of tree growth in the Amazon jungle. The issue has no practical relevance for the job at hand. If one spends quite a bit of one's working time with lathes, routers, planes and such like, there may be little time during the working day to reflect on Amazonian bio-diversity, even though it might have implications for the long-term prospects of the job. So responsible carpenters might divide up their knowledge along lines of relevance contoured by narrower or broader projects. All of this is practical knowledge of course, though some may be more properly termed 'knowledge of practice' and some a broader kind of information which could be called 'intellectual knowledge'.

Intellectuals likewise derive forms of attention from the pattern that emerges from their various purposes-at-hand as they go about the tasks of their work. But the fact that reflective intellectual knowledge *is* practical for this task means that they give value to their work by reversing the importance of situated knowledge. True as with the carpenter, so here too; attending to the practical work of reflecting on a research issue the intellectual cannot afford to be distracted. But the supposed distraction takes the opposite form. The *intellectual* value of the practice derives from the degree to which it appears to be undistorted by prejudicial (lit: pre-judging) factors – practical matters like who is paying for their work, or what the immediate impact of the knowledge it produces might be. In Bachelard's words, 'the world in which one thinks is not the world in which one lives' (quoted in Bourdieu 2000: 51). We know this to be untrue (and here I mean we *all* know, both intellectuals and everybody else), but it is a misrecognition that we must retain – what Bourdieu calls the fallacy of 'scholastic epistemocentrism' (ibid.). There is nothing especially radical or new in this discovery of the peculiar social setting of knowledge production. Roseberry, for example, spoke of it in terms of 'academic enclosure' (Roseberry 2002). But the training needed to acquire the necessary skills here does not rely simply on the enhancement of reflective techniques and communicative skills in a general sense for the study of different moments of reality (even if reality is sometimes cast as the sublime): for science the material world, for art the acuity of insight, for social analysis 'the immanent tendencies of the social world' (Bourdieu 2000: 5), and so on. These may be what are found in the rule book but not the rules you need to know to achieve a certain goal, and we can assume that the goals are not the same for all intellectuals. They are all in search of the best leverage for making their ideas effective but the ends they serve will vary.

Because I don't entirely reject this rather Bourdieu-ian way of thinking about what intellectuals are and what they do, I see the challenge to be how people who concern themselves with the 'critical' study of social reality might make their contribution to 'praxis'. How do they address the immovable object of conditions and the irresistible force of the possible – not just the parameters of people's agency, but the especially acute kind of agency that can shift the very structure itself: praxis – a term to which I will return later. And then, engaged as they are in exploring the possibility for praxis of others, how might they understand what constitutes the praxis of the intellectuals themselves? Not just the practices they perform in their everyday work, or simply the agency necessary to make their mark in their careers, but the kind of contribution their praxis can make to comprehend so as to change the limits of the possible? 'The existence of a concrete relationship with a set of people (defined as public, class, group, sex or whatever) forms part of [the] self definition [of critical theories of domination]' notes Luc Boltanski; '[t]heir aim is to *render reality unacceptable*' (Boltanski 2011: 4–5. Italics in original).

Such a project creates precisely the opposite relationship between intellectuals and the practical work of other 'sets of people' to what Gramsci called 'traditional intellectuals', and we can learn quite a lot from what he says about them. His particular concern was with the role intellectuals played in allying the coercive resources of the state to a broad array of integrative functions (organization, education, culture, and so on) to produce a more or less lasting hegemonic field. This involved the use of formal culture and the various sites of its production, but it also involved intellectuals' participation in the sites of practical sense. One feature of what he called traditional intellectuals – those aligned to older dominant blocs – was the way in which they drew upon what Ernst Bloch called 'non-synchronous' sentiments, both in terms of the formal culture of Catholicism, older forms of schooling, literature and so on, and at the level of what he called the common sense of the past. The overall effect was to give people tools for rendering the practical world coherent in the way I have discussed above and, as a result, giving pertinence to an older kind of collective subject with its attendant institutions and forms of organization (see Chapter 5).

This can be seen at the level of popular discourse, folklore, forms of respect and so on, but it also plumbs deeper by authorizing sets of social relations: the landlord–tenant and patron–client relations of course, but also the hierarchical relation between the traditional intellectual and his passive flock. It is easy to note that such intellectuals preached a certain gospel because of the supposed interests of their paymasters but, apart from being a rather crude way of thinking about the relationship between intellectual production and its social setting, this tends to obscure the degree to which it was the vision of the world, the language, the keywords that had the effect of producing a certain kind of culture that then made older relations taken for granted. It was not just a question of the dominant ideas of the dominant bloc being transmitted through a brain-washing formal culture. Far more importantly it was the way in which intellectuals then threaded their way through daily life to endorse the common sense that then fuelled Bourdieu's 'causal probability'. As Bourdieu notes, jokes, addages, old wives' tales and so on are all means of transmitting the probabilities of lives lived by a certain class to their practical ways of setting about the tasks of their livelihoods.

This suggests that the ability of the intellectual committed by contrast to rendering such a reality unacceptable by enhancing the critical intervention of individual and collective subjects is greatly dependent upon the work to be done on what Gramsci would call organic links. One of these has to do with the assessing of the opportunities and limitations thrown up by the current conjuncture – what I encapsulate in this book by the phrase 'the conditions of possibility' (Braudel 1992; Bourdieu 1990a). The other has to do with the organization of popular mobilization and discussion of strategy for effective praxis. The first, a focus on vertical linkages, serves to tie emergent collective projects to 'the immanent tendencies of the social world' in Bourdieu's phrasing. 'One way in which Gramsci conceptualized the character of any given political event, social relation, social group, etc, was in terms of whether or not it was organically linked to that which was fundamental, in other words the basic economic structure of society' (Crehan 2002: 23; Smith 2004a, 2006). This of course means intellectual work assessing the nature of the current conjuncture and the conveying of that assessment to people with less access and time to do such work.

The second serves to enhance the connectivities among people both through formal culture – education and other forms of cultural production – and, with a focus on horizontal ties, working to make links across different people's practical sense as each tackles the concerns of their differing tasks. This kind of work, by all involved, takes place across a threshold because it involves a perpetual assessment of how the specific balance between intellectual reflection and practical work is embodied in multiple sets of people. In so far as everybody is an intellectual at some moments in their day or their life, so there is always this balance to be gauged. It is surely across just these thresholds that there is room for a fruitful dialogic conversation that would help to build bridges between one situation experienced in a micro-setting and over a limited temporal scale to other similar experiences, hence one role for the intellectual seeking to make organic connections – that is, an organic intellectual.

Much of the sensitivity intellectuals have now developed to perform in this way derive at least in part from the work that has been done in the areas gathered under the broad rubric of cultural studies. But, especially in anthropology, this has tended to be at the cost of critical analysis of the objective relations that arise out of the principles for reproduction on which our societies rest. So it is not enough to celebrate the wisdom of local knowledges or to disparage the imperialist purposes of universal rationality while inserting oneself among people faced with the pressing concerns of daily life. To this we need to add the special leverage gained from an intellectual's objective assessments, (a) of the potential for the formation of collective subjects over the long term (i.e. issues of appropriate organization for popular mobilization); and (b) of the possibilities for the achievement of their goals through praxis (see Chapter 4).

Both Bourdieu and Williams were provoked by the absolute necessity of exploring the difficult terrain between an intellectual moment and a practical moment: 'embodied practices' for Bourdieu, 'changes of presence' for Williams. They saw the fruitfulness of the terrain but also the tensions and difficulties that arose from traversing it. Both insisted that there *is* some kind of distinction between the two. Bourdieu, for example, notes how statistical probability has a reciprocal relationship with grounded practical sense, the success of practical moves producing the statistics that form the ground that make a move practical as opposed to impractical. 'The causality of the probable', he called it. And both *Homo Academicus* (Bourdieu 1988) and *Weight of the World* (Bourdieu 1999) can be seen as studies of what happens when disjunctures arise between the practices arising from assessments of probability and the actuality of probability. For Bourdieu this meant that precisely the fruitfulness of the intellectual enterprise lay in taking advantage of these two forms of attention. Intellectuals must not forget, 'what I know perfectly well … but only in *the practical mode*, namely that they do not at all have the project of understanding and explaining which is mine as researcher' (Bourdieu 2003: 288. Italics his).

In my view, Bourdieu is arguing against a prevalent anthropological bias by suggesting that we can, indeed we must, step back from our desire to experience 'the natives' point-of-view' and instead (or in addition?) set that point of view in its material conditions of possibility. In this sense we are not measured as better anthropologists because we return home understanding better how the natives think, but precisely by taking advantage of the fact that we can take an intellectual perspective distinct from theirs. The difference between ourselves and the other means that there are limits to how we understand their practical sense, but there are advantages to be gained from the distinction: not between 'them' and 'us' but between practical sense and intellectual reflection.

Not surprisingly for Bourdieu the sociologist, the arrow – of probability – points forwards. For Williams the arrow of time points backwards. 'Practical consciousness is what is actually lived, and not only what it is thought is being lived' (Williams 1977: 130–31). The methodological issue that worried him is not Bourdieu's. It was rather that when social analysts name elements of the world that are most acutely experienced when lived at *that* moment in the present, they lose the substantive quality of present experience: as though the word we use is like the fetishized commodity that obscures the actual practices that it represents.

> The mistake as so often is in taking terms of analysis as terms of substance … All the known complexities, the experienced tensions, shifts and uncertainties, the intricate forms of unevenness and confusion are against the terms of [this] reduction and soon, by extension, against social analysis itself. (Williams 1997: 129–30)

Obviously we are seeing very different configurations of what I am glossing as practical sense here. But what matters is that the two authors are trying to stretch beyond a kind of settled, perhaps slightly self confident, conceptual armoury in social and cultural studies. Each of them is challenged by the limits intellectuals have in recording and interpreting the way people engage with the practicality of life. The result in each case is to produce a fruitful reflection on a threshold that arises when a student of social and cultural practices both uses the practices of their own kind of work and discovers the disturbance that results. Rather than settling the disturbance it might be possible to use it as a way of getting at how this troubled kind of enquiry has useful political value.

For I think a kind of perspectival positionality is important here. What I try to show in this book is that when the purpose at hand begins from the perspective of a philosophy of praxis, that is to say from a motivation to enhance the leverage of radical democratic interventions in history, then the forming of the intellectual problem takes a particular shape. Certain questions are given high priority while others are reduced. This is not a dogmatic or rigid position. Time and again we see social analysts, from Marx to Gramsci to Foucault, when faced with a recalcitrant social world, reshaping the form their critique takes. So the possibility of praxis requires continuous assessments of the leverage gained from manoeuvres within this threshold arena.

Historical Realism

Although there is a major bias toward anthropology in this book I quite intentionally avoid restricting what I say to people in that profession. Rather I see the anthropological stance as a useful entry point for interrogating a broader array of critical social analysts. For example, there is a sense in which, often without realizing it, anthropologists began with a suspicious glance at the kind society they came from (e.g. Levi-Strauss 1973). From its beginnings anthropology's characterizing of most of its objects of study in contradistinction to modernity, capitalism, urbanism and so on, almost became its line of distinction from the other social 'sciences'. Its peculiar techniques and reportage – condensed in subsequent generations as the *doing* of 'fieldwork' and the *writing* of 'ethnography' – attained their special characteristics, such as they were, from the need to probe the cryptic mysteries of the social relations, practices and beliefs supposedly qualitatively different from the world that produced the anthropologists themselves. Yet today, unlike the period when the distinct disciplines of social analysis arose at the end of the nineteenth century, we live in a kind of global society in which capitalism is (or capitalisms are) geographically pervasive. Even the spheres of intimacy and affect, like the family or friendship, seem from day to day to bend ever more under the weight of capital's fierce demands.

The mysteries awaiting discovery now therefore appear to be those of capitalism itself – how it works, what it does to us, what we do with it and so on. And this is so not just for those long associated with this kind of society – entrepreneurs and workers – but the vast array of people who find themselves at the beginning of the twenty-first century caught one way or the other in its tentacles, be they slum dwellers in Mumbai or illegal immigrants in Milan. It is almost as though the challenge of demystifying the remotely placed unfamiliar has been reversed; tools need to be found to demystify the shape-shifting placelessness of the here and now. This, in turn, means that the praxis of intellectuals, especially those familiar with the use of fieldwork and ethnography, are perpetually called into question. Let me suggest some of the ways these questions might arise.

The first has to do with the scale at which we do our work: the size of the space of the social world we see to be our appropriate ground of work and also its temporal span and its particularity as opposed to its generality. Ever since I first saw it when I was about fourteen I have always been fascinated by *The Third Man*: by its location on the boundary – geographically of course, between East and West, but also between the dubious Harry (Orson Wells) who makes things happen and the upstanding Holly (Joseph Cotton) who can't seem to make anything happen at all, least of all get Alida Valli to fall for him. As a boarding-school wimp I was annoyed by my sympathy for Holly and secretly but deeply in love with Harry. Anybody who has seen the film can't forget the scene in which Harry takes his old school pal, Holly, now confused and disillusioned with his one-time hero, up on the giant wheel. As the cage rises in the air, Holly asks his friend the crook how he can stomach what he does, the deaths he is responsible for. By the time Harry replies they are high above Vienna looking down at the people who look now like nothing but dots. Harry, annoyed by the question, threateningly throws open the cage door and forces Holly to look down: 'What difference would it make if a few of those dots stopped moving', he asks. Then the wheel descends and they are back on the ground, two coated and hatted men in the close setting of a street corner. 'In Italy, for thirty years under the Borgias, they had warfare, terror, murder and bloodshed', says Harry, 'but they produced Michelangelo, Leonardo da Vinci, and the Renaissance. In Switzerland they had brotherly love, they had five hundred years of democracy and peace, and what did they produce? The cuckoo clock.'

The wrap-up is what we all remember and it impressed me the more because it was Wells himself – Harry, of course – who wrote the lines, as Graham Greene later recorded. But the move from the ground up to the perspective on high and then down to the street again, that is what I want to convey here. It's the way of the film as a whole too of course. Greene has the micro drama of Holly, like the anthropologist perpetually and anxiously in search of his 'subject', Harry, who is seen in momentary fragments and whose real character eludes Holly until Harry is finally killed off and Holly can return home still puzzled but at least a little wiser. But taken out of its larger setting of the emerging Cold War, the story of a couple of ex-school buddies wouldn't amount to a hill of beans as Bogey famously put it.

Starting on the ground, steadily rising up in the cage to get a wider – though less 'human' – perspective, only to return slowly back to the street corner, this is what historical ethnography can do I think. Too often I hear my colleagues assuming, almost without question, that the task of anthropology begins and ends with the intimate world of 'ethnography'. 'It's what we do', I am told. Why? Apart from the fact that it's not even true – ethnographic fieldwork played a miniscule role in the contributions of some of the anthropologists I most admire – surely the task is to come to grips with historical reality, through whatever methods that requires.

It could I suppose be argued in the spirit of the age that there is room for variety: some do one thing and some another. But two things need to be said about this. In anthropology there isn't a very balanced distribution between the study of the intimate spaces of what is taken to be ethnography and what might be called a more global kind of project of the kind we saw for example with *Sweetness and Power* (Mintz 1986) or *Europe and the People without History* (Wolf 1982), and we see currently in the work of people like Andreas Wimmer and Nina Glick Schiller (2002) and Jonathan and Kajsa Friedman (2008a, 2008b). I am not making the case for *just* anthropology on some grand kind of scale. We would all acknowledge that monopolization of one scale without reference to another is absurd. But training in most of the anthropology departments that I know is directed a great deal more at the intricacies involved in occupying the same spaces as the people being studied than in addressing the issue of how historical forces expand and contract those spaces and engineer widely distinct kinds of articulations between and among them. I am told that there simply isn't time for it all – for either the period of training or for the period of research. And I understand this, at least as an initial problem. But this doesn't quite explain the continued celebration of the microscopic among my older colleagues; thirty or forty years at the job doesn't seem an especially restricted time period. Perhaps broadening our horizons would broaden our minds.

I am inclined anyway to insist on attention to articulations between different spheres of social interaction; articulations whose reciprocal causalities are a function of specific historical conjunctures – what Don Kalb calls 'critical junctions' (Kalb and Tak 2005: 1–27; Kalb 2005). The pertinence of one scale of interaction and how it articulates with another will vary from one time and place to another, as I note especially in Chapter 2. But this will also vary, depending on what level of social reality we are referring to. And this raises the second issue: is there a certain level of social reality that has become especially privileged in anthropology? Perhaps we shouldn't speak of articulation between social relations and practices on the one hand and interpretations and structures of feeling on the other. After all, disentangling the one from the other can do more harm than good to our understanding of the real world. But the extent to which anthropology has become so deeply committed to the interpretation of experience means that anthropologists only have something to say about this expressive level (and increasingly even the inexpressible level), whatever scale we speak of.

The expression 'political economy' in the context of anthropology was initially supposed to counter this kind of culturalist fixation. It was used in the sixties, in North America at least, to distinguish a certain approach simultaneously from the vulgar materialism of cultural ecology on the one hand and from Geertzian cultural anthropology on the other. It has had an odd and unruly upbringing since its entry into the family. Not the least of its difficulties was the fact that its early usage was the result of self-censorship on the part of those in the United States who were inclined towards a greater influence from Marx than from Durkheim and Weber as mediated by Talcott Parsons, who anyway had consigned anthropology to the study of culture alone (Roseberry 1996, 2002). Two problems arose from use of this code. One was the loss of clarity in the use of concepts and the difficulty in sorting out the ill match between historical materialism and the prevailing notions of socio/cultural totality prevailing at the time (Roseberry 1978; Wolf 1978; Mintz 1978). Another was that it lumped under the unspoken Marxisant banner anthropologists with wildly different explanatory tools – from newly enlightened ex-cultural materialists and social evolutionists to anthropologists especially interested in Marxist historiography.[5]

These were early days. Political economy really meant Marxism and Marxism really meant materialism, whatever that might mean. And we can imagine that it could mean quite a lot of different things if we think of Marvin Harris's crude functionalism on the one hand and those influenced by Althusser and/or world system theory on the other. But the trouble was that Marx, especially as interpreted by 'Western Marxists' (Jay 1984; Anderson 1976), was as much a phenomenologist as he was a materialist, as useful for the hermeneutic sciences as the social sciences. And meanwhile the very success of the hitherto disguised U.S. Marxists had given Marxism a huge caché in the academy – as well as the debates enlivened by the almost endless years of U.S. military defeats in South East Asia of course. The result was a boom in Left cultural studies engaged in a vast array of Marxist approaches (see Grossman and Nelson 1988). Meanwhile across the Atlantic, two figures, one associated with the history of the working class (Thompson 1968) and the other with the history of the novel (Williams 1973), were used to add purchase to the explanatory and interpretive value of culture by understanding it in profoundly historical terms. So the two features of 'political economy' – its distinction from cultural determinism and its concern with historical ethnography – were now echoed in fields beyond anthropology.

As we approach the present therefore, two apparently mutually contradictory problems with use of the term 'political economy' for describing a particular approach or school of thought in anthropology arise. One is the association of the term with its early suspicion of cultural determinism. This has resulted in use of the term in anthropology generally (i.e. well beyond the U.S.) as a form of denigration: an anthropologist hopelessly incompetent in the study of culture's niceties. In response some have been persuaded to add a descriptor, hence: 'cultural political economy' (or even 'political economy of culture'). The second works against this. Given its continuing association in some vague way with the Left, many anthropologists feel that making some allusion to themselves as political economists shows evidence of progressive scholarship – this despite only a vague familiarity with historical materialism and a deep and abiding disgust for economics in any form.

While there are occasions throughout this book when I use it, there are then good reasons, at least in the anglophone world, *not* to use the term. My use of the term 'historical realism' however is not only to distance myself from these confusions. I also think there is something to be said for the term in itself. It serves to emphasize the fact that society and culture, whether at the level of the field site or at the level of the world system, can only be studied historically. And it also serves to clarify my belief in the relative weight of historical reality over the constructedness of history. In the pages that follow it will become abundantly clear that I am fascinated by the way people think about history. But I think that, in their preoccupation with this important issue, writers in anthropology and cultural studies have tended to downplay the extent to which people's concern with history has to do precisely with their recognition of its gold standard in reality. One of the most mistakenly cited books in the early years of my career was Hobsbawm and Ranger's (1983) *The Invention of Tradition*. It was almost always cited to suggest that there was a sleight of hand involved. There was tradition and then there was 'invented' tradition. I don't know Terence Ranger, but I doubt very much if Eric Hobsbawm would be comfortable with this kind of radical distinction. Of course there is a sense in which much of tradition and much of history depends in some way on invention, on construction on narrative form and so on – and this should not be downplayed. But failure to come to terms with the materiality of the past can leave you very bruised and battered as you make your way across a town – across a rural landscape too, come to that. It is this reality that I refuse to downplay or give up on.

But there is another inclination I want to highlight by use of this expression about history's awful – or perhaps the better word today would be awesome – reality. Although the advocates of contingency would be horrified to be associated with such an expression, we are back again with the idea of history as 'one damned thing after another'. The problem is not with contingency as such – no cyclist gets to work in the morning without taking it into account. The problem is with the 'all'; or at least 'all that really matters' (is contingent). Given the state of finance capital and indeed capitalism more generally over the past few years, bankers would love intellectuals to assure the world that it was all contingent. *But it wasn't!* Except in quoted dialogue this is the only time I will use that punctuation mark. But it really is needed here, especially because of the culturist bias in so much anthropology today, not to mention critical analysis more generally. It didn't happen (just) because of traders' wet dreams. It didn't even happen (just) because of the duplicity in the top ranks of Lehman Bros, Goldman Sachs or Bear Stearns – though a pretty good case could be made for their responsibility. The major reason it happened was because of the way in which the society we live in reproduces itself or, to put it more precisely, because of the way in which a dominant class bloc intervened in the logic of capital reproduction to ensure the perpetuation of their class position.

It is true that the interconnectedness of the issues makes it tempting for the intellectual equipped with any one skill set to retreat into the secure arena and collegial atmosphere of his or her own discipline, pleading for the limits of their own naivety. Anthropologists, cultural theorists, cultural historians, discourse theorists, political scientists and old Uncle Tom Cobley and all, may each have their own special 'expertise', their training. But this odd combination of timidity and hubris calls into question precisely what the responsibility of intellectuals as experts is. Mushroom pickers need to know which ones are poisonous. People who teach them, but only tell them about the ones that taste good and bad, are irresponsible. People could get sick – some could even die. Social and cultural analysts who justify their positions as intellectuals and who feel that position is one of responsibility and still yet insist that they are better to stick with what they (like to) know may be a bit like the mushroom pickers' gourmand teacher. Making a living out of teaching students about desire among rag pickers, or the humour of pastoralists, while feeling that it is not within one's mandate to understand the fundamentals of the society in which we all live … well that seems to me a bit like forgetting to tell people about the mushrooms that make them die. I have recently been told that scholarship in anthropology is best advanced by 'making original arguments in the area in which you are most qualified', rather than straying off into the territory of 'economic and political processes involving the state', in which, not being properly trained ourselves, we simply repeat the findings of others (Gupta 2010: 179). This seems to me to make the issue of intellectual responsibility a little too precious, driven perhaps more by the concerns of professionalization that have become so central to graduate student training than by responsibilities coming from beyond the academic enclosure. As Raymond Williams said with some heat during an interview, 'Well, if you tell me that question goes outside your discipline, then bring me somebody whose discipline will cover it, or bloody well get outside the discipline and answer it yourself' (Williams 1989a: 157).

Whether working in anthropology, cultural studies, political philosophy or what have you, we do have to bring the greater picture right into our own concerns, from the beginning when we start to formulate our questions and then returning again and again to reformulate those questions. What we will find as we explore the complexities of capital's reproduction and transformation will be neither entirely the outcome of some kind of iron logic but nor will it be fruitful to give up the game and call everything contingent. Seeking to expose the logic by which different kinds of capital are reproduced doesn't pre-empt taking into account a wide variety of contingencies. Indeed the word only has meaning in reference to what is not contingent. One part of the job is disentangling contingent moments from moments that emerge out of the logic of expanded or concentrated reproduction. Another job is understanding how this process is steered – through planning, management, risk avoidance, coercion, terror and so on – and knowing who is on the bridge doing the steering. This brings us to questions of critique and of politics.

Critique and Counter-politics

It is of course tempting to argue that global capital is so big and so complex that it's not really worth trying to determine if some people have a greater influence on the rudder than others. And if this seems a little unsatisfactory one can always turn away and simply blame 'the state' for the whole mess. And it is quite possible, indeed likely, that the risk strategies of finance capital and the scenario planning of dominant states are so wildly overdetermined that nobody has control over everything (did they ever?). But from one cluster of forces to another, from one complex of supply chains to another, from one regional combine to another, there *are* people together on the ship's bridge – identifiable class fractions seeking through alliances to control fields of force so as to ensure the expansion or reproduction of surplus production and extraction. There are ways we can speak of this. We can speak in spatial metaphors (Smith and Katz 1993) such as economic society and political society seeking to discover the particular interlacing of say production, finance and extractive capital in a given setting, as well as the institutions through which policy is made, possibly by the state and its various appendages and/or suprastate formations. We may be able to identify classes that arise in one arena and the alliances they need in another to ensure their position through the reproductive cycle and so on. It is quite obvious that, even beginning with such simple thought experiments as these, we arrive at a point where a whole variety of social, political, cultural and religious forms of power come into play in the Gramscian hegemonic sense, in the more Foucaultian cellular sense or the Deleuzian rhizomic sense. These in turn give rise to multiple conjunctural contingencies. But these multiple forms of power are not to be found floating off across the city, each on its own magic carpet.

The task of political economy 'as critique' is to expose the immanent properties embedded in the reproductive and transformative features inherent in the different relations of capital (see Chapter 2), and to thread these through the constraints and contingencies of politics as expressed in those multiple forms of power. To get at this I find it useful to use the term 'politics' in this book in a number of ways – not all of them consistent. While meanings of the word are almost infinite, four sometimes overlapping usages are worth noting here. One is the rather general usage as you might find in a comment like, 'I used to be quite political but over the last few years I've lost interest in politics'. Here politics is used to mean some form of participation in the formal political institutions of the society in question, voting in periodic elections, debating the platforms of the established political parties and investing in the belief that shifts in personnel – Obama versus Romney for example – or in the priorities of one party over another are important. This is the first and most obvious usage.

It is no doubt connected to the second, but it is not quite what is meant by some writers when they speak of the end of the political. Two slightly different things are being alluded to here – one somewhat more Foucaultian, the other more Marxian. In the first case what is being alluded to is the way in which social issues hitherto understood to be a matter of politics and perhaps to be addressed differently according to political allegiance are now rendered in technical terms and become problems amenable only to discussion and solution by experts (Dean 1999; Mitchell 2002). Such people may either be employed by those in political office or may themselves be holders of political office. Mario Monti, the prime minister of Italy for two years recently, is literally such a person, having been appointed in his capacity as a financial expert. But the argument goes further. It is that all social issues are now rendered in technical terms to the point where a cadre of professional, though elected, politicians take on the role of expert over and above the role of democratic representative. The more Marxian reading associates the absence of politics with the absence in public discourse of reference to the ineluctable class element and hence inevitably *conflictual* character of contemporary societies (Wang Hui 2006; Zizek 2011). While each treats the absence of politics in a distinct way they both understand the absence in terms of a deficit in democratic sovereignty and this provides a frequent provocation in the chapters that follow.

Quite often in this book I make use of a third meaning of the word political by referring to 'political society'. This can be an awkward term if seen as a compartment alongside 'economic society' and 'civil society' in which exclusive functions are assigned to one arena or another. I do not use the terms in this way. Instead I use the term to refer to state-like moments in a social formation, though they may not in fact be undertaken by the sovereign state. The European Union would be one such example. But we need not be speaking of an actual fully formed institution. Political society refers to the political controls necessary for the reproduction of a given economic system. These are frequently the apparatuses of the state in a quite extensive sense – that is state organs and also private institutions and apparently 'non-governmental' organizations. But to avoid assuming that all these features take the form of state apparatuses, I use the term 'political society'.

The final meaning of politics I want to speak of motivates the particular shape this book takes. It can be summed up in the expression 'the philosophy of praxis'. Two historical forces become the focus of attention: the immanent features inherent to capitalist society and the counterforces that can be mustered against those features. So I make a distinction between criticism in this regard and critique. The former can take a critical stance towards prevailing society, finding it wanting for example in terms of inequality or injustice, and from the package of criticisms thus gathered a package of solutions might be suggested. Critique however refers to an attempt to understand the immanent features of a social phenomenon so as to find within those features their own negation. The assumption here is that social relations through time produce elements that effectively aid in their reproduction but also through the same cycle produce counterforces which find political expression in praxis.[6] These kinds of politics then emerge along two interconnected fronts. One is a kind of politics that intervenes in and against the dominant features of the society of capital by negotiating within its own terms.[7] I refer to this throughout the text as a politics of negotiation. Another kind of intervention denies the legitimacy and authority of the society of capital and hence also a kind of politics that can be negotiated in that society's terms. I refer to this as counter-politics.

As I have said for the expression 'political society', so here too: I am not speaking of compartments into which one or another actual political intervention can be assigned. Instead I find it useful to begin the exercise of radical intellectual enquiry into current society by asking how praxis might be enhanced. And I understand the end point of that praxis to be a rejection of the society of capital, i.e. counter-politics; but along the way are the multiple forms of negotiated politics. It is my proposal that it is by focusing on the potentialities that can arise from the threshold between a politics of absolute refusal and a politics of suspicious negotiation that intellectuals might make a contribution to historical praxis.

This position is certainly influenced by Rancière's use of the term 'counter-politics' (Rancière 1999; Deranty 2003); but unlike his, my position is far more strongly embedded in a critique of political economy and does not identify counter-politics so strongly with voice and with the notion of *la politique du tort* (Rancière 1999, 2004, 2005). At various places through the following text I identify three elements which I believe to be the necessary foci of intellectual enquiry concerned with praxis. I refer to these as: the conditions of possibility, popular mobilization, and strategic action (sometimes I refer to this as leverage). The chapters that follow can be seen as triangulations of these three concerns, some referring to one or two of them, some to all three. Their points of reference are quite obvious I am sure. By conditions of possibility I mean the need for intellectuals to make a contribution to praxis by assessing the structural and conjunctural conditions that limit or set possibilities for praxis. Popular mobilization refers to organizational issues as well as matters having to do with the relationship between individual and collective subjectivity, while by strategic action I mean the need to assess the leverage that can be achieved through a particular political strategy. Rather than expand on these matters here I will rely on the various chapters to flesh out their pertinence, and will return to them in the Conclusion.

* * * * *

The book is divided into three parts. The bulk of the chapters, those in Part II, fall into the category of historical ethnography. It could be said that each is tethered to a spot whose scale is usually associated with ethnography, that is to say a temporal scale embraced by short- and long-term fieldwork and a spatial scale that finds the enquirer living and working among the people being studied. But in fact I see these chapters as essays – attempts – to query what scale and the contemporary articulation of scales might imply for the way we do ethnography. Not surprisingly along the temporal scale I find myself in conversation with historians, while along the spatial scale geographers have been useful guides. Because these are ethnographic kinds of social enquiry, place becomes both a constant presence and a troubling puzzle. Because I tend to enter the problem I am trying to address as one which has to do with the limits and possibilities of praxis, so place and politics get threaded into one another. As will be seen this is not a comfortable cloth to wear, but I still think that – globalization and the supposed society of flows notwithstanding – 'place-ness' is an aspect both of material reality and of intercommunicative subjectivity that we cannot easily dispense with.

Wrapped around these chapters are two others (plus a Conclusion) that would not conventionally be seen in terms of historical ethnography. The first of these, in Part I, is an especially long and necessarily abstract chapter. Readers familiar with *Capital* or who have read much more comprehensive introductions or guides might wish to skip this chapter, or perhaps confine their reading to the final section on Finance.[8] But I would defend its importance in this book on two grounds. The first has to do with my sense that many people in anthropology, cultural studies and political philosophy understand themselves to be speaking in some way about capitalism, sometimes to the point of simply naturalizing what that implies, but they do not understand capitalism. And I think it is important that we should be quite clear about what that kind of society is. The second reason is that it is from the baseline of this way of thinking about the society that we live in that I start all my enquiries. So it is as though I am providing the reader with what in later chapters I take for granted, what for me goes without saying. So this second reason points to a cautionary note. Chapter 2 is not so much an authoritative account of the sociology of capitalism to be endorsed by all who work in the Marxian tradition. Rather it is simply – or perhaps not so simply – the tool kit I carry into the field.

The bulk of Part III is taken up with a chapter in which I seek to assess the conditions of possibility in the current conjuncture. As a result the scale at which the enquiry is set differs from the ethnographic chapters, and I freely admit that the assertions as a result are more provocative than sensitive to historical and geographical particularities. The purpose of this chapter conforms most closely to the epigram by Sebastiano Timpanaro that opens this book, 'to fulfil a provisional function of critical stimulus'. Yet I believe that some of the provocations, rather than leading to empty spaces devoid of evidence or guidance, do in fact lead back to possible re-explorations of the ethnographic chapters. Set in the past as they are, they are about history and, as Gramsci remarks to his son, as such they are about living people.

By calling this part 'Politics' Edge' I have wanted to call up the various invocations of that word, 'edge': something beyond the centre, perhaps that darkened and dangerous place on the edge of town; the edge that cuts; and the irritant captured in the word 'edgy'. These senses all emerge by the end of Chapter 6. I take up questions of the edge in the Conclusion, or rather of two edges. I am interested in why, on occasions throughout the writing of this book, I have found myself drawn to the notion of 'threshold'. Perhaps it is that refusal to give up on place while even so being pushed out of one place and not yet arriving in another that explains it. Perhaps it is an awareness of the strength and comfort that comes with securing oneself in a place, a comfort zone, if not among friends then at least among people, things and ideas with which one has become familiar. Movement across the threshold formed by two edges (perhaps more) of ideas and positions that have a clarity of their own but a troubling discomfort as we cross between them – this seems a useful non-place for both intellectuals and counter-politics to be.

Notes

1. Adorno wrote this in the 1950s. It bears comparison with these remarks made by Aijaz Ahmad in the 1990s: 'there has grown, because of equal allegiance to irreconcilable pressures, that same kind of eclecticism among the politically engaged theorists as among the more technicist, conservative ones; it is not uncommon to find, say, Gramsci and Matthew Arnold being cited in favour of the same theoretical position, as if the vastly different political allegiances of these two figures were quite immaterial' (Aijaz Ahmad 1994: 71).
2. There are a number of overlapping terms here, each of which produces its own effect: intelligencia, intellectual, academic, scholar, expert, and so on. There is even an extension towards the party functionary and the bureaucratic policy wonk in one direction and towards the artist in another – Zola being perhaps an early example of the engaged artist in the setting of the Drefus affair. I don't want to lose these connections entirely (as I think Gramsci also did not), but 'intellectual' covers the most ground in what I discuss below.
3. I find this idea of *leverage* useful and expand on it further at various points throughout the book. I have no doubt that there are monastic kinds of scholars whose sole concerns are the niceties of scholarship for its own sake, but I don't think most of us are of this kind. I think most of us want our work to have some kind of leverage; this may be confined to enhancing one's status within a certain set of colleagues but mostly it is somewhat more than that. What that 'more' actually embraces will obviously vary, but I do want to extend this desire for leverage beyond those who are branded 'political' or even 'radical' by their colleagues. It seems important to recognize that the pursuit of leverage is not confined to the self-consciously politically active intellectual.

4. I am quite aware of Deleuze and Foucault's (1980) dismissal of the role of the intellectual, but I would agree with Radhakrishnan's assessment that, 'In the guise of retiring the "universal intellectual", Foucault retires the entire cadre of the intellectual and the many typologies that comprise that cadre. Of course, we are left with the specific intellectual, but this intellectual is "always already" dispossessed of macropolitical intentions' (Radhakrishnan 1996: 40).

5. In his review of three generations of 'anthropological political economy' in the United States, Bill Roseberry suggests that 'political economy has had two different but related meanings' (2002: 61): the one referring to the study of capitalism in its various regional and historical manifestations, and the other to 'explicit use of Marxian perspectives within anthropology. The second … offers a particular theoretical approach to the substantive questions juggled by the first', and notes that the generation of the Sixties 'stands as the political economy generation *par excellence*' (ibid.). He then notes a drifting away from the centrality of capitalism and class for writers still frequently claiming allegiance to political economy. I take my intellectual history on this topic from Bill's various reflections (see also Roseberry 1997), but I think the word 'explicitly' is misleading (as he himself notes elsewhere [1978]. See also Vincent 1990). Many radical anthropologists of the 1960s were unfamiliar with the work of Marx, and this was frequently out of choice rather than neglect. Despite the cultural capital to be gained in that, and in the next two decades from citations of Continental Marxists especially, many professional anthropologists were still aware that the paranoiac atmosphere of the previous period might return (and they were right). 'Marxism without guarantees' probably captures well the sentiments of those who preferred to stand on the sidelines cheering cautiously, and genuflecting at the right moments, but ready in due course to move on, less for intellectual than for professional reasons. For a discussion of anthropological political economy outside the United States, see Narotzky 2002.

6. My use of 'praxis' here is quite close to Rancière's use of *la politique*: 'Politics exists when the natural order of domination is interrupted by the institution of a part of those who have no part. This institution is the whole of politics as a specific form of connection' (Rancière 1999: 11). My usage does not conform perfectly to Rancière's way of understanding politics, as I note below. By 'praxis' I mean the ability of people as collective subjects to become a force in history, not merely the objects of other people's history.

7. I use the expression 'society of capital' here to avoid confusion. A more usual term would be simply 'capitalism' or 'capitalist society', but there are occasions in the text where I argue that capitalist society includes social relations and associated values and ideas that may not themselves be capitalist. So capitalist society may exhibit and provide opportunities for politics expressed in terms other than those of capital. The term 'society of capital' refers to a society whose reproduction serves the purpose of reproducing capital in its various forms (see, for example, Sanyal 2007).

8. Four books which complement one another in this regard are Harvey (2010) which takes us carefully through Volume I by helping us to grapple with Marx's argument rather than simplifying it as I do here; Balibar (1995) which is a wonderful critical engagement with the way Marx thought; I.I. Rubin ([1928] 1973) which is a mind-blowing engagement with what he calls 'commodity-capitalism'; and Harman (2009), which begins with helpful remarks on Marx's work but takes us further, dealing with finance in the last sections of the book.

PART I

INTELLECTUAL INFRASTRUCTURE

– Chapter 1 –

CAPITAL
Structural, Phenomenological, Financial

$\mathcal{C}\!\!\sim$

[I]f capitalism has all but disappeared as a subject and object of political theory … capitalism is and remains our life form … [C]apitalism arguably remains the dominant force in the organization of collective human existence, conditioning every element of social, political, cultural, intellectual, emotional, and kin life … This is not to say that capital is the only significant social power afoot in the contemporary world … [but] Marx's insight into capital's awesome power to drive human history and contour agentic possibility is not diminished by them. …our averted glance here … prevents us from grasping the extent to which the dramatic alterations in the configurations of the political … are themselves effects of capitalism and not simply secularization, disenchantment or contingent human invention … Thus, to theorize the politics of recognition, the sexual order of things, the nature of citizenship, or the reconfiguration of privacy, without taking the measure of their historically specific production by capitalism, *is literally not to know the constitutive conditions of one's object of analysis* [italics added].

– Wendy Brown, 'At the Edge'

Introduction

One reason I made the decision to get a degree in social anthropology was so that I could avoid doing any more economics. It went something like this. I had been in an investment bank on Wall Street and then in Montreal working in what today is rather cryptically called 'the financial services sector', when I became interested in initiatives poor people were making to change their lives – mostly in what we then called 'the Third World'. I applied for a variety of jobs and found that I was always offered a desk job as some kind of economist (I had a degree in Economics and History). I realized, to use another current expression, that I needed to 'rebrand' myself. This may explain why, once I made it to my field site to understand peasant resistance, I was so determined that no part of that understanding would involve economics. It was not just that temperamentally I didn't like doing economics; it was also that I felt determined to dispense with the dominant role economic issues played in people's lives. More accurately, I got these two things muddled up. Not enjoying economics, it suited me to propose that economics was not important. The book I wanted to write would be called *Peasant Resistance and Politics in Central Peru*.

Unfortunately the people I lived with for two years, first in the Andean highlands and then in Lima's inner city slums and shanty towns (*coralones, callejones* and *barriadas*), didn't agree with me. Their discussions perpetually interwove the *political* issues that revolved around securing the basic means for maintaining their way of life – pastoral land in the highlands, a secure place to live and access to sites for petty commerce in the city – with the *economic* issues of livelihood concerns – how to find and maintain lines of credit, acquire skilled labour and so on. Much as I wished to understand their culture and politics in terms relatively removed from the economy, narrowly or broadly conceived, they themselves kept pulling me back. Moreover, two years after the original fieldwork I returned to the *barriadas* to explore how interpersonal credit networks were affected by Peru's shift from a fixed currency rate that limited inflation to a floating rate that stimulated it.

So in the end the book that resulted had to carry the title *Livelihood and Resistance: Peasants and the Politics of Land in Central Peru*. Not only had livelihood and land crept into the problematic; it was impossible to understand resistance, politics, livelihood or 'land' without seeing them to be thoroughly interlaced with one another. And attending to the issues relevant to livelihood was not simply a matter of taking account of local 'economic' practices,[1] it was also a question of exploring shifts at larger scale levels – in the regional, national and global economies – noting how shifts at one level required responses at another.

Part of the point of this story is to show how unwilling I was to come to this conclusion. Having gone to considerable effort to get away from capitalism in its various sites and manifestations, I was not filled with joy at the discovery that coming to grips with the realities of life for the people I had lived with obliged me to take into account those very sites. I stress this unwillingness to obviate the suggestion that only social analysts with certain inclinations *choose* to address the issues of the specific nature of the capitalist economy. As Wendy

Brown makes clear in the epigraph to this chapter, for the responsible scholar there really is no choice. Indeed she makes clear that in fact we are not talking about an isolatable sphere that we might call the capitalist 'economy', rather we are speaking of a particular kind of society in toto (see also Streeck 2012).

At least since 1991, when the Soviet Union collapsed followed by various of its satraps and then more recently by the shift to 'capitalism with Chinese characteristics', it has become tempting to naturalize capitalist society – or at least to see capitalism as the inevitable end point to which all societies tend. While talking about any one of the issues that are the concern of this book, however, I wish to tug us back – perhaps as reluctantly as I had felt those years ago in Peru – to the specificities of capitalist society. As Wendy Brown notes, features that distinguish the age we live in may include the politics of recognition, the sexual order of things, the nature of citizenship, or the reconfiguration of privacy, but their constitutive conditions lie in their embeddedness in a specific kind of society; one in which daily life depends on commodities whose production and circulation are achieved through the normatively sanctioned pursuit of profit through capital (Harvey 2001: 312).

I am interested in a variety of relations that arise in the reproduction of the kind of society in which commodities are produced and circulated in the pursuit of profit. For this process to unfold, a series of relations must arise – between people and tools, between people and the things they consume, between people and other people, between things as they circulate through exchange, and so on. We can identify some of the most fundamental of these relationships and we can follow them as they are reproduced or undergo modifications through time. In so doing we can identify moments of potential tension and contradiction as well as the means by which these tensions might be resolved or apparently overcome to provide bases for a renewed cycle of reproduction.

In this chapter I set out some of the most pervasive of these kinds of relations, tensions and contradictions. An exercise of this kind runs the risk of appearing overly formulaic and even deterministic, especially when stripped down in the way I do it here. I admit to the straitjacket tendency in viewing our society in this way. Clearly the flesh and blood that comes with the skeleton I describe is what real societies are all about and, as Wendy Brown notes, we are interested in all these elements of the social world. Nevertheless I insist that we do need to know about the quite specific way in which capitalist relations are reproduced, even if, once we understand them and take them into account, we can as it were complicate the picture. This is especially so because recently scholars have either lost interest entirely in the specificities of the kind of society we live in *qua* a capitalist society, or they have begun to speak of capitalisms in the plural without specifying what characteristics of these various kinds of society allow us to speak of them all under the rubric 'capitalism'.

Along with these disappearances of capitalist society we are in danger of also losing the social grounding not just of the subjectivities, practices and relations we study in our work, but the social grounding too of our own practice of critique. Everything becomes contingent and the dialectic that constitutes phenomena through the relations among them in a dynamic of reproduction/transformation is reduced to the placement of events, spatialities, regimes of rule and what have you in assemblages whose juxtaposition has no emergent property but is rather a convenient portmanteau for the analyst. This is not to say that such authors deny social causality but, in reducing the characteristics of capitalist society to a series of features of no greater significance than any other phenomena, they are denied the possibility of exploring the ways in which the immanent features of capitalist reproduction relate to the contingencies of specific histories. This linking of critique to its specific social setting (within capitalist society) and thence to the immanent features of that society's reproduction is what I turn to now.

For Marx the practising subject is always historically and socially constituted. If there is some trans-historical essence distinct to the human being, such as manipulating symbols to inform practice (that is, 'culture' as understood by some anthropologists), it is of no particular epistemological or political importance. 'Consciousness can never be anything else than conscious existence, and the existence of men (sic) is their actual social process' (Marx, quoted in Williams 1989b: 207–8) In Balibar's words (1995: 25), 'the subject is practice'. So we need to ask what might be the socio-historical basis of a counter-politics under capitalism. Where does such a counter-force to the dynamic of capitalist logic come from? For Rancière, [counter-]politics is not socially grounded at all, rather it is a kind of radical democratic imperative across history. Others would make the case for the contingency of counter-politics: the existence of a collective will that counters and disrupts the logic of capital or the iniquities of power cannot be captured by reference to any useful set of social determinants: either the very notion of 'will' works against such a formula, or counter-politics are always so overdetermined that the exercise is futile.

For Gramsci by contrast, answering the question 'Is this the right time to strike?' meant studying a historically specific society to assess the conditions of possibility for a counter-politics. But if we stick with the notion of the socio-historical constitution of a practising subject, then an assessment of capital's domination and weakness is not sufficient. We need to show how this domination produces such a practising social subject. It is at this point that we confront the issue of immanence and, by extension, the role of a particular kind of critique of capital. Not just a criticism on moral or ethical grounds, not even a criticism that suggests that there are practical problems with capitalism that need addressing (social differentiation for example), but rather an immanent critique.

> The real consequences of social and political actions are always codetermined by the context within which they take place, regardless of the justifications and goals of such actions. Inasmuch as immanent critique, in analysing its context, reveals its immanent possibilities, it contributes to their realization. Revealing the potential in the actual helps action to be socially transformative in a conscious way. (Postone 1996: 89)[2]

Marx recognized the implications of his insistence on historical determination for the social practice of critique itself: there could be no 'outside' of capitalism from which one could critique capitalism, no well-placed redoubt from which one could view the battle beneath from some kind of intellectually isolated position. But, in his view, this did not mean that the dominance of capital simply meant the moulding of the subject *positively* into its logic. And this was because of the contradictions inherent to capital itself. So,

> Marx now feels compelled to construct his critical presentation of capitalist society in a rigorously immanent fashion, analysing that society in its own terms as it were. The standpoint of critique is immanent to its social object; it is grounded in the contradictory character of capitalist society, which points to the possibility of its historical negation.[3] (Postone 1996: 140)

But note, this is absolutely not a form of historical determinism. As Postone is careful to say here, capitalist society does not produce its own negation; it produces the possibilities for the *emergence* of a politics counter to its domination, what I am calling a counter-politics. Subsequently the historical specificities of its actual contradictions condition the possibilities of the *outcome* of those counter-politics. None of this suggests that the use of immanent critique leads inevitably to a kind of 'iron logic of predetermined history'. Rather it simply proceeds from a series of logical moves: that social reality cannot be understood statically – it needs to be understood as a historical process (of dynamic reproduction); that the specific form capitalist society takes makes this dynamic reproduction inherently contradictory; that the subject is inseparable from historically specific practice. There is no ahistorical subject and there is no subject prior to social practice. It therefore follows that the practice of critique itself arises specific to its historical context. Critique must therefore attend to the immanent features of social reality that make it possible.

In this chapter I do no more than lay out the baseline for an understanding of capitalist society in terms of the characteristics of its social reproduction and transformation. To do this I change the order of Marx's presentation.[4] I divide the discussion into two sections in which I discuss the two essential features of capitalist society: the peculiar feature of *capital* and the peculiar feature of the *commodity* (in that order), followed by a final section on finance capital. So, in the first part, I treat capital as a rather mechanistic set of social relations that need to be reproduced through time, ending by showing how reproduction produces tensions and contradictions that, through moves to resolve them, then reconfigure the process for another round (transformation). Then, in the second part, I change the angle of vision from the mechanics of social reproduction to the phenomenology of commodities. If the importance of Part I is that we understand the social world in terms of tension-filled reproduction, the importance of Part II is that we understand ideology, not as an issue of mind, separate from or determined by the mechanics we have seen in the previous part, but rather as inherent to the practised relations of what I.I. Rubin (1928) called 'commodity-capitalism'. In these two parts I seek to provide a fairly straightforward and I hope uncontroversial summary of the 'elementary structures' of capitalist society as Marx drew them out. In the final part of the chapter, however, I move beyond the kind of capitalism that most drew Marx's attention, and make some introductory remarks about the nature of finance capital. This section is especially relevant to the argument I make in Chapter 6.

The challenge to understanding a society dominated by social relations reproduced for the purposes of capital is to attend to the dialectical production of what appear to be three levels, or moments, of social reality but in fact cannot be thus compartmentalized.[5] These are: immanently produced relations among people, the imaginary associated with the commodity form, and the irresolvable tension between two kinds of power. These are not separable spheres of social activity – social relations/practices, ideas/subjectivity, agency/

constraint – rather they are mutually producing phenomena, and we need a methodological frame that allows us to see them as such. So this is what I seek to do in what follows.

The Structural Features of Capitalism

'Production in general' is an abstraction, but it is a rational abstraction … Yet these general or common features discovered by comparison constitute something very complex, whose constituent elements have different destinations. (Marx 1973: 85)

So we begin with social relations and we are especially concerned with understanding the principles by which they are reproduced: how, as these relationships are put into practice over generations, they are reproduced and possibly transformed.[6] This process of social reproduction gives rise to tensions which, in turn, call for the need for resolutions and, if those fail, then possibly to a major transformation in the way social reproduction takes place.[7] From this point of view social relations are not thought of through the metaphor of a structure – the parts of a bridge that hold it together, making it rigid and stable – but rather in terms of formation and re-formation. Movement takes precedence over stasis in the model we use to try to understand the parameters of social relations and practices. The practices of key social relationships in our society meet with tensions and contradictions that give an immanence to their outcomes. Nonetheless, immanent features of these relations provide us with only the warning signs of what we need to look for. This is just a preliminary – an elementary – task. The way tensions and contradictions are resolved cannot be predetermined: rather they result in multiple outcomes, the variety of which are one element (and only one element) of what we know as history or, perhaps better put, histories.

The fact that what we are trying to understand is the process of a society's reproduction, not that of its stable equilibrium, means that we are faced with a carousel that will not stop. So we need to choose the moment we jump on, recognizing that, had we jumped on elsewhere, we would be starting our enquiry from a different place. Others trying to describe capitalism would start elsewhere – Marx for one. Indeed the elementary game plan laid out in what follows is a terrible corruption of Marx's processes of thought and even his means of evolving concepts (Sayer 1979, 1987). Again the carousel image is useful, or perhaps a wheel would be better. As the wheel of our discussion rolls forward, notions that were overly simple can be rendered more complex. This chapter then is first and foremost an attempt to begin an understanding of capitalism aided by Marx (not an introduction to Marx). One final point has to be made before we proceed. What we are about to discuss is nothing like the way an actual capitalist society works, only an extrapolation from a characteristic feature of its reproduction: its 'imperative to unlimited accumulation of capital' (Boltanski and Chiapello 2005: 4). Subsequent chapters provide evidence for real, historical and varying actuality, but they are grounded in an understanding of the society we live in, in the terms laid out here.

Marx begins a short reflection on his approach by stressing that his subject is not individual actors, or people's subjective consciousness, or even the economy narrowly understood, but rather society as a whole – 'the subject, society, must constantly be kept in mind as the premise from which we start' (Marx 1904: 295, quoted in Rubin [1928] 1973: 3). In the case of capitalist society this means that the entire package of social relations are so regulated as to reproduce themselves. Thinking again of the carousel, the circuit of reproduction can be understood very simply as 'production → exchange → consumption', the last of which can be thought of as resetting in motion the first, literally productive consumption, hence the circularity.

As in all societies social reproduction both produces and depends upon differences among people or, to put it in a more extreme form, the production of different subjectivities – 'the constitution of the world is not, for Marx, the work of a subject, but a genesis of subjectivity' (Balibar 1995: 67). Anthropologists are especially attuned to this in the matter of exchanges between sets of people. In societies where merchants operate as intermediaries by bringing cash to markets, we might imagine an artisan also coming to market but with a pot, as well as a peasant coming with a sack of corn. By the one selling the pot to the merchant and the other the corn – while the merchant sells the corn to the first and the pot to the second – they both go away having rid themselves of something they needed little for something they needed more. It matters not at all how any of the three actors felt towards one another. They were, in the jargon, 'indifferent as to person'. Yet the exchange could not be conceived of without it both generating differences and also relying on prior differences. The merchant, for example, arrived at the market with a sum of money and would have spent a wasted day if he left it with the same sum. This feature of the merchant's position – what makes him, at least at this moment and for these purposes, a merchant – is the nature of this relationship: that by the different wants of two separate people, he is able to make a profit. Formulaically, for both the artisan and the peasant, their products (P=pot and C=corn respectively) became money and then the money became another product (P→C and C→P), while for the merchant money (M) became a tradable item, which then was traded again to make more money (M^1).

If merchants are not often the favourites of artisans or peasants it may be because of the transparent fact that the merchant has got a bit extra while the other two have simply exchanged one thing for another. It may also be because of the fact that s/he seems to have done it simply by being in the right place at the right time – the market or the *entrepot* as it could be called – while the other two sweated away making pots and growing corn. Be that as it may, what we need to note for the moment is that while the merchant did indeed make a profit, he did not do so through the use of 'capital' in the strict sense of the word.[8] His intervention between artisan and peasant did not add anything to the overall worth of the things involved.

For this to happen, we need to add a relation of 'production' into our game plan and we will do this by imagining first a relation of simple production and reproduction, and then a relation of expanded production and hence a somewhat transformed reproduction. But first we need to pause to reflect on what we have learned about the implications of social reproduction for differences among people – social, possibly even cultural, differentiation. And then I have to say something about what the word 'exploitation' means to me – and I introduce myself here, because the word has very emotive connotations among many of us, and its more technical use is disputed among social analysts.

All we need to note about social relations and differentiation here is that many relations and differences that mostly refer to one element of the social or cultural world may carry with them elements of what we saw happening in the market as it were 'behind the backs of the actors' (the expression in this context is Marx's). We may speak of age relations, patriarchy, race and gender; we may speak of the homeless and the unemployed and so on. While in none of these cases are we talking precisely of the kinds of relations this very small scenario has enacted, it is at least possible that traces of them could be found were we to 'go behind the backs' of some of these terms that we use in contexts far removed from what we think of as the economy or the market. The important point is, then, that a wide variety of ways in which the process of transferring value from one person (or group of persons) to others will create differences between people as well as relying on pre-existing ones. How these differences are felt and expressed – as differences of gender, of culture or of class – will depend on a whole series of factors that require empirical investigation in each instance.

As for exploitation, we need to understand it as a technical term referring to a particular characteristic of relationships between sets of people. The essential feature of a relationship of exploitation is that in working, a person produces something (it could be a leather belt, or it could be a service, like washing clothes). At the end of a day or a week, that person could go home with the full value of whatever it is they have produced. For example, if the person walks home with the belt on, then they are wearing the value of the raw materials, the tools and the work they put into making the belt, and that is it. If that person ends the day with something *less* than the full value they put into it, then the difference between that full value and what they actually take home is the rate of exploitation.[9]

We need to get away from the idea that this is necessarily always a bad thing. If the belt maker comes to my house and uses my leather-working tools, he may produce a better belt than if he stays at home and uses his own pocket-knife, or he may produce the same belt more quickly (thus freeing him up to do something else). If I pay him for doing this while he is at my house, using my tools, and then I sell the belt for a bit more than I paid him, then he may say he is exploited, even though he may still go home better off, having thus been 'exploited' by me, than if he had stayed at home and – unexploited – spent three days producing his belt. And anyway I may say that all I have done is charge him a rent for using my tools. The fact that we cannot agree about this may not mean that exploitation is or is not taking place, but that there is no abstract norm or value we can use to find a balance – except the relative worth of our inputs, his labour and my tools, which is of course a circular argument.

Simple Reproduction

With the issues of difference and of exploitation behind us, let us turn for a moment to a very simple case where production and regulation are tied ineluctably together. In the highland area where I worked in Peru, one source of livelihood for local people came from their household plots of arable land. In the years before I arrived in the area the small unit of the farm with its household labour reproduced itself by mobilizing labour through the domestic relationships in the household and putting them to work on the plot of farm land.

Typically a husband and wife with their unmarried children – who begin as dependents and soon grow to become workers – constituted this labour force. Initially any exploitation (as we have defined it) that occurred took place within these domestic relations: the way in which the household head could use his naked power, together with gender and familial ideologies, to hold back resources produced by the labour of others in the household could be the crucial levers on which exploitation occurred, suggesting that buried within these apparently cultural distinctions there was a class relationship in general uses of the term 'patriarchy'.

But isolated farmers who own their own land and produce for their own subsistence are rare. For one thing, what I have described here is a static version of social relations, not one that takes reproduction into account; clearly over time, children got married and moved out of the household to form new units, just as their parents had done before them. Once such units are set within broader relationships, a complex set of exploitative possibilities arise. In the case of these people in Peru we can explore this through the way the in which labour was mobilized to cultivate the community's 'common land'.

Within the bounds of the community, arable land was divided between the household plots we have just discussed and larger plots cultivated through the use of the collective (communal) labour of household members known as the *faena*. Produce from this land, at least in principle, could be used to cover the needs of old people perhaps, or orphans – community members, in other words, whose households had insufficient land or labour to survive by themselves. Or produce from communal land could be sold and the proceeds used to roof the school or repair a road. One way to think of this is that the labour given to these community *faenas* is a kind of rent paid (in labour) to the community for the right to household arable land. Many expressions, stories and jokes served to obscure this interpretation, but at least two features give it some purchase. First, the amount of labour required from each household for the *faena* was based on the number of its active workers. From time to time the community adjusted the amount of land a household had access to in accordance with its size. So in effect, more labour rent in the form of the number of people working on the *faena* meant more land for the household. Second, with the coming of cash into the community, some household heads got into the practice of paying the fine levied for non attendance, rather than losing the labour from their own small plots during the days of work on community land. What they were in effect doing was paying the community for the work their offspring gave to the household on that day. In so doing they translated a child's concrete labour into a money value, thereby turning labour rent into cash rent.

The example is only illustrative, but what it shows is that even in relatively simple circumstances, the channels for passing 'value' from one group of people to another can be multiple (Turner 2008). These channels are by no means smooth and clear, letting something called 'the economy' flow easily through them. Rather each of these relationships flows through a complicated set of differences between [groups of] people.

By the time I was living in this area, villagers had migrated to other parts of Peru returning with their earnings, and produce from both the common land and from at least some of the household plots was being sold in local markets for cash. As a result, all the older relationships now had their mirror image in a cash version. This in turn led to a whole series of immanent changes that occurred 'behind the back' of the people involved. I have written about this elsewhere (Smith 1989), but the point to be made here is that we can imagine all these sets of relations – intra-household relations, inter-household relations and household-community relations – reproducing themselves over time without the necessity to expand the circuit of this reproduction. Changes will undoubtedly occur, but they will be historically contingent.

Yet the kind of agriculture I have described here does not exist in a world dominated by similar kinds of social relations of production, rather it exists in a world that is dominated by a set of social relations in which expansion is inherent to their reproduction, as we will see below. It is quite possible that rural societies the world over have become so chaotic that it is increasingly hard to see the kind of framework I have outlined here. On the other hand we do need to at least ask whether it is not also possible that an apparent state of rural chaos is not as much the result of the chaos of rural societies as it is the result of deficiencies in the tools we use to understand them. It might be said that 'The crisis of the countryside is so rampant in the global south today that no relations as you describe them here can ever be *reproduced*'. This may indeed be so, but apart from the array of contingent factors that have produced today's vast swathes of rural poverty, we need at least to understand such contingencies in terms of the relations of simple reproduction that make such small-scale producers inherently unable to survive within a world dominated by expanded reproduction (Kahn 1980; Friedmann 1978; Smith 1985; Lem 1988). Otherwise we run the risk of offering apparent solutions that will not stand the test of time, not just because 'history' is against these people, but because scholars fail to take their models through the stages of their reproductive logic.

To see why this is so, we need to move to the basic features of 'commodity-capitalism' itself – the expression coined by Rubin (1928).

Expanded Reproduction

There are many features of capitalism that make it simultaneously transparent and opaque. Some of these have been around for a long time; others are a product of the kind of capitalism that has developed in recent years.

Long after his death, the 'dark satanic mills' of Blake's prophetic poem seemed to be a striking feature of capitalism – when Engels wrote about Manchester in the 1840s for example. Today the role of rapidly processed information through new technologies, together with the fact that so much wealth can be accumulated through speculation, seem the most obvious features of capitalism and just as satanic as Blake's mills. It is almost as though the carousel is now spinning so fast that jumping on it inevitably leads to dizzying obscurity.

Lewis Carroll suggested that you should begin at the beginning and when you get to the end, stop; but that is a difficult business with a carousel. The most striking ways in which money is made today – from retailing, to advertising, to entertainment – seem a long way from those dark satanic mills of Manchester. And yet it was part of Engels' point that, although the smoke and grime of the North of England were a symptom of industrial capitalism, to focus on them alone was to focus only on the symptoms of the disease and not its pathology; we could say very much the same about our own vision of current capitalism's ephemera. So we need to begin somewhere else, and that place is where material goods are produced through people's labour.

For despite the easy visibility of these spectacular realms of capitalism, at bottom capital derives its value on the production of *material* goods. You might develop a machine that allows you to make a car out of less and less steel or using less and less petrol, but your car will always be dependent on some material goods and some form of energy. So at root 'wealth' must be based on the efficient production of material items *somewhere*. Even if we can trade our expertise in piano playing or making video games for a pair of shoes, in the last analysis we are all dependent on the production of those shoes – not to mention the piano and the video console.[11]

> **Modern societies depend on the efficient production of a number of *material* items:**[10]
>
> 1. Extraction from nature (mining, oil wells, etc.) → raw materials. Appropriation from nature (interventions through agriculture) → agricultural products.
> 2. Processing into steel, refining into gasoline, etc. Processing into food.
> 3. 'Consumption 1' → of steel into machines, for example. 'Consumption 2' → of food by people.
> 4. Machines (Constant capital) + People (Variable capital) → Final Goods
>
> **Stages of Material Production**

Capital and Labour

Shoes of course have been made for quite a long time, certainly well before capitalism came along. But in most cases today this production takes place in firms whose owners undertake to produce the items so as to make a profit, and whose workers undertake to work to make a wage. In a sense this is about interest and interests. Put bluntly, if high interest is paid on a stock it increases its interest (for those who may buy it). Thinking in these terms only, we can note certain features of profits on the one hand and wages on the other that might incline those tied to the one or to the other towards different interests. In this sense there is an inherent tension in the way profit rates and wage rates are arrived at, and this forms one axis of competition in a capitalist social formation; we might call it the 'vertical axis of competition'. It is not the only relationship where competition is decisive in these kinds of societies, as we shall see.

A firm, let us call it I-Bum, produces goods over a year, which it sells. Generally it divides up the returns for three purposes: to re-initiate production by buying more raw materials, fixing or improving machinery and so on; to pay interest to the owners of shares; and to pay wages to the workers. Indeed the first of these three 'costs' can act as a pivot that can control the balance between the other two. In seeking to improve profits, directors will seek out the most productive machines for producing goods. Workers meanwhile will make demands to improve both their working and their living conditions, and so increase 'the wage bill'. If the firm can introduce a more efficient machine it will produce more and hence be able to pay higher wages, while also retaining the level of interest it is paying to shareholders. Everybody is happy.

Yet, if we think about these three elements, we soon realize that they can be reduced to two. After all what we are seeing here is that a bargain is being made on a basis not dissimilar to the exchange between artisan and peasant in which one had something the other needed. In this case workers have productive energy (labour power) which they cannot put usefully to work because they lack machines; capitalists have potentially productive machines which they cannot put to work because they lack labour. The interest paid by the firm to the (share) owners might be seen as a rent paid for the use of the machines they own. The wage likewise might be seen as a rent paid for the use of labour power. Now, if we return to the strategy I have imputed to this firm – of buying better machines – we see that the long-term effect is to increase the value of what the owners are bringing to this bargain. Were the firm to invest instead in public health, safety features and an increased wage, effectively one might say that they were increasing the 'value' of labour power in this bargain – though in truth, our own society works on a principle of property ownership such that, in so far as the workers do not have ownership in the firm, the paying out of higher wages appears as seepage, rather than 'good investment'.[12]

There is then a tension between the two groups over the 'just' division of the social wealth produced by their respective contributions – the one providing machines and materials, the other labour power. While there are endless ways of 'resolving' this tension – we have already seen one, the use of more efficient machines to increase overall productivity – ultimately it is a form of competition, based on the respective leverage, or power, between the two parties – between capital and labour. 'Hence, in the history of capitalist production', notes Marx, 'the establishment of a norm ... presents itself as ... a struggle between collective capital, i.e. the class of capitalists, and collective labour, i.e. the working class' (Marx [1867] 1976: 342–44).

Competition between Firms

A second form of competition – we will call it 'horizontal competition' – sets one firm off against another. To illustrate this we will introduce a second firm which we will call I-Pud. Both raise capital through selling shares (of ownership) and employing labour by paying a competitive wage. At the end of the first year, confident that its machinery dominates the sector, I-Bum pays a healthy dividend to its shareholders and raises the wages of its workers. I-Pud pays barely any interest at all and holds back on a wage increase, but buys some very sharp new machinery. As a result, at the end of the second year, I-Pud produces more computers more cheaply and, feeling generous, pays out interest to shareholders and a wage increase to workers, thus keeping these potentially conflictive partners momentarily content. I-Bum, on the other hand, still lumbered with klutsy machinery, fails to do either. With a discontented labour force, it finds shareholders are more attracted to I-Pud shares. As a result their shares get a higher market value, while I-Bum's slip down. I-Pud has now increased its capital value (actually it has increased its ability to extract labour power from its workers). This means that, should it want to, it can even go to the bank and borrow money (to buy still better machines) at a lower rate than I-Bum, by using its higher-valued shares as collateral.[13]

Once again I need to emphasize that there may be numerous contingent factors that modify this scenario, but the essential point is that it is not possible, given the fact of vertical and horizontal competition, for a firm to simply stand still. It must aim for ever-increasing 'economies' – ever-greater 'productivity' – by combining better machinery with each unit of labour. This is not simply coincidental. It is built into the system. 'The constant reintroduction of capital into the economic circuit with a view to deriving profit – that is to say, increasing the capital, which will in turn be reinvested – is the basic mark of capitalism' (Boltanski and Chiapello 2005: 5). The improvement in machinery has allowed the firm to extract more labour value from the worker in the same amount of time, thereby increasing the amount of value pumped out of the one for the benefit of the other. This constant drive to heighten productivity, to increase the rate of exploitation,[14] gives the entire process a tendency towards expanded (rather than simple) reproduction.[15]

A vastly simplified model such as this directs us to certain forms of enquiry and away from others. First, it suggests that criticism of 'bad' companies in moral terms fails to note that – in terms of a kind of society in which the production and circulation of commodities are achieved through the normatively sanctioned pursuit of profit through capital – there are in fact 'good' companies. Put another way, while it may not direct us entirely away from conspiracy theories about unfeeling company directors – who continue to drive down labour costs, strip nature by seeking out ever cheaper raw materials and endanger the atmosphere by encouraging the use of their products – at least it helps us to understand the web that the spiders have set for their prey.

Second, it encourages us to try to distinguish between contingent problems, which can be solved with little adjustment to the fundamental relationships involved, and problems which are immanent to expanded reproduction. I say 'try' because, since Marx's day, capitalist social formations have gone through such a vast array of resolutions that many authors have taken the view that, far from being threatened by crises and criticism, capitalism thrives on crises and is renewed through criticism (e.g. Boltanski and Chiapello 2005).

The actual resolutions we find to the crises of capitalism are legion, but if we stick with the schematic framework I have so far been using, we can begin by identifying three types: technical (as we have seen a new technology might offset the class tensions between wage earners and shareholders, but we can imagine technical resolutions extending across a broader range of production and reproduction tensions); institutional (for example, through the introduction of various forms of welfare state which might subsidize the cost of reproducing labour and offset the iniquities inherent in the capital–labour relation);[16] and spatial (where increasing costs of local raw materials and labour, for example, lead to displacements of capital, leaving 'rust-belts' in their wake). Referring specifically to the last of these, David Harvey has used the word 'fix', an especially apposite term, since it draws attention both to mending something before it breaks, and also to the kind of fix we associate with addiction – one which does no more than take we the addicts to another day.

More recently, anthropologists and cultural theorists have turned to the role of spectacle, desire and consumption, the argument being that 'culture' plays a greater role today in the reproduction of capitalism than in the past. The result is a proliferation of studies on 'the culture of capitalism', understood as a kind of superorganic phenomenon deracinated from the grinding dictates of relations of production. The problem with these perspectives – that culture is more inherently a part of capitalist processes than hitherto, and that capitalist culture can be understood sui generis – is that the phenomenology of capitalism has always been deeply embedded in its material reproduction – through the commodity.

The Commodity

It is hard to read Marx's thoughts on the role of the commodity in political economy without being reminded of his profound influence on Foucault and the latter's determination to shift the vector of force that gives us our modern history. The shift was to substitute this new kind of raison d'état for Marx's *burgerliche Gessellschaft* (bourgeois society, i.e. market society) as the central gravitational pull of the newly spinning world whose centripetal force drew in human raw material and 'socialized' it. And yet what makes Foucault's understanding of the particular features of emergent bourgeois society so radically distinct from Marx's is, ironically, the way he learned from Marx. Foucault argues that what we see changing, as we survey a range of institutions which (were their totality known to us) would constitute a state, was the way in which 'power-as-knowledge' produced a form of government – govern-*mentality* – whose effect was the production of modern subjects. It is fruitless, he argues, to seek out a set of key agents, assess their intentional strategies, and thereby arrive at understandings of how power affects the world we live in. The shift Foucault made then was from 'commodity-capitalism' as the key figure of modernity to forms of 'governmentality' as its key figure.

There was nothing new in this focus in itself. Social analysts, including Durkheim but especially Weber, had been interested in what it was, beyond naked violence, that produced the 'domination-effect' on citizens, from 'conscience collective' to *Herrschaft*. Following Weber, they shifted attention away from 'the economy' towards a broad set of criteria, key among them various forms of social 'power'. Subtracting force majeur and rejecting the ideal of consensus[17] left these writers with the need for some notion of subjectivity that would account for a domination, a collusion of consciousness – in short, ideology under various guises (spirit, *conscience*, culture, etc.). This need for something that must be added *ex machina* runs the risk of making that add-on do overly heavy amounts of work in the supposed determination of social conduct.

What makes Foucault different from these figures is not his concern with power and governance, but his sharing with Marx a refusal to take individual or collective consciousness as an element sui generis in our understanding of social being. The challenge then, is to understand how the historically formed social subject can be studied without resort to dominant ideology.[18] For Foucault it was the peculiar features of modern power and of the new governance that began to arise from the eighteenth century onwards; for Marx it was the peculiar features of the 'commodity'.

What then is this thing, 'a commodity'? Is it not simply something, an item of goods, which is produced by a firm and then sold on the market for a price? Indeed this is so, but we need to be a little more precise; for a product to be termed a 'commodity' it must be produced for the sole purpose of being sold on the open market, and the price it gets has to be the result of its potential open exchange with all other items that are for sale in the market. This latter point means that the commodity-feature of this product (its exchangeability) has absolutely no connection with its physical nature. A commodity then, simultaneously has two 'realities', one is its concrete nature – as a clock or computer – the other is its abstract exchangeability with all other commodities, testable (theoretically realizable) only on the market (Marx 1976: 164).[19]

If we go back for a moment to Part I two things covered there are useful at this point. First, if we go to the box entitled 'Stages of Material Production', we can see that a physical item which arrives at our factory floor – perhaps as some raw material, perhaps as a machine to modify that raw material – is in fact a materialization of an earlier stage when it too was being produced by human labour: if you like, from miners, to steel workers, to machine-tool makers, to auto workers. It is almost as though it does not matter how far back you go, somebody before you put tools and labour together to make the thing you are about to use. This helps us with the first point: *a commodity is the condensation of the quantity and quality of the actual working activity that went into it.* And when we forget this – as we mostly do – we value only the thing, thereby devaluing the work that went into it, a kind of fetish.

Second, we can recall the discussion of firms which ended up with a firm producing and then selling a product, the product achieving a value only when it went through a market transaction. We can recall too that this 'value' reverberated back on the two firms effectively allowing them to 'evaluate' the worth of their machines and their workers. What the physical features of that commodity actually are may be of little concern to the worker. In fact s/he may be making a digit having no idea of what its end use will be – its use value. Meanwhile, within the firm itself, different people are doing a wide variety of different jobs, each with its own special characteristics – some for example requiring more skill, others more drudgery; some more mental work, others more manual. These are the different forms of concrete labour – the use value of each contribution if you like to the final product. As the magic moment arrives when the commodity is exchanged on the market for money, its exchange value has the effect of giving real, measurable value to all those qualitatively different tasks and relations of work, homogenizing their variety into abstract labour whose form of value is the only value that will matter to both the worker and the capitalist.

So a commodity does not just act as the mask and material condensation of the practices and relationships that went into its completion, it also (and this is the second essential point), at the moment of its sale, *establishes the value of all the multiple activities that brought it to this point* within the commodity sphere.[20] Social relations are not just 'symbolized' by becoming things (my first point), they are only 'realized' when they become things. Moreover, just as turning an item into a commodity in this way transforms its use value into an exchange value, so when its sale transforms multiple concrete labour into measurably abstract labour, labour power itself becomes a commodity.

And what if we turn for a moment to the 'consumer end' of this process? Marx (1976: 165) notably remarked that 'definite social relations between men themselves … assumes here, for them, the fantastic form of a relation between things'. And this applies to more of our lives than might at first appear, because we have just learned that among these 'things' is our own labour power itself. So one way of describing what people do when they buy something is 'they appropriate the produce of the labour of others, by alienating that of their own labour' (Marx quoted in Rubin 1928: 15). The alienation, in other words is two-way: it occurs as the producer loses what he has produced to the market, and as the consumer loses the fruits of his labour also in that market. So, perhaps without us realizing it, an extraordinarily large arena of our social relations in a commodity-capitalist society is one of relations between owners of commodities, one of these being labour power itself – our productivity and creativity. Moreover though this is not a long-term kind of social relation but rather a relation that happens only at that moment of exchange, it nonetheless is one in a series of endless fragmented snap-shot relations that take on a coherence of their own.[21]

In other words, the effect of commodity relations is not to give an organic character to our social relations, thoroughly interweaving us coherently into the sum of the social whole, as Durkheim would have it; nor might we understand a crucial feature of modernity to be the 'disenchantment' that Weber alluded to, in which cold reason takes over from enchanting faith. Rather, if indeed there once was a realm of the world that we understood to be enchanted, we have dispensed with it only to replace it with another.

Why does this matter? Is it not just a complicated way of talking about consumer society's fetishism about commodities – something most of us are surely only too aware of? I have so far avoided the word 'fetishism', partly for this very reason. Marx had his reasons for using the term at the time no doubt, but it runs the risk of implying too much or too little. By saying that there is something akin to magic about our thrall for commodities it says too much, and by becoming just another way of saying 'Live to shop', it says too little. These views separate the 'idea' – envy and desire for commodities, or expressing one's 'self' through commodities, and so on – from the essential character of social relations and their reproduction, making it appear as though this 'new' consumerism is a pathology, an added perversion. Indeed it may be all these things. But we need to situate it within the unfolding ordinary practices and relations of our society, or as an extension of them – not as an entirely different phenomenon in another realm, fascinating and magical, and qualitatively different from what might be 'healthy' or 'normal'. This is why it is a mistake to label what we have so far been talking about as 'economic relations' or even to understand the term 'production' in a narrowly material and economic sense. For better or worse Marx was the quintessential holist, the only subject he speaks of is 'society' – the whole set of activities of production, exchange and consumption, the combined effect of which is perceptible to each person outside himself as a 'natural' property of things (Balibar 1995: 67).[22]

Fetishism, used in this way, is not just the fixation on things that we associate with today's shopping mall. It is and was essential to the way political economy worked from the outset – essential not because the commodity is just a thing on which we fixate to the exclusion of the social relations it masks, but essential because the commodity is simultaneously a representation and a material object in its own right. How does this affect the way we might configure an enquiry into 'the culture of capitalism', let's say, street art, music, or mountain biking? If we take as axiomatic that the simultaneous mystification and materiality of the commodity is at the root of capitalist political economy (as Marx did), and not a superstructural add-on to its essential workings, how might that inflect the way we do cultural studies of capitalist societies?

I have already juxtaposed it to Foucault's 'governmentality'. Governmentality addresses the question of regulation and freedom, or perhaps better put, regulation-through-freedom. It comes at an understanding of our historically specific kind of sociality through a theory of the technologies of governance, or what Gramsci would call 'political society'. Marx too was concerned with the peculiar nature of regulation and freedom or regulation-through-freedom that characterizes our historically specific kind of sociality,[23] but for him the key element in this is the constitution of the world of subjects and objects inherent in social relations expressed through the exchange of something quite particular – the commodity. This produced a 'civil society' whose norms had to be coherent with those of the market.[24] Here is Marx then, in a tone dripping with irony, referring to the sphere of culture:

> This sphere ... within whose boundaries the sale and purchase power of labour-power goes on, is in fact a very Eden of the innate rights of man. There alone rule Freedom, Equality, Property and Bentham.[25] Freedom because both buyer and seller of a commodity, say of labour-power, are constrained only by their own free will. They contract as free agents, and the agreement they come to is but the form in which they give legal expression to their common will. Equality because each enters into relation with the other, as with a simple owner of commodities, and they exchange equivalent for equivalent. Property because each disposes only of what is his own. And Bentham, because each looks only to himself. The only force that brings them together and puts them in relation to each other, is the selfishness, the gain and the private interests of each. (Marx 1976: 280)

Clearly then, one would have to be an especially unworldly academic to propose that a person who perceived the world in terms of these notions of freedom, equality, property and the individual was suffering from false consciousness, or was the victim [*sic*] of a dominant ideology since, were that person to join the academic in his 'enlightenment' s/he would lose all practical effect in society: s/he may prefer being a rich fool in fact than a wise pauper. It is to get beyond this 'either/or' way of thinking (either you are mystified and therefore act foolishly, or you see things clearly and so act in your best interests) that, however reluctantly, we need the term 'fetishism'.

Fetishism is not a subjective perception felt by a person beyond the realm of social relations, nor is it a false understanding of those social relations; rather it is the only way a certain kind of social form can but appear. Indeed without having such a view it would be impossible for one to function in society and impossible for society itself to function – 'to suppress the appearance would be to abolish social relations' (Balibar 1995: 61). Moreover we see too how commodity relations become simultaneously a mechanism of subjection, a form of regulation, and a facilitator of productivity and creation; indeed it is through the effectivity of production organized in this way that regulation occurs. Yet there is nothing 'natural' about the kinds of freedoms or rights we are talking about here; they are thoroughly stamped with the press that produced them: 'What becomes central is … the direct correspondence established between … the egalitarian form of exchange and that of the contract, the "freedom" to buy and sell and the personal "freedom" of individuals' (ibid.: 77).

It is then quite impossible to disentangle the ideas and mystifications involved here from the way in which the social relations necessary to this kind of society are produced and reproduced in the most mundane elements of everyday life. If we want to talk of 'subjectivity' then we need to recognize that for Marx the essence of our subjectivity is not some inner voice, spirit, soul or mind; it is our practice, *tout court*.[26] Because it is our doing that is the only evidence of our being, and because there were others before us, so there is no natural human essence, no *tabula rasa*, but only the historically produced social subject.

The power of this understanding of the commodity is that it refuses to disaggregate regulation through symbolic means from the perceptions, habits and norms which are not tacked on to, but are themselves the practice of social relations actualized through the complex weave of configured and contingent conditionalities.

Understanding the role of symbols, culture and ideology in the exercise of power may in no way be explained in its entirety by these means. It would be absurd to argue that any responsible scholar would suggest so. But so complete has been our shift away from this kind of approach that now perhaps the shoe should be on the other foot: theories of culture that leave the features of commodity-capitalism's social reproduction entirely unexamined, need to be asked how this enhances their analyses. And this seems especially true since the financial crisis that began in 2007. Indeed the prior comfortable neglect of the particular form of our society as specifically a capitalist kind of society means that these intellectual jugglers and acrobats are now obliged to have something to say *a propos*, but end up making it look as though the mystifications now so evident arise superficially from the snake oil used by speculators rather than from the deep principles of capital reproduction. Capitalism has changed vastly of course from the baseline skeleton I have provided here. Given its chimeric complexities today it is tempting to resort to explanations that speak of contingency, a runaway world, and so on. But if we substitute contingency for an understanding of the immanent features of capitalist society I have so far discussed here, then a vast sphere of social process and historical dynamism disappears from enquiry.

Finance

So far we have looked at capitalism as though it were a system that brings machines and raw materials together with labour power in a particular way to produce goods. This 'particular way' arises from the primary purpose of the relationship: extracting surplus value from labourers in the form of profits which are garnered by those who control the machines and raw materials. The pursuit of this goal makes the actual goods, crops, services and so on that result a matter of indifference. While Marx had much more to say about many other facets of capital in his work with that name, this was his baseline point of departure. Among those other facets, he dealt with an especially significant moment in the reproduction of the cycle of capital: the pursuit of finance when the productive firm needs to seek investment in its operation. Recently however this financial moment has acquired a powerful centripetal pull on the reproduction of capital as a whole.

As I noted in the Introduction, the vantage point from which I take my perspective on each of the topics in the chapters that follow is the one I have outlined here. By the time we reach Chapter 6, the topic is entirely threaded through how we might understand contemporary society and its politics in terms of a critique of the political economy of contemporary capitalism. To illustrate what it means to take such a perspective one could contrast it with an argument about the rule of experts in a kind of society with a distinct form of technology of rule and the kinds of subjectivities that result (e.g. Dean 1999; Rose 2000). In this case however the argument is about the form that contemporary capitalism has taken as a result of the projects of recently composed dominant blocs, and the very different kinds of class relations that arise. This framework then shapes the questions that need to be addressed for an effective counter-politics.

Contemporary capitalism has changed from the era when Marx wrote but, contrary to the views of many writers, it has not changed 'out of all recognition'. One especially significant way in which capitalism has changed has to do with the now pivotal role particular kinds of finance play in the reproduction of capital. The hitherto discrete but essential working of Wall Street suddenly came into full view, rather as though the spotlight had suddenly and unremittingly fallen on Rasputin rather than the despotism of the Tsar. There were two immediate effects – both in the media and in the academy – each of them unfortunate. First it was suggested that the crisis arose as a result of some unduly greedy capitalists, as though no such crisis would have occurred had such people behaved as normal, proper capitalists. And second there was continual talk of speculation, casino capitalism and so on, as though it were something entirely separate from what was actually referred to as 'the real economy'. Both these propositions are misleading if not downright false. Finance capital *is* part of the economy, and the problems this creates (as well as the solutions it offers) have little to do with the character traits of its major players.

In the remainder of this chapter I will try to take us for a ride into the world of finance capitalists, because what can be learned from this ride will be helpful in the chapters that follow and essential for the penultimate one. That is my sole purpose. This section should not be read as a textbook introduction to finance or an exposé of the financial crisis (of which there are now a vast array). Rather it simply provides a series of signposts and navigational instruments for getting into the ethos of contemporary finance capital. Though some of the social and political implications of this ethos are touched upon, these are taken up more thoroughly in a later chapter.

With current finance capital and its various instruments there are so many mirrors and lights that the eye wanders, and so I will try to introduce a little order by focusing on some of its tools. Perhaps the first thing to note is the way in which investment and finance address the issue of time that capital faces, notably the time between the putting together of the package necessary to produce something and the moment when that something achieves a return by being sold on the market. Clearly the owner of a small firm can put up some of his or her own money for this purpose and perhaps even call on his or her extended family too. But in the previous sections I have spoken of the competitive advantages of making the production process work more efficiently, of which the magnitude and speed of the operation are often key elements. The ability to acquire the necessary money beyond family and personal networks is clearly an advantage under these conditions, and there are various commercial institutions for this purpose, from stock exchanges to investment banks.

One way to raise money through these channels is to borrow it at a fixed rate of interest. The advantage for the firm owner here is that s/he remains the full owner of the firm, simply making interest payments to a bank or a bond holder from one year to the next. The disadvantage is that whether or not s/he has a good or bad year, s/he will still have to produce the dividend payment for the loan. An alternative is to sell shares in one's company, thereby raising capital through the initial floatation (say, on the New York Stock Exchange). The advantage here is that you are not committed to a fixed dividend payment on a bad year, since you now share ownership of your company with other shareholders. You may see the disadvantage as the fact that you now have to share your profits with others. Of course the point of a place where stocks of this kind can actually be exchanged is that, after the initial floatation, shares in your company can now be traded, the initial purchasers now selling their shares to others, hopefully for a profit. If these 'others' perceive your firm to be doing quite well in the Darwinian world of companies, then they will likely pay the initial buyer of your shares something more than you first received from your floatation.

This may seem a little unfair in view of the fact that you (and if you are feeling generous or possibly honest) and your employees did all the work. But if we now move on a few years and we find you in need of more liquid cash for your operation, either through borrowing or through a second floatation, then the existing market price of your outstanding shares will affect how cheaply or how costly that new money will be for you. If your future looks good, you can pay low interest on your bonds or you can float your new shares at a good price. So the 'real economy' that you with your now growing firm participate in is intricately tied to the world of finance. And the converse is also true. Ever more intricate and possibly even intimate details of the operation of your firm will become of great interest to the various kinds of agents in the business of 'advancing' money to you – bankers, brokers and so on. You must of course convince the people who buy your widgets of their superb worth. But if you want to stay in business you must also convince the people of finance of the value of your future.

But I have been taking the perspective of the initial manufacturer trying to get his or her business off the ground and then moving on to greater things. But this section is about finance and so we should change the direction of our gaze. It may be helpful to make a strange move in doing so: to filter a political economy understanding of finance through Foucault's insights about government and the populace. In his later writings Foucault asked how we might think about government in a situation in which the ideal was now seen to be limiting its purview. The answer, he suggested, is that the citizen should regulate her or himself. How might this be done? Foucault (2008: 119–84) argued that one answer was provided by German economic theorists (the *Ordoliberals*) who early contributed to notions of neoliberalism. Their answer was that such regulation can occur when we all act as though we were buying and selling ourselves in a market which itself would then 'self-regulate'. In such a view of the world, we do not find on one side people with labour power selling it to people with machines, the owners of enterprises; rather on both sides of the relationship the parties possess capital, for some it may be material, for others it may be human.[27] Human capital, like any form of capital, must be nurtured to enhance its value and, like any enterprise, people must then go out into the world and exchange the 'capital' they have for what they want or need. Here there are no workers and capitalists, just possessors of capital of different quality coming together in the market place for exchange to their mutual advantage – say human capital on the one hand and manufacturing capital on the other. Self-discipline then serves the same purpose as factory discipline. It is a means of maximizing market price in this case of the human understood as a kind of capital. This does not mean that regulation beyond the self disappears; it means that institutional forms take shape from those principles.

Let us now take Foucault's argument and apply it to a narrower constituency – finance capitalists. It is misleading to speak in general terms of a regulated or unregulated market or economy. Since it is evident that *some* regulations must always be in place for transactions to occur over time, the issue is what has to be regulated and how. For much of the history of capitalism a great deal of this regulation was undertaken by national states: writing the necessary laws of property, establishing a uniform exchange rate for the currency, mediating the forms of contract among players, and so on. If, as Foucault argues, a neoliberal ideology seeks to constitute a world in which the interventions of the state must be quite different and if anyway capital flows themselves are becoming so global that they break the bounds of the state, then where some regulating is seen to be necessary appropriate tools must be found to do so. Many of the current instruments of finance capital are precisely designed to serve this function.

The result is not the absence of regulation (the so-called de-regulated market) but rather the use of various market devices for the purposes of reducing the hazards of the market while of course accepting the winds and currents that provide its opportunities; in other words, turning fate into chance and then intervening – to insure against it or to speculate on it. As with everything to do with market participants, what is insurance for one is speculation for the other. From the point of view of regulation, what is given with one hand is taken away with the other.[28]

One way to talk about this is to follow the path of the now infamous 'derivative'. The first thing one is likely to know about a derivative is that it is an instrument that 'derives' its price from an underlying asset. For example if a farmer wishes to protect himself against the price of his crop being very low at the time of harvest, he can go to a commodities market and buy a 'future' from a trader. What he is buying is the guarantee of a certain price, no matter what the actual price of corn will be on the day he sells it. And the value of this derivative depends on what traders estimate the price of corn will be in a few months time. If for example indicators suggest that it will be quite stable, then the cost of the farmer's insurance may not be very high, but if prices are very volatile then the cost of this derivative – the 'hedge' the farmer is making against the ups and downs of the market – will be quite high. Moreover, once this instrument is a piece of paper that can be exchanged among traders on the commodities market, then we can see quite easily that, if the holder of the contract with the farmer actually stands to gain quite a lot because now prices have gone up while the farmer is tied into the price he agreed on when he bought the 'future', then obviously other traders will pay a good price to buy that derivative from the trader. It is gaining a value independent of the purpose for which the farmer originally bought it – though not, it should be noted, why the trader sold it to him.

The second thing we need to know about derivatives is that they are an especially useful instrument for leverage – that is, getting hold of money at a fixed rate in order to use that money for returns at variable rates. In our case above, the farmer has used a small amount of money to buy a hedge against the loss of a much greater amount of money. We can see better how leverage works if, for the farmer, we substitute an investor who wants to provide himself with at least some protection for his investment. In fact it may not be quite 'his' investment. He may be an investment banker charging a fee to invest somebody else's money, a fee that may in fact be a commission tied to the profits he makes for his client; or he may be acting for himself but having borrowed the money at a fixed rate, in order to get leverage. At this point we can use some very straightforward maths to see how leverage works ... and where it might take us.

Let us say that he borrows $90,000 at 5 per cent, and puts up $10,000 of his own money, investing the $100,000 in a stock he thinks will be worth half as much again next year. To cover himself in case he is wrong, he buys a 'hedge' in the form of a $10,000 option to sell the shares if they go below $104,500 on the day he has to pay back his loan. If his shares do not do as well as he had expected, he can use his option to cover his loss. So this option is almost the same as the farmer's 'future', but here there is a difference. If his shares do as he had anticipated, he does not have to exercise his option. He has wasted $10,000 to buy something he will not use, but hey, who cares? His shares went up and he got his commission, or levered his meagre $10,000. In fact, he did quite well. After all, his $10,000 brought in $150,000, so although the share price only increased 50 per cent, he made fifteen times his money. Well, not quite. He still has to pay 5 per cent or $4,500 to his creditor – still, not a bad year. Of course, he could have been wrong, but then he would have exercised his option which would cover his debt and leave him with his original investment ($90,000 + $4500, plus his own $10,000 = $104,500).[29]

But the term 'hedge' is rather like the word lift (or elevator) or the 'Start' button on the Windows programme; it refers to only one part of what could be involved. Imagine that this investor is so sure that this stock will go up by 50 per cent that he buys an option for $10,000, not to *sell* if it does not go up, but to *buy* when it does. Now he is using his $10,000 to buy an option that will be worth $50,000 if he is right. But why not do what he did before: borrow $90,000 and now buy not the *actual* shares but simply the options to buy them. Now he has used the total amount available to him to buy $1 million shares which, if they go up, will bring in $500,000. He now pays back his loan and walks away with some 400 per cent on a position of his own of just $10,000 – on a share that only increased 50 per cent.[30]

What we see here now is not a hedge at all, but its opposite. And this is really the problem with any use of the market to do one thing; it can almost always be made to do the exact opposite as well. This is not some awful pathology but is precisely what makes the market, for those committed to it, attractive as a means of mediating social relationships. Nonetheless, even though this derivative may not be doing what we originally had in mind for it – to secure something in the present against the uncertainty of the future – it is, if we care to dig deep enough, still at bottom a derivative in the original sense we gave the word. There was an underlying value from which the final profit was made – however far down we have to go.

But the third thing we need to know about derivatives is that for the vast majority of them their prices are not, in any useful way, tied to the value of any underlying asset. This does not mean that they are in any way fictitious or 'virtual'; it means simply that their prices (should) reflect the function they perform and that function has become much more multiple, serving many more purposes, than in our original scenario. Two things have happened to derivatives since those watershed years of the seventies. We might think of these as a vertical feature and a horizontal feature.

The vertical feature is that the purpose served by the relationship we have seen between the farmer and the trader can be extended to pretty much anything. Why should we need to think of an 'asset' as a material thing, like corn, with an unknown price some time in the future? Why not just think of anything whose worth in the future is not fully known? This after all is what life insurance was always about. If we can go to an insurance company and buy insurance against our early death, or debilitating illness, then why should we not do the same with a trader – which anyway is what the insurance company then does, to hedge its *own* position? And if we can do this with our health, why not do it for anything else? Why not the weather on my holiday (or, more seriously, if I am a utilities supply firm, against a warm or cold winter)?[31] In a sense we still have here the original 'vertical' meaning of the word 'derivative' – the price of the future we are buying is derived from an underlying value, just as the corn was. But so enmeshed are we now in a monetized way of evaluating our lives, we need to note an important slippage here that we might not have noticed. How are we to place a price on the asset in question, so that the derivative that is traded against that asset can also be priced (as we saw for the corn)? We know that the corn will ultimately be traded on a supply/demand market, but is that the case for my health, or the possibility of a world war before I die? So the first thing we need to note is a change in the vertical dimension of derivatives.

Besides this vertical dimension we can add a horizontal dimension – the way one derivative relates to another. We have just noted that there is something quite significant about the ability to translate a quality like future health into a quantity that can then be traded on an open market – what we call a 'commodity'. Now we can note that, once this has happened, there is no reason why we should not trade a health derivative for a corn derivative. Indeed, if I am a trader with a large holding of futures on a population whose health begins to look risky, I might want to 'hedge' my exposure by buying some corn futures, something I will expand on in Chapter 6. Nonetheless, while this too may (nowadays) seem quite commonsensical to our ever more commodified reasoning, we do need to note that there is no obvious or straightforward way of finding a proper exchange price for two such widely different items as health and corn. This is not to say that such trades will not take place. After all, any trade is always possible. But as we have already noted, contained in the meaning of the term 'commodity' is the fact that it is a global phenomenon, not something locally exchanged between two or three traders. If there are no common means for comparison, what we would expect would be a wide variety of exchange prices from one place to another. If, however, we could come up with a formula that would indeed make it possible to make relatively accurate assessments of value on either side of the trade, then hitherto rather anachronistic and localized gambles could be smoothed out – arbitraged – and such a set of prices would become truly globalized, fully commodities. The Black-Scholes model, published in 1973, did just this. Indeed, in one sense, we do not have to conclude that Black-Scholes actually did solve this problem – turning apples into oranges, perhaps even lead into gold – we only have to conclude that in the apparently unregulated derivatives trading climate of the eighties the model was universally believed to have resolved this problem. Lanchester (2008: 10) writes, 'Within months, traders were using equations and vocabulary straight out of Black-Scholes ... and the worldwide derivatives business took off like a rocket.'[32] In fact, most traders did not have to master the niceties of the model itself since software programmes made it possible to apply the model without grappling with its workings (Sassen 2008: 350). So while this particular model allows for what one author calls a kind of 'market Esperanto' (MacKenzie 2008a: 25), permitting people to discuss often quite different situations[33] in a mutually intelligible language, what it referred to often remained obscure.

Models also served another purpose. They acted either as a substitute for the history of a situation, or the absence of the 'relevance' of history (cf. Ouroussoff 2012). Imagine, for example, that we are talking about the possible bankruptcy of General Motors against which various packages of derivatives are being sold. Such an event is so 'big' that there is no useful history that would help us to make a 'rational' decision. Models, then, can stand in for the qualitative elements of histories: a mathematics of the future stands in for the non-comparability of the specificity of the past.

If uncertainty, exposure and volatility need to be counteracted, then derivatives rely on a form of 'planning', specifically the securitizing of risk, based on modelling.[34] Yet modelling, like the discipline of economics itself, is always vulnerable to its own hubris – a kind of disciplinary imperialism. The very value of economic models depends on their claims to account for an ever wider swathe of variables. We see this especially clearly in the case of another kind of model designed to help with a different kind of problem.

Imagine that you are a bank holding corporate bonds – contracts in which a company undertakes to pay a fixed interest to the bearer. Unlike an equity, the interest or dividend is not now based on the growth potential of the company, so much as on its collateral – what it would be worth if all of its assets had to be sold in the event of default. In order to cover yourself against over exposure to such a risk, you can pay others to take on the risks of the loans you have made by selling them on as packages (called Collateralized Debt Obligations or CDOs). The price paid for such packages is greatly dependent on the ratings the packages are given by companies that make a living from assigning them scores (such as Standard & Poor's, or Moody's).[35] Again, models are used for this purpose. One variable will be the extent to which a default might be an isolated event (resulting, let us say, from the bad management of a company) or a result of something affecting the whole sector of which the business is a part. This is referred to as a correlation, and again there is a model that claims to assess the degree of correlation (The single-factor Gaussian copula model [MacKenzie 2008a: 24]). Clearly, in a relatively healthy economy, we would expect these kinds of clusters to be quite isolated from one another, but one way to think of a generalized economic crisis is when they begin to get connected up, one cluster having a knock-on effect on others. Put another way, when the overall economy begins to go to pot the clusters being modelled lose their independent integrity. As the increasing waves of hitherto external variables rush in, the ability of the models to capture the reality deteriorates. As this becomes evident in market sentiment so specialists have less and less faith in what such a model might be telling them. Yet here the wave can become tidal because, as we have seen, the models are the only language with which specialists can talk to each other about very different things. But what the 'words' in this Esperanto actually mean become ever more tenuous, and model and reality part company.[36] The value of the derivative package is shaky – simply because the variables have now become so widespread.

It is extremely misleading to speak of the neoliberal regulation of the individual subject as 'the self-regulating subject' as though Freud had crept into the game. A more heuristically useful exercise is to identify the new means for regulating the world that displace much of the managerial planning that took place in social institutions. This disappearing of 'society', if you will, gives the appearance of the individual unmediated by the social. The subject has not been set free from a sense of embeddedness in society by neoliberal ideology. The issue has to do with the operational field necessary for the reproduction of finance capital as I have described it here and, of course, a vast array of extensions thereof. Loosened from the tethers of any one state, global finance has produced instruments which have broken out of the kinds of regulation that could be carried out by any one state. This in turn has meant the need for some instruments to be found within that system itself. Early derivatives could serve this purpose but they created their own logic of and for capital – requiring new forms. On each occasion what we see is a fundamental contradiction in the sense that instruments that do one thing either do its opposite themselves, or generate further instruments for that purpose, and so on.

I will discuss the historical conditions that gave rise to this most recent dominance of finance capital in Chapter 6. Suffice it to say here that the earlier ascendance of finance in the first three decades of the twentieth century was halted by the social interventions (and attendant juridical forms) that came into force following 1929. Attempts were made to regulate the financial sector by carving up different elements of its operation, assigning them to different kinds of finance and restricting the overlap among them. In the United States this was achieved in 1933 through the passing of the Glass–Steagall Act. Commercial banks concentrated on investing the deposits of high-street customers so as to pay them 'interest', while investment banks concentrated on underwriting the floatation of equities on the stock market to raise capital for production enterprises, and insurance companies sold policies to offset risk. Laws restricted poaching from one area to another.

From the 1970s however and the end of the gold standard the proliferation of monetary instruments, as we have seen, made obsolete the old distinctions between loans, securities and deposits. Old-style high-street commercial banks especially were pressed to increase their hitherto conservative returns on people's bank deposits as other kinds of financial operations targeted their customers. The security arising from social regulations that enforced separate functions from one type of firm to another could now be achieved by repealing the act. This was so because, it was argued, by breaking up a firm (say a bank or an insurance company) into fire-walled departments, their very different functions would produce security through diversification. This breaking down of older institutions into their functional parts as defined by market performance is a feature of a kind of capitalism that makes profits through transactions. And the fragmenting and diversifying that enhance these possibilities spread well beyond commercial institutions, as I will argue in Chapter 6, to reconstitute the realm of the social in ways that are crucially important for politics and counter-politics.

The purpose of this chapter then has been to provide the intellectual infrastructure that becomes a kind of 'taken for granted' point of view in the chapters that follow. For me, historical materialism must take into account these three moments in the production and transformation of capital: the production of goods through the bringing together of labour and tools controlled by the capitalist; the form these goods take as commodities; and the role finance plays in channelling surpluses.

Notes

1. I write 'economic' in quotation marks here because in fact there is no way to thus separate that part of real people's practices that are supposedly economic from those that are something else.
2. In a later essay, Postone argues:

   > Marx's analysis implies that the overcoming of capital entails more than overcoming the limits of democratic politics that result from systemically grounded exploitation and inequality; it also entails overcoming determinate structural constraints on action, thereby expanding the realm of historical contingency and, relatedly, the horizon of politics. (Postone 2006: 93–110, 96)

3. Postone (1996) argues that it was only the older Marx, from the *Grundrisse* on, that grasped the fact that immanence was a feature of capitalist society, not of transhistorical reality. The younger social evolutionist Marx was replaced by a mature historical specificity Marx.
4. David Harvey's *A Companion to Marx's Capital* (2010) provides a much more detailed introduction and retains the order of *Capital* Vol. I. See also, Chris Harmon's (2009) *Zombie Capitalism: Global Crisis and the Relevance of Marx*.
5. What is proposed here has especially important implications for studies claiming to explore the way capitalism is *experienced* as 'the *culture* of capitalism' apparently separable from the materiality of capital. Such writers commonly accuse Marx of hopeless materialism (suggesting that when Marx turned Hegel on his head, he became a materialist). It is much more fruitful to understand Marx's Capital as a kind of ethnography. As Raymond Williams (1977: 90) notes, 'Marx analysed "capitalist production" in and through its own terms'. Thus perhaps the most damning evidence of Marx's slavish material determinism, the relationship between [economic] base and [ideological] superstructure, Derek Sayer (1979) argues was to draw attention to what anthropologists would call bourgeois emic categories, not to assert a set of transhistorical concepts (see also Postone 1996).

   As is often noted, Marx begins his study of *Capital* with a discussion of the commodity which is simultaneously a fictional idea and an inescapable (and material) fact. Because Marx began as a continental Hegelian whereas I am assuming that most of my readers begin as dogged Anglo-Saxon analysts, I have reversed his order of presentation. But these peculiarities of the commodity were fundamental to his understanding of capitalism and make understandings of ideology as uniquely a form of (individual or collective) subjectivity incoherent. 'Production thus not only creates an object for the subject', Marx noted in the *Grundrisse*, 'but also a subject for the object' (Marx 1973: 92).

6. The term 'transformed' needs to be used here with caution. A full transformation would mean a change in the fundamental relations of capital (see Postone 2012).

7. Social reproduction is often used as distinct from production – for example, the latter taking place in factories, while the former takes place in families and households and has to do with the [re-] production of the social persons who arrive at the factory gates. I do not here use the expression in this way. Rather I use it to draw attention to the transgenerational nature of the circuit of production-exchange-consumption.

8. This reflects Braudel's (1982: 228) distinction between market economy and capitalism, a distinction retained by Wolf (1982). It is not however the way in which the word is commonly used in everyday language. There 'capital' is any asset that generates a rate of return (as in this case the money has for the merchant, but the pot and corn have not for the artisan and peasant, making the merchant a 'capitalist', something that neither Braudel nor Wolf would accept. The problem with this usage is that, first, it would mean that any society in which there was an intermediary in an exchange might be called capitalist; and second, it implies that inanimate objects carry within them the ability to generate value (see the entry 'Capital' in Bottomore et al. 1983). Marx's point was that it was only the commodity 'labour power' that could generate value. Why this is so becomes clearer in the discussion that follows.

9. This actual rate can only be established through socially generalized exchange of items valued through an open market as 'commodities'. We will come to this in a moment, but it is for this reason that it can be argued that exploitation *strictu sensu* is only possible through the commodity form.

10. As well as a vast array of services that make this process possible.

11. Raymond Williams (1977: 33) criticizes Marx for his remark that a piano maker is a 'productive' worker, but a pianist is not, suggesting that to take any other position ends up with a kind of bourgeois materialism that leaves us with a base and superstructure. The problem that Williams seeks to address here has to do with an expansive understanding of the word 'production' on the one hand, which both Williams and I would agree is the one best suited to Marx's epistemology (one which would include 'creativity', for example), and 'productivity' on the other. Of course the piano would be of no value to society were there no workers called 'pianists' to give it a use through their concrete labour. But the point here is that the pianist performs the task of *realizing* the value of the piano as a commodity through her abstract labour.

   Shifting away from the actual relations involved, Marx made an observation that perhaps would have been less troubling to Williams: '[A] schoolmaster is a productive labourer, when, in addition to belabouring the heads of his scholars, he works like a horse to enrich the school proprietor. That the latter has laid out his capital in a teaching factory, instead of a sausage factory, does not alter the relation' (Marx 1976: 644).

12. We see this in popular discourse. We find nothing odd in the expression, 'General Motors is in dispute with its workers', despite the fact that 90 per cent of the population in a GM factory is the workers.

13. The logic described here becomes problematic in conditions discussed in Chapter 6.

14. Sticking with the definition of exploitation we are using here, it will be clear that another way to increase its rate would be the sweatshop solution: not to improve machinery but to sweat more labour out of the workers, through longer hours and increased use of violent means, for intensifying the work done in each hour.

15. The contrast here of course is the simple reproduction described by use of the Peruvian example. In fact, in the last part of that example, we saw a moment when the seeds of expanded reproduction could be planted. All households were obliged to divide up their labour between the household plot and work on the communal land. I suggested that some households might hold back their family labour from the *faena*, finding it beneficial to use that labour on the household plot and pay a fine to the community for non-compliance.

Holding back labour in this way would be especially beneficial if the household owned some means of production not available to the communal work team, such as a small mechanical tiller or a concrete irrigation ditch. This in turn would make the household more productive than either the community *faena* as a whole or the average productivity of all the neighbouring households: land, tools and labour in this household produce more value. The increase in value makes it possible for such a household to expand by buying less-productive land from others, resulting in polarization (Lenin 1956).

16. This inherent polarization Marx described as follows: 'The worker becomes poorer the more wealth he produces, the more his production increases in power and extent. The worker becomes an ever-cheaper commodity the more commodities he produces' (Marx 1967: 39).

17. The early years of social theory in Europe, from the turn of the century to the beginning of the Second World War, can hardly have given much empirical evidence for the notion that social cohesion resulted from some form of consensus!

18. Marx began his life fascinated by ideology, but as he took flight from 'the misty realm of religion' towards 'a critique of political economy', he ceased to resort to explanations in which 'the products of the human brain appear as autonomous figures endowed with a life of their own' (1976: 165), and he never used either the term 'class consciousness' or the evaluative term 'false consciousness'. Indeed he slipped into a playful way of writing when discussing other writers' dependence on the notion, skewering in the process, the hubris of intellectuals vis-à-vis ordinary people. 'Let us liberate them from the chimeras, the ideas, the dogmas, imaginary beings under the yoke of which they are pining away … Let us teach men, says one, to exchange these imaginations for thoughts which correspond to the essence of man, says the second, to take up a critical attitude toward them says a third … Once upon a time a valiant fellow had the idea that men were drowned in water only because they were possessed with the *idea of gravity*. If they were to knock this idea out of their heads … they would be sublimely proof against any danger from water' (Marx and Engels 1970: 23–4).

A number of writers have argued that Marx made a radical shift in his early (Hegelian) ontology in the latter part of his career, most notably Althusser. As noted above, I follow the position taken variously by Williams (1977), Sayer (1979) and Postone (1996) that the epistemology Marx employs in his later work is best understood as a series of ethnographic concepts appropriate for the study of mid-nineteenth-century capitalism.

19. In providing a rather succinct discussion of the commodity and fetishism I have ironed out many of the complexities. Rubin's discussion, 'Marx's Theory of Commodity Festishism' in his 1928 book remains unsurpassed. A more sophisticated discussion than my own can be found in Harvey 2010: 15–53.

20. I need to add 'the commodity sphere' because there are many activities, such as the child-rearing and home care that produce and maintain the worker which are essential to the production of this commodity but are either not themselves commodified or are commodified in highly complex ways. In Chapter 6, I refer to these as 'complexly commodified relations'. A number of writers have noted that a feature of contemporary capitalism is the extension of the commodity sphere into a wide arena of hitherto non-commodified social spaces from the public arenas of the city, to health care and education, and to what becomes a second nature. See inter alia: Lefebvre 1970; Smith 1984; Harvey 2003, 2005.

21. '[While] not creating a permanent connection between them … these *momentary and discontinuous* transactions, taken as a whole, have to maintain the *constancy and continuity* of the social process of production' (Rubin [1928] 1973: 16. Italics in original)

22. The remainder of this section is especially indebted to Balibar 1995, Chapter 3.

23. I recognize that 'sociality' is an awkward word. But there are problems with terms like 'the subject', 'the person', 'the agent' etc., which I wish to avoid at this point.

24. This is not to say that they will in fact be so. Hence simply refusing to 'act thus' is itself a kind of resistance to the dominance of this kind of society.
25. By Bentham, Marx meant to refer to the idea that the greater good might be achieved were all *individuals* to pursue their own interests.
26. It is this understanding of our expression as social being entirely as praxis that gives a very catholic meaning to the notion 'production' – a kind of human activity broader than the material or the economic. Production in this sense may simply be a sub-category of human practice, but in being an especially fruitful one it is the baseline of humans as the makers of their own history. Moreover if the essence of man is expression-through-practice over time – 'As individuals express themselves so they are' (Marx and Engels 1970: 32) – then there really is no bedrock essence of man, rather it is constantly a function of history. Hence, as Marx shifted his interest from ideology to commodity fetishism, he was no longer concerned with an essence of man that became alienated in some way; there was no 'natural man' that some epiphany might take us back to.
27. Note that 'capital' here is being used in the way I hitherto criticized.
28. Bryan and Rafferty (2006) make a convincing argument that the possibilities for regulating financial markets through state or state-like institutions is extremely limited: the task of Sysyphus in fact. For evidence of some of the issues, see MacKenzie 2013.
29. It is worth noting that he is not entirely 'unexposed'. His stocks may not increase at all. They may even go *down* 50 per cent.
30. If he was in fact using the capital of his employer (a hedge fund or bank) he may even be given one of those exorbitantly big year-end bonuses – and may even think he earned it.
31. The reason such items are available is because different counterparties have different needs, the trader acting as an intermediary between them – a transport company wishing to hedge against a rise in oil prices, an oil company wishing to hedge against a drop in the price and the trader offering the service that allows both parties to be satisfied.
32. Black-Scholes was initially used for a rather more mundane version of cross-local heterogeneity. While throughout the world arbitrage trading took place daily between one currency and another – and indeed the entire justification for the practice is to retain across the globe a flexible relationship among currencies – the model was able to identify so accurately the value of one currency against another that minute gains could be made simply by trading on the 'sticky-ness' of currency trades in the multiple sites across the world – with the promise of there being no risk involved.
33. Different 'situations' both in geographical terms – exchanges of local conditions on opposite sides of the globe, and in sectoral terms – exchanges among market sectors understood by one set of specialists but less so by another.
34. For the way in which models have been extended to 'scenario planning' well beyond the financial sector, see Cooper 2010. She writes, 'In the era of capital market liberalization, political and economic power lies in the art of leveraging the event, of harnessing debt accumulation to determine the shape of possible future worlds' (2010: 181). For an equally provocative (and troubling) extension of financial modelling, see Haldane and May 2011.
35. Conflict of interest meant that the accuracy of these ratings came into question after the 2008 crisis since sellers of CDO packages were actually paying the fees of ratings companies to rate the packages they were selling. Far from regulating against the possibility of a bubble, they were themselves inflating it. Subsequently, fearing the economic chaos that would result, sovereign states used their resources to save key sectors of finance capital. Partly as a result of this move, by late 2011 ratings agencies were downgrading their sovereign debts. When the accuracy of such ratings was questioned, given the failure of ratings agencies three years earlier, they responded by referring precisely to the fragmentation of a company into isolated functions that their risk models had produced. Alluding to the assumptions underlying the repeal of Glass–Steagall, they said that the conduct of one department had no effect on that of another because they

were walled off from one another: the CDO raters had no connection with the sovereign debt raters.

It is quite staggering that the conflict of interest of ratings agencies has not produced more media scandal or political enquiry. As early as 1896, another era of high finance, the risk of ratings agencies manipulating ratings for the benefit of those who paid them was seriously questioned. 'For instance, if they were associated with credit insurers, would not rating agencies be encouraged to give low grades so that credit insurance would be more profitable?' (Flandreau 2013: 42).

36. It is this threshold moment that encourages discussions about the 'performativity' of statements in economics. Are economic models constative statements that do the best they can to describe what 'is' and hence serve a useful if limited purpose? Or do economic models become so pervasive a feature of knowledge about the social world that the world is folded into what they say. While this is a useful discussion to have, the point I am stressing here brings in the issue of temporality and faith (cf. Guyer 2007). The performativity effect of economic models may be punctured at unpredictable moments when their claims to be accurate descriptions lack aura.

PART II

Scales of History and Politics

– Chapter 2 –

THE SCALES OF ETHNOGRAPHY
Periodizing Spatial Coherence in Early-Twentieth-Century Spain

e~っ

> It is necessary ... to reconsider relations between places and transplace or supraplace organizational forms and, finally, across national boundaries, to imagine alternative possibilities in the reorganization of spaces. Such alternatives may be novel products of contemporary circumstances or they may draw upon and rework ... earlier organizational forms that have been marginalized and condemned to oblivion by modernist regimes.
> – Arif Dirlik, 'Place-based Imagination: Globalism and the Politics of Place'

The Problem of Place

Over the past decade, 'ethnography' has spread beyond its home in anthropology to become a popular form of research for the social sciences generally, the latter joining history where its attraction has been more long standing (Sider and Smith 1997).[1] There is no question that this recent popularity is the result of the limitations of macro accounts in capturing the complexity and heterogeneity of contemporary social formations as well as the sense that the causal force of global interlinkages anyway limits the value of 'methodological nationalism' (Beck 2002; Wimmer and Glick Schiller 2002). Yet, there remains a certain irony in the fact that this attraction is growing at just the time when an older assumption – that people's identity with a place was obvious – is more and more difficult to sustain (Gupta and Ferguson 1997). My own experience seems quite symptomatic of the issue.

The idea of ethnography among the people who trained me in social anthropology was that you went to a place – it could be a Johannesburg slum, a highland village in Nepal, or a tin mine in Bolivia – you found some people there and you studied their social relations (if you were American, you studied their 'culture'). In many cases, you found yourself actually having to study elsewhere too of course. George Marcus (1998), notwithstanding multi-sited fieldwork, was in fact more the rule than the exception a long time ago. But the point is that within this rather taken-for-granted protocol, the *association of people with a place* was pretty much assumed. Even if people migrated, what they did was leave one place and go to another place, possibly to many other places. As we shall see in subsequent chapters, in the case of my fieldwork with the huasicanchinos of central Peru, there would be little provocation to examine this assumption – since they shared it. They called themselves by the name of the local area, they were engaged in a violent struggle against others over the place, and they were quite nasty to people who they thought had no claim to belong to it – not just the nearby haciendas but neighbouring communities too.

Some years later, however, I began to study people in the Bajo Segura region, south of Alicante in Spain. The question that drew me to these people reveals the plasticity of collective sentiments revolving around 'place'. It was provoked by the Peruvian experience. The question that had arisen in Peru was how migrants in the slums and shanty towns of Lima, the mines of La Oroya, and the coca fields of the high jungle were all drawn into the land recuperation struggle, despite their dispersal and their extremely varied occupations. It was this that drew me to ask what some kind of working class consciousness would look like where the industrial working people had never been concentrated in mass production factories and had never been 'freed' (as Marx put it) from their ties to land. This is why I chose this region of Spain, which had a long history of dispersed manufacturing activity threaded through farming.

Yet increasingly, as I began to do the research with these people, the issue of 'place' seemed to be problematic. This is not to say that the sentiments of belonging to a place or the materiality of 'place-ness' in terms of work sites and circuits of the economy were not relevant. This was not some society of flows, some marvellous network floating untied to place or space, as Castells (1996) and numerous others would suggest. The problem was that 'place-ness' mattered, but it was by no means as obvious as it had been in Peru.

When I first began working in this area in the 1980s it had many of the features of what people like Castells and Portes were calling 'the informalization' of Western economies (Castells and Portes 1988). Labour-intensive irrigated horticulture – artichokes, melons, tomatoes and citrus fruits – took up many people's labour, with further activities in the shoe and carpet industries. Perhaps 75 per cent of the agricultural land was in the hands of quite large- and medium-sized farmers who relied on day labour. As for industry, factories of perhaps two hundred workers put out work to semi-legal workshops and to women in homework – so a few people had factory jobs, but most worked in small shops or at home. While locally organized, all these activities were crucially tied to the fluctuations of exterior markets for supplies and for sales.

Moreover, prior to this period, multiple factors had served to destabilize the area. Persecution following the Civil War (1936–39) created political factors that exiled people from place, while the black-market economy of the 1940s and 1950s, with its plundering possibilities for the victors and its haphazard volatility for working people, produced their own instabilities. The migration that resulted did not take on the institutionalized and vaguely predictable characteristics that I had found in Peru (Smith 1984) but instead was both wrenching and haphazard. One elderly woman for example told me of her father's experience migrating for agricultural work in neighbouring provinces:

> They went once in winter and once in summer. In winter it was for the pruning of the vines (*la poda*). A few went, ten maybe twelve. It was work for those who understood how to do it. More went in summer, in June and July, if they had previously got work there. Just 2 or 3 months, although some who went for the pruning stayed on (*en la siega* [*sic*]), and were there for 8 or 9 months. [Fieldnotes 1978] (Narotzky and Smith 2006: 42)

Throughout the 1950s and 1960s, and well into the few years before my fieldwork, people found jobs off and on in Germany and France as well.

Even when locality did appear to be an important factor in the economy, as happened in the latter years of my fieldwork, it was imposed from outside when, together with a number of other areas in the European Union, it became part of development strategies to produce 'regional economies' – clustered small-scale units whose dynamism supposedly was closely tied to features of 'the local culture'. Local people's sense that with appropriate strategizing something, somehow could be gained from manipulation of this newly imposed place-ness however resulted more in puzzlement than a suddenly rediscovered sense of local identity.

And yet, in a sense, and looking back to past eras, there was nothing entirely new about this external forming of the contours of local spatiality. In the final chapter of *The Country and the City* (1973), Raymond Williams captures quite well the sense of what I am saying here when he refers to a 'response to a whole way of life largely determined elsewhere' (ibid.: 290):

> [[W]hen forces that will alter our lives are moving all around us in apparently external and unrecognizable forms, we can retreat, for security, into a deep subjectivity, or we can look around us for social pictures, social signs, social messages, to which, characteristically, we try to relate as individuals but so as to discover some kind of community. Much of the content of modern communications is this kind of substitute for directly discoverable and transitive relations to the world. It can be properly related to the scale and complexity of modern society ... [This] *unevenly shared consciousness of persistently external events ... is then a specific form of consciousness which is inherent in the dominant mode of production, in which, in remarkably similar ways, our skills, our energies, our daily ordering of our lives, our perceptions of the shape of a lifetime, are to a critical extent defined and determined by external formulations of a necessary reality*: that external, willed reality – external because its means are in minority hands – from which, in so much of our lives, we seem to have no option but to learn. (Williams 1973: 295–96. Italics added)

Williams' admonitions here notwithstanding, the tendency in anthropology and cognate disciplines like cultural studies has been to explore the ephemeral nature of place in our lives in almost uniquely experiential terms. The world is on the move, it is said; things, people and symbols are caught up in so much movement and plasticity that the sense of space and place is experienced in entirely new ways. In another version it is often then suggested that, restrospectively, perhaps ethnography was always distorted – amalgamating cultural identity with locality, as I have noted above. While it is always heuristically useful to challenge the assumptions of our ancestors, there is something about this cultural determinist version of modernist teleology that is eerily similar to the distaste for local sentiment – the insistence that it should pass – that was a characteristic of republican rationalism in the state-building projects of the nineteenth century (see, for example, Weber 1976).

The most influential in the cultural determination of place and space has been Appadurai (1996), for whom people's *experience* of space is decisive, the various folk-imaginations of space (ideoscapes, ethnoscapes, etc.) becoming primary foci. 'The only processes allowed to be determinative are cultural ones concerning the flux of feeling. The overdetermining and equally dynamic processes of economic and political geographies thereby [are obscured] by his overweening account of the imagination' (Sparke 2006: 65). When history is alluded to it is always a teleological history and one experienced homogeneously by all. When new kinds of understandings of place and space appear to arise they are said to be the result of 'deterritorialization' – itself the result of 'globalization' – making the argument circular. Denied a periodization of the social formation in terms of what I would call a 'realist history', the quite specific ways in which current capitalist and state forms reconfigure space are left unaddressed.

So what Williams insists we note has been lost here: that is, the way in which people's sense of how their physical situatedness relates to a broader field of spatiality and their conversations about the shifting shape of place, are related to the historically changing political economy in which they are found. 'The task is therefore twofold', as Claudio Lomnitz-Adler notes: 'On the one hand we need to explore the "political economy" of regional culture … and on the other we must explore the relationship between space and ideology' (Lomnitz-Adler 1991: 196). Yet here Lomnitz-Adler is speaking of a relatively identifiable and coherent 'region';[2] but in my case, since the degree of coherence of the region as a distinctive political economy is itself in question, we need to explore the ways in which a broader arena of social reproduction has, through history, given rise to changing articulations of spatial scale (Friedman and Friedman 2008a, 2008b).[3] Only then can the profound complexity of people's sense of space and place be understood.

The challenge then, is to try to connect up the habitus of place-ness as it was accumulated through 'experienced history', and the 'material history' that shaped the articulation of spatial scales. In many ways this is quite reminiscent of the way Eric Wolf understood the shaping of different kinds of rural communities in Mexico (Wolf 1956, 1957. See also Carbonella 2005). There he set out to understand these 'communities as outcomes and determinants of historical processes; to visualize these processes as intimately connected with changes in the wider economic and political field; and to understand cultural structures as growing out of these involvements over time rather than in terms of culture content' (Wolf 2001: 161). Wolf argued that the character of the geographically situated social relations of the closed corporate community arose in response first to the *hacendado* power bloc and subsequently, as a result of a broader array of forces, to the building of the post-colonial Mexican state. In a similar spirit, Winnie Lem has used Robert Brenner's (1985) discussion of the French case in his study of the transition from feudalism to capitalism to show how the role of the French state conditioned the historical formation of rural politics in Languedoc (Lem 1997, 1998).

The way in which such studies insist that the character of what Wolf calls 'cultural structures' to be found in our ethnographic field sites emerge out of the tensions and outcomes of history over a wider terrain provide a useful starting point for rethinking ethnography, place and space in Spain. What they show is the way in which fields of force through time give rise to compacting collectivities of people – something conventionally referred to as 'communities'.[4] But I need something a little more. I need to think about how place-ness can become an instrument for or against particular collectivities of people, and I need to periodize the waxing and waning of the differing conditionalities at a broad scale that make possible openings for sustained practices at a narrower scale. As a result I find that the kind of historical political economy of Wolf, Mintz and those who followed in their footsteps can usefully be enhanced by perspectives embedded in a similar intellectual and political tradition, but arising in geography.

We do not have to move back too far in time to note how the Keynesian national welfare state was organized in terms of nested scaler units, from the central planning state to its regions, municipalities and so on; and then to note how current forms of the state have off-loaded many items of planning and have prioritized *competition* between regions over the *coordination* of regions to offset the distributional shortcomings of the capitalist economy (Jessop 2008). Shifts in the way different scales articulate with one another in this way then clearly become an important question for the historical periodization of space and place in a given setting.

Neil Smith's (1984) original study of uneven development showed how economies – in fact capitalist economies – must on the one hand overcome the stickiness of place, facilitating movement; and on the other hand contour physical sites in the production of what he called a 'second nature'. David Harvey (1982) referred to something similar in terms of the 'spatial fixes' capitalism uses, like a heroin addict, to resolve ongoing tensions and contradictions. This contouring of social and physical space as a result of the contingencies of capitalist reproduction in a given social formation are not some kind of bedrock on which culture arises, rather they are part and parcel of the practices – habituated and inventive – that give rise to the experience of place (or its absence).[5]

Such a framework would involve periodizing the way in which social and economic reproduction, through time, generate different articulations between various scales of a social formation. This is a difficult and time-consuming task and certainly not one immediately attractive to the scholar who through temperament has chosen to do ethnographic work. But what is relevant to the enquiry, our competence to undertake its study, and our inclination to do so, do not necessarily nicely match up. Meanwhile all the indications are that in the contemporary world ethnography does need to problematize the ephemeral ways in which place-ness morphs from one shape to another. And not just overall – in a rather general and vague sense – but appearing to be of urgent moment at one time in terms of collective sentiment, at another in terms of economic strategy and still another in terms of the exercise of power. In what follows I try to begin such an exercise because I think the urgency of the task requires at least a first step. Nonetheless, by the very way in which I have framed the problem, it is obvious that I can only offer a highly abbreviated version of what would be a more thorough examination.

The Framework

In different periods of the Spanish political economy, overarching institutions of economy and regulation resulted in scales of spatial coherence. It should be possible to identify periods when forms of the economy and institutions of regulation induced such patterns. And it should also be possible to note breaks in the trajectory of a pattern with shifts in features of the economy and breaks from one regulatory regime to another, while also making ourselves aware of the path-dependency one period brings to its successor.

Throughout the nineteenth century in Europe there was a tension between the building of a modern state on the basis of the national-popular, in which the state becomes the condensation of popular sovereignty, and what Henri Lefebvre (2001: 774–75, also 1977) called the 'productivist' state, in which 'the State takes charge of growth, whether directly or indirectly'. For many European states there was a growing tension between the state as the condensation of popular will and the state as enhancer of national productivity – the latter increasingly, if unevenly, through capitalist production. The way this tension worked itself out varied from one state to another. In Chapter 6, I will use this tension between *demos* and *tecnos* to expose changing features of recent forms of capitalism and regulation. Here I use it as part of a framework to get at historical changes in the articulation of scales in Spain.

Lefebvre was concerned with the spatial implications of a social formation seen in this way. Along similar lines, David Harvey (1982: 422) refers to 'nested hierarchical structures of organization which can link the local and particular with the achievement of abstract labour on the world stage'. In his early work Harvey focused especially on how the relationship between fixed and mobile capital gives rise to relatively coherent, provisionally stabilized territorial configurations. Neil Smith was especially clear about how this produced different scales within a social formation:

> the drive toward universality under capitalism brings only limited equalization of levels and conditions of development. Capitalism produces distinct spatial scales – absolute spaces – within which the drive toward equalization is concentrated. But it can do this only by an acute differentiation and continued redifferentiation of relative space, both between and within scales. The scales themselves are not fixed but develop (growing pangs and all) within the development of capitalism itself ... But the necessity of discrete scales and of their internal differentiation is fixed. (Neil Smith 1984: 147)

Smith's early work tended to stress the logic of capitalism at the expense of the way the political forces produced by the conflicts and alliances of capitalism also invoke scale. Regional class alliances, for example, are only made possible by a prior setting of spatial coherence, but then themselves become factors as '[r]egional difference reduces internal competition among producers in favour of cooperation, while it increases external competition at the expense of cooperation' (Smith and Dennis 1987: 168).[6] What Eric Wolf helped us to do was to see the production of spaces of, and in, the state as the effect of a series of successful or failed power bloc formations. Grafting Smith's observations onto this insight, highlights the way in which the formation of *regional* class blocs play a role in the way different scales of a social formation are articulated. Lefebvre's (2001) 'provisional stabilization' of spheres of spatial coherence are first the result of attempts to manage productivity at different scales of the national geography, but they then take on further form as a result of struggles within and between scales.

In Spain the continual failure of a 'state-productivist' project was a direct result of the particular way in which the demos/tecnos tension played itself out. Autocratic projects to enhance production had as their primary goal precisely the offsetting of popular sovereignty, and this in turn produced a particular configuration of scales.

Beginning after the loss of the last colonies in 1898 with the group of intellectuals and politicians known as the 'Regenaracionistas', technicist interventions in Spain's geography were projected to enhance her physical 'nature' so as to improve her social nature without any significant readjustment of the class structure. Whether full-blown projects, integral ideologies or piecemeal reactions to crises, they all shared the goal of finding fixes that would obviate the need for thoroughgoing social reform, let alone revolution. Periods in the Spain of the twentieth century can be understood in terms of changing packages of 'fixes' in Harvey's sense, beginning with the period immediately following 1898.

The Scales of Autocratic Governance

To begin with, it is important to note that right up to 1960 Spain was a predominantly agricultural country. So attempts on the part of a state in pursuit of modernity to enhance productivity meant, for most of the last century, the productivity of agriculture.[7] This is especially important for questions of spatiality, because there are features of agriculture that make its role in 'place-making' quite particular.

First, agriculture is fixed to place, not just in the cultural sense, but essentially in the physical, topographical sense. This explains why, for southern Spain, the delicate health of the nation-state was configured as a question of Spain's deficient geography; specifically its perpetual thirst for water. Hence, second, if state productivity meant agriculture, then agriculture meant hydraulic engineering. Thus the great regeneracionista Joaquin Costa remarked, 'To irrigate is to govern' (quoted in Swyngedouw 1999: 456). So we see from the outset how closely the pursuit of a productivist state was tied up with notions of physical space and what Neil Smith (1984) calls 'the second nature'. But to these we must add a third factor. The low productivity of Spanish agriculture was, in fact, profoundly an issue of social structure, one in which the access to the means of violence by dominant regional class fractions was the principal factor shaping social relations of production.

So we should expect these three intertwined elements to play off one another in the constitution of place: first, the materiality of place in agricultural; second, at the broad level of the state as a whole, the association of good governance with interventions in physical geography; and third, at the scale of profit-seeking enterprises, the use of force for regulating labour. So if we are to note the importance in Spain of both autocratic rule and the pursuit of productivity, then we need also to note that the one generates contradictions within the other and these contradictions produce spatial configurations. Attempts to enhance the national project at the level of the state through technology may generate problems at regional levels, where profits are enhanced not through technical advances but through increasing the level of violence for the extraction of absolute surplus value from labour.

At the broader scale we might say that progressives initiate and reactionaries react. The century opened with the regeneracionista debates in the early part of the century. These were debates among progressive political intellectuals who sought to marry technical engineering projects to some form of popular education. Because they never received the endorsement of a class bloc, their initiatives largely remained on the drawing board; still less were they able to turn their projects into state programmes. When remnants of regeneracionista proposals did become part of the state's agenda, it was during the long reactionary periods of dictatorships (briefly interrupted by the Republic from 1930 to 1936) when technicist adventures arose, not as idealistic proposals but rather as piecemeal responses to the crises resulting from the low productivity of primitive labour conditions. Paraphrasing Polanyi's (1957: 141) famous remark, we might say that during these periods an autocratic state was planned, a technicist state was not. For this reason, we need to be careful to distinguish between these often fatuously ambitious projects to manage uncertainty by producing a 'second nature' and the actual historical emergence of that built landscape. Thus Vilar (1977: 68) notes that little research was done to back up Joaquín Costa's early-twentieth-century irrigation programme, while even by the time of Primo de Rivera's dictatorship in the 1920s, '[t]he plans stayed on paper and the [irrigation] *Confederaciones* were covered with the same discredit as the dictatorship itself' (ibid.: 88).

In fact Vilar also ascribes failure to the fact that the state was weak and local vested interests got in the way of these programmes. Given my interest in the articulation of scales within the social formation, I want to be more specific about 'local vested interests' by referring to the area to the south of Alicante, where I have done my own fieldwork. For the century from 1860 to 1960 this was an area where one commercial crop succeeded another: silk-worm cultivation and silk-spinning; vines into wine; hemp into ship's sails, ropes, nets, sandals and rugs; and citrus fruits, above all oranges.

Two things are striking about these products. First, unlike some of the poorer regions of Spain, all of these goods were produced for external markets – the broader national market and, crucially, international markets.[8] This meant that the region's economy was an especially 'open' one and, unlike Catalunya, in Valencia (of which Alicante is the southern province) no power bloc had been successfully formed to handle this. Openness to national and international markets gave especially good value-added to state-directed infrastructure improvements in this region, from port facilities at Alicante for the international market, to railway and road construction for the national market.

Second, all of these agricultural crops, except citrus fruits, involved some form of on-site processing prior to sale, giving rise to a complex interweaving of agricultural and non-agricultural labour processes with their attendant forms of organization and skill. It was around the class issues related to this labour process that the politics of place was played out. Broadly speaking most of the best land was controlled by large owners, while perhaps 30 per cent was occupied by smaller farmers often dependent in one form or another on the larger owners,[9] plus a large day-labour population.

As this infrastructure increased so too did the potential for people to move around in the 1920s and the elite responded by fetishizing place, giving it unique, even atavistic characteristics. To do so they invoked an ideology of local autonomy which was patently a mystification given the reliance of the region on external markets and the benefits it derived from the advantages of better communications. As towns in the region, such as Alcoy, Elche and Elda, shifted from artisan to manufacturing production, their demand for labour made the threat of outward movement quite real. And as infrastructural advances did occur – albeit unevenly and, by the standards of other European countries, rather pathetically – these tensions increased, with greater movement putting pressure on the need for a defensive response on the part of the agricultural elite.

One kind of development literature might see this in terms of a modernizing project that fails in the face of the backward 'traditions' of a region, yet notions of tradition seem to obscure more than they reveal. Another kind of literature might shift quickly into a discussion of the tensions between the regional elite culture and national programmes of rule in terms of conflicting discursive practices. But again I think this allows us to skip over a more complex understanding in terms of antagonistic fields of force that arise out of the specific spatial contours of the political economy. After all we are discussing here autocratic rule at the national scale and selective violence at the regional scale. To leap immediately to issues of discourse at this point would be to give undue weight to discourse's determinative role.

Instead we need to uncover a series of articulated elements in a social formation, and I am defining a 'modern' social formation as one in which national productivity becomes central to state programmes.

This means that we have to think of the scales in the social formation in terms of different forms of capital and how these produce different kinds of place-ness. In *The Limits to Capital*, Harvey talks of three circuits of investment, the primary one being that which directly produces surplus value (Capital 1); these are the enterprises to be found in the Bajo Segura and surrounding regions. The secondary refers to investments in the fixed capital of the built environment (Capital 2), that is the Spanish state's encouragement of railway and port building projects and so on; while the tertiary involves investment in such things as education and social welfare (Capital 3), elements starkly absent from the Spanish state's project, as we shall see.

In terms of Capital 2, with the coming to power of Primo de Rivera in the 1920s, and then the destruction of the Second Republic by the Franco dictatorship in 1939, the progressive component of the regeneracionista project to redeem Spain through the mastery of the physical land mass had become entirely corrupted, abandoning entirely even the pretence of investment in Capital 3. At the national scale, grand infrastructural schemes now served these autocratic regimes simply as spectacular images of modernity that obviated the need for real *social* change. Franco is exemplary here. As one highly conventional economic historian notes of Franco with some despair, '[What] political propaganda tried to represent after the fact as a planned sequence of events' had in fact only one unwavering goal, 'to keep the dictator in power at whatever cost' (Tortella 2000: 449). For both dictators, domination through force remained a primary tool of government, providing openings for local-level regulation through selective repression by regional bosses. State endorsement of these techniques allowed heads of enterprises to respond to the pressures of international and national markets – not through the greater productivity of capital but rather by ever more draconian means for the repression of labour. This heavy reliance on labour relative to technical equipment within the sphere of Capital 1 then led to what Lefebvre calls the contradiction between what is 'transient' and what is 'durable' (quoted in Brenner 1998) – in this case the inherent transience of actual labour and the potential durability of fixed capital.

Because actual manual labour could be squeezed tighter and tighter through the whip hand of fear, there was little inducement to invest in material items such as farm machinery or improvements in local irrigation systems, to increase productivity.[10] This in turn affected the physical character of place-ness, shaping the regional landscape. In short, landscape, as a concrete abstraction that silently conditions the possibilities of life, was the historical product of class relations. The local power imbalance meant that collective labour was unable to drive up labour costs to the point where owners would seek a resolution through investment in the means of production. As a result, investments in the fixed environment – roads, railways and so on – advocated by certain class fractions at the level of the state, not only had little effect on this primary sphere of investment (specific farms as well as firms processing agricultural produce, especially hemp), but, by advancing communications, they actually intensified the violent means by which local *patrones* sought to restrict the mobility of labour.

Lefebvre, Harvey and Smith each note, in their different ways, the importance for the production of space, of the fixity and mobility of capitals: the distinction between capital-fixed-to-place and freed-up capital. But in this case what we are seeing is the articulation between two different scales of 'fixed' capital. At the broader scale there is some degree of fixed capital in the form of infrastructure. But at the level of the sub-region of the Bajo Segura the almost complete absence of advances in fixed capital – made possible by the legitimizing of local-level violence – meant a reliance on labour, by its nature transient and always potentially mobile. Then the fact that labour was not fixed, as capital could be, meant resistance to anything that would 'unstick' that labour from the locale.

To show how this worked I need to say something about the way in which inherently transient labour power is transformed into durable capital. Actual, concrete labour power is energy that can be used only at the moment that workers engage, through tools, with material. The tools they use today however are the materialization of a previous round of labour. Seen in this way, this kind of capital is like the freezing of the flowing stream of labour into ice cubes of capital that can then be stored away for later use. Put another way, by thus 'alienating' the labour of workers in their possession of the capital tools they produced, the capitalist releases himself not just from some of his organic ties to the worker, but also from the inherently temporal, transitory nature of concrete labour itself. This means that in the ratio of labour to capital, the lower the ratio of capital to labour (a low composition of capital) the more the production process is determined by the temporal and spatial dictates of living labour[ers].

Conversely (that is to say, what *didn't* happen), when surplus is transferred into the primary sphere of investment (tools and machinery, upgraded fields and irrigation ditches) it effectively fixes units of labour power in material tools which allow the capitalist to 'release' the value of that labour, now as capital, whenever he pleases. In this sense Harvey's 'Capital 1' helps to reduce the degree to which production depends on the dictates of labour, both temporally and spatially, the trade-off being the embedding of physical capital in place.

So as one or other of these patterns works itself out through time, the result will be a topographical and social shaping of place. Where *capital* advances in the capital–labour relationship, we see this *physically* in the building of a material landscape of ditches, walls, pathways and fields; where labour advances in the capital–labour relationship we see this *socially* in the sites and institutions of collective labour – syndical halls, places of public sociality, festivals that celebrate those things that enhance human capacity, and so on.

The fact that the dominant class were able to use violence to repress labour meant that they had little incentive to replace that labour through more productive tools. Yet this placed even greater pressure on them to prevent labour from moving to areas where productivity was higher, because they could not replace that lost labour with capital tools. This regional power relationship then, produced a different form of capital to the form of capital at the national scale and, because it relied so heavily on labour – which could so potentially become mobile – it also produced a specific articulation between scales, differences that would be quite visible in the physical landscape in the first half of the twentieth century.

At a broader scale, state projects tended to respond to external international pressures and the persistent threat of internal social upheaval, with technical fixes through investment in the secondary sphere (Capital 2) – the built environment: roads, gigantic hydraulic reconfigurations and schemes for the colonization of supposedly upgraded land. If we try to understand cultures of place-ness in terms of different scales of spatial coherence, the implications when the state seeks greater productivity through investments in this secondary sphere are that capital is embedded in the national territory as a kind of 'second nature'. It is as though autocratic forms of governance that prioritize a technicist, rather than a 'social' path toward modernity, will produce a particular kind of fetishism of the physical geography of the national body. As a parliamentary document of 1912 stated, '[n]ot a single drop of water should reach the Ocean without paying its obligatory tribute to the earth' (quoted in Swyngedouw 1999: 453).

But I have argued that, at least for the Spanish case, it would be a mistake to separate the fixation on technicist solutions from the particular forms of power that go along with it – not a reach for the *demos* through hegemony but essentially rule through naked domination or *force majeur*. Here lies a fundamental contradiction, and this was expressed in the articulation between the national and regional scales.

At the level of what Harvey calls 'Capital 1', the state endorsed regional capitalists' use of personalistic and random fear to control labour. This reduced their need to invest in fixed capital to enhance profits through greater productivity. Instead local capitalists took the route of increasing the extraction of absolute surplus value through actual or threatened violence. This in turn produced a different kind of fetishism of place-ness – now at a narrower scale of spatial coherence and one which was not shaped so much by the fixity of capital in physical place. Rather it was shaped as a result of the particular character of labour, its elusive transientness and the consequent need to fix it in place through an ideology that fetishized local particularism, playing on the 'corruption' that awaited anybody who crossed the nearby horizon into the impure lands beyond the sub-region. To leave was to return a suspect (Narotzky and Smith 2006).

But, at this level of the sub-region, we can move beyond the physical landscape to explore how concrete abstractions play a role in the emergence of social institutions as well. We see this especially clearly in the disputes and discussions that arose during the Republic around the issue of rural labour laws (Narotzky and Smith 2006: 105). Owners of farms sought a relatively flexible labour force that they could hire and fire over the course of the agricultural (and processing) annual cycle – and the ordinary *jornal* (day-labour system) served this purpose quite well. But, by the nature of things, demand for labour, and especially labour with specific agricultural or processing skills, arose at the same time for all local farms.

One way in which this was handled was for owners to use a core of workers who, while remaining day-labourers, nonetheless had some kind of tie to the owner. This arrangement, the *aniaga* (usually the provision of a minimal small plot of land for household consumption), also involved other more personalistic kinds of relationship. The contract between *patron* and family patriarch actually tied all members of the household and possibly other destitute kin into an integral hierarchy of dependence such that the interests of life and work were tied organically to those of the *patron*.

Day-labourers unable or unwilling to enmesh themselves in these kinds of ties faced a slightly ambiguous set of interests. On the one hand they wanted to be free to move from one municipality to another to maximize their opportunities for employment. On the other hand, the profound threading of interpersonal relations and at times even local kinds of labour-capital compacts – what E.P. Thompson (1968) would call a kind of 'moral economy' – promoted an interest in heightening the importance of everybody's loyalty to locality in an attempt to prevent owners from hiring at will beyond the municipality and thereby side-stepping the rigours of this local compact. The result was a perpetual dialogue over the pertinence of place for the shared business of livelihood security. The contradictions of this situation came to a head during the Republic of 1930–36 when the government sought to pass a series of agricultural labour laws that would supposedly protect local pools of labour. *Jornaleros* responded in different areas, depending very much on whether these so-called protections aided the owners in preventing the mobility of workers, or protected workers from owners importing essentially scab labour.

Here we are especially reminded of Williams' insistence on divisions within rural communities. It is not hard to see that – even leaving aside other kinds of divisions, like those between men and women, between young and old and between a scrapbag of trades not mentioned here – *patrones*, *aniagueros* and untied *jornaleros*, through their livelihoods and disputes over the conservation of the conditions that made the specific practices of those livelihoods possible, produced a configuration of place. Some of this was a kind of unintended by-product of the disputes and conversations amongst the actors, and in that sense a kind of shared atmosphere of place. But it is equally clear that quite distinctive senses of place coexisted. The way heads of enterprises that relied on large amounts of low-paid labour employed strategies that hindered workers' movement to the close-by small manufactories gave rise to a highly partial sense of place. Likewise the integral sense of patron-patriarch-family of the *aniagueros* when extended to the broader community invoked a sense of organicism unshared by the untied *jornaleros* who nonetheless themselves invoked their own insistence on the particularity of place in the pursuit of their own form of livelihood.

But these overlapping and conflicted structures of feeling cannot be unmoored from the physical landscape that different people's practices produce. The degree of power held by *patrons* vis-à-vis workers and the form that power took – personalistic, violent and endorsed by the state – gave rise to a particular coefficient in the ratio of capital instruments to living labour. A greater investment in capital would not have prevented disputes between capital and labour of course; it would simply have changed their terms. But the ratio of fixed capital to transient labour produced a certain kind of 'place' that went well beyond what people thought about it, to include both the physical landscape and the embedded social institutions. Taken together within the sub-region, these had the effect of shaping the character of place-ness.

But place-ness is produced in another way too, in the dialectical articulation between scales. As forms of production and forms of regulation at the level of the Bajo Segura achieved their albeit transient coherence through a period of market stability and/or political rigidity, so they came up against the ability to produce a coherent modernist project at the scale of the overall polity through tecnos. This was neither a question of recalcitrant traditional culture versus rationalist modernity, nor regional parochialism versus raison d'état. The features that produced the internal properties of regional place-ness, as well as the specific articulations among scales, were a product of the contradictions of the Spanish State and the country's particular form of primitive capitalism in the first half of the twentieth century.

Conclusion

What does this highly schematic journey through history tell us about ethnography and place? I have voiced a discomfort with anthropological discussions of supposed deterritorialization and the ephemeral nature of contemporary place that rely pre-eminently on cultural sensitivities. I have suggested that Raymond Williams' project in *The Country and the City* and elsewhere in his writings (see Harvey 1996: 19–45; Higgins 1999) was not simply to write about changing cultural dispositions through different epochs, but rather to try to understand those changes by reference to shifts in the political economy. The work of Henri Lefebvre and a number of geographers who wrote after Williams' major work, on the way in which the political economy gives rise to certain kinds of spatial patterns and shifts the way spatial scales of a social formation articulate with one another, makes it possible to think about place in terms of the kind of cultural materialism that Williams advocated.[11] Unlike Bourdieu (e.g. 2000), who was prone to hubristic claims to have overcome some of the perpetual dualisms of social theory, Williams did not purport to have overcome the tensions in materialist versus idealist epistemologies. Rather he asked us to think about the way in which cultural practices and expressions might be framed by and have implications for material elements of the world. The result of such a way of thinking is to oblige us to work against a comfortable compartmentalization of the two, as well as against a temptation to make the one (materialism) or the other (idealism) dominate our epistemology.

Williams himself was a specialist in the study of English [language] literature. I have therefore sought to push beyond his focus by turning to the geographers for balance. In doing so, I may have overcompensated to the discomfort of many of my anthropology and more culturally inclined colleagues. But I think it is not unreasonable to argue that we see in this chapter precisely the kind of cultural materialism that Williams was seeking. I have tried to resist the temptation of placing situated ethnography within a social formation made up of nested scales, in which the fieldworker metaphorically works 'upwards' and 'outwards', and then back again to the site of his/her work. Instead I have argued not just that scales need to be understood dialectically, taking form from an ongoing process of articulation, but that the ways in which that articulation takes place are likely to change with shifts in the form of economy and the regime of regulation.

The understanding of historically produced space in terms of the social relations between people pursuing their livelihoods exposes the interweaving of their varying projects, their individual and collective practices, and the physical world that is formed through history out of those projects and practices, just as it comes to condition them in the present. How we find people and places working upon one another in the present may appear chaotic and ephemeral, as I have noted it was for me when I began my work in the Bajo Segura. But the beginnings of insight will only arise from understanding the specificities of that 'present' in historical terms that attend to this intertwining of the interpreted, practised and physical world.

Notes

1. I use quotation marks here, because what is taken to be ethnography in disciplines like political science and to some extent sociology would often strike anthropologists as rather thin.
2. In a sense Lomnitz-Adler's problematic is the reverse of my own, since he finds a sense of region and seeks to account for it; I find the sense of region uncertain and need to understand using the lens of historical realism.
3. What I here call 'changing articulations of spatial scale' is one of the key components of the 'critical junctions perspective' proposed by Don Kalb. See especially Kalb 2005.
4. The assumption I make here is that within any 'community' there is division and a variation in consciousness that goes along with the variation in lived, worked and

propertied worlds. 'In the village as in the city there is division of labour, there is the contrast of social position, and then necessarily there are alternative points of view' (Williams 1973: 166). We do not therefore speak of the broader forces that give rise to local community as consensual collectivity but rather of the ephemeral bindings arising in social relations of multiple division.

5. The character of a specific lived 'place' then can be discovered through a combined enquiry into the material history that produces spheres of spatial coherence and the study of instituted practices and communicated interpretations that then occur therein. In Narotzky and Smith 2006, we concentrate mostly on the latter, while providing the historical material that would make the former possible.

6. Discussion of Neil Smith's developing views is to be found in Marston 2000; and in Marston and Smith 2001.

7. Tortella (2000: 294) remarks, 'Spanish agriculture remains as much behind the European norm as it was at the beginning of the [twentieth] century'. The low organic composition of capital is reflected in the fact that, while agriculture contributes only 7% of GNP, it absorbs 18.5% of the population. The figures for the EU are 6% and 8% respectively (ibid.: 295). Illiteracy rates in Spain at the beginning of the twentieth century (compared to France) were very high: 1890: 61% [22%]; 1910: 50% [13%] (ibid.: 13). In 1960 agriculture accounted for 33% of gross national product but only 13% of total investment (Vilar 1977). During the Republic there were over 4,000 tractors in Spain; by 1945 there were just 59 (ibid.: 285). This grew to 260,000 by 1970, but investment was still only $15 per hectare compared with $60 for Europe (Vilar 1977).

8. Alongside these predominantly export crops could also be found olives, wheat and various fodder crops for local livestock.

9. Dependency came in at least three forms. The need for processing facilities for agricultural crops, the fact that many farmers had access to land through various forms of tenancy, and the additional fact that most plots were insufficient for family income, obliging people to sell their labour at various times through the year.

10. The argument I am making in this paper relies on a distinction between the specifics of Valencia's irrigation system, and projects for a national hydraulic infrastructure that would carry water from one territory and deliver it to an irrigation network in another. The Bajo Segura relied on an ancient set of irrigation channels minimally requiring cleaning and clay relining. My argument is that their potential for intensifying agriculture through engineering improvements beyond this (such as the use of concrete channelling and mechanized gates) did not occur until the late 1950s, as sales resulted in the transfer of land from larger owners to tenants managing and working their own *fincas* (see Narotzky and Smith 2006).

11. I am referring here specifically to Williams' use of this expression; but absolutely not to the epistemology of Marvin Harris, who used the same term for his own work.

– Chapter 3 –

POPULAR STRUGGLE, INTELLECTUALS AND PERSPECTIVES IN REALIST HISTORY
A Case from Late-Twentieth-Century Peru

℮∽

It is safest to grasp the concept of the postmodern as an attempt to think the present historically in an age that has forgotten how to think historically in the first place.

– Fredric Jameson, *Postmodernism, or the Cultural Logic of Late Capitalism*

How one does history shapes how one thinks about politics, and how one does politics affects how one thinks about history. [Italics in original]

– Fred Cooper, *Colonialism in Question: Theory, Knowledge, History*

Introduction

Although we may be well past the postmodern era, interpretations of the popular movements scattered across the globe in the past couple of years do seem to remain 'in an age that has forgotten how to think historically in the first place'. Pushed to 'elaborate more clearly what they think the ideal relationship between scholarship and politics should be' (Maskovsky 2013: 128), anthropologists need to be careful that they do not present the past as a savage, albeit noble, slot rather than in terms of careful historical specificity (Trouillot 2003). Yet, in the elusive pursuit of relevance, anthropologists have found a good trade in snake oil: the charms of cultural distance as the source of insight, not so much for the purposes of strategy – which reeks of an older kind of protest – as to provide us with what Will Self (2013) has called 'comfort savagery'.[1] In lieu of plants whose roots lie in the rich earth of their own history, popular movements, quickly branded romantically as having an anarchist sensibility, are offered hope and vision through potential crossbreeding with the exotic plants of a revived romantic primitivism. Speaking of an analogous move in respect to 'autonomous' economies, Narotzky remarks, 'there is a kind of reification of these "other" economic relations that tends to endow them with a "moral" (i.e. good) aura that refers to the primitive or primordial slot where they have been positioned before the "fall" into capitalism' (Narotzky 2012: 245).

And yet even if we leave aside the nastier parts of anarchism's propaganda by the deed, confining ourselves instead to horizontal consultation and inclusive participation, rejection of organizational infrastructure, refusal of established political parties or institutions, and rejection of the state or state-like forms (see, for example, Graeber 2013), there is still much to learn from history and not just from anarchist history – a great deal to learn from historians too, and anthropologists concerned with people's specific histories and not their distinctive otherness. Rejection of the practices and ideas of our intellectual and political predecessors need not include a refusal to learn from them.

Motivated by a wish to address Maskovsky's question, in this chapter I want to discuss how different kinds of scholarship about political protest may arise from an author's assessment of the political conjuncture in which s/he writes. There has long been a dialogue between Left historians and Left anthropologists that, whether explicitly or not, addressed these kinds of questions (Cohn 1981; Medick 1987; Sider and Smith 1997). And of course the dialogue changed from one generation to another, as did the broader political conjunctures when they wrote and the narrower developments in each of the disciplines. The people I discuss here were motivated by a kind of intellectual – even political – dissatisfaction not dissimilar to what many people feel today. Their assessment of a conjuncture obliged them to turn over the settled ground of older political and historiographical interpretations to explore questions that had been left on the edge of existing agendas. Then as newly emerging dissident intellectuals built upon the projects shaped by an older generation they found themselves in a different social and political conjuncture. As a result, how *they* did politics affected how they thought about history. But the academy they worked in and debates within their respective disciplines had also changed. So questions arising within the politics of the Left were addressed by different generations of historians and historically inclined anthropologists. This affected what they chose to look at. But it also affected 'how' they chose to look, and it is this difference in ways of looking and hearing, that crosscuts developments in history and anthropology, which mostly concerns me.

Some thirty-five years ago, the historian Eric Hobsbawm published a review of Piven and Cloward's *Poor People's Movements* in the *New York Review of Books*. It was entitled, 'Should Poor People Organize?' (see Hobsbawm (1978) 1984: 282–96). In looking at four different movements, two before the Second World War and two after, Piven and Cloward found that initially vigorous and, from the point-of-view of the establishment, dangerous movements were essentially tamed by the institutional organizations that began to take hold of them as they developed. After extensively assessing this conclusion by reference to various movements in terms of the specific historical conjunctures in which they arose, Hobsbawm decides that 'their book is enormously instructive. However, it is also inadequate, because *its field of vision is extremely restricted'* – restricted I think, in part, in the way Jameson is noting above. Yet Piven and Cloward were not anthropologists and their book was not an ethnography, so Hobsbawm's assessment as a historian could make an anthropologist working with the quite limited field of vision of ethnography a little nervous, however committed to history. How would a historian who looked at popular movements from this perspective assess the value of the scale at which ethnographic research is conducted, however historically motivated?

As it happened, Hobsbawm's review was written just a couple of years after he had published an article entitled 'Peasant Land Occupations', which focused on the region where I was doing fieldwork as he wrote the article. So it is possible to answer this question quite specifically – or at least one instance of it. This would seem to allow us to assess the strong and weak points of a study by a historian and a study by an anthropologist of roughly the same material.

But what was Hobsbawm's unease with the book he was reviewing? What 'the stage armies' (as he calls them) of popular protest can do is they can 'disrupt and *rely on the political reverberations of their disruption*. [But] this does not give them much leverage' (Hobsbawm [1978] 1984: 291. Italics in original). Indeed he suggests that in most cases through history, authorities can deal with spontaneous popular pressure by concessions combined with face-saving punishment for the 'agitators'. And then they disappear, often leaving little to memory. 'It is *organized* popular action they seek to prevent' (ibid.: 293. Italics in original). And so he concludes, 'any subaltern group become[s] a subject rather than an object of history through formalized collectivities, *however structured'* (ibid. My emphasis). Only as we move into the nineteenth century in industrialized countries and 'movements become an institutionally organized force', do we see evidence of their effectiveness.

For the younger reader this conclusion may not be especially surprising, coming as it does from an old Marxist historian. But it was not Hobsbawm who caught the fancy of Left anthropologists in the 1970s, but Edward Thompson. And for every time Hobsbawm may invoke institutions and organization, Thompson would invoke experience and culture. This is what I mean by different ways of looking: both historians, both interested in the formation of popular movements, but for Thompson what 'made' the English working class goes a lot further back than 1800 or even 1750; channelled through the multiple expressions of popular culture the making of that class is indistinguishable from the waxing and waning of what Raymond Williams would call an emergent 'structure of feeling'. Hobsbawm must surely have been snubbing his nose at Thompson at least a little when he wrote an article whose title speaks of the making of the working class '1870–1914' or, in case that did not quite catch, then another that confines 'the formation of British working-class culture' pretty much to the nineteenth and early twentieth centuries (see Hobsbawm 1984).

My point is that as engaged anthropologists we could usefully have a dialogue with dissident historians, even of the same generation, but we would not get quite the same perspective from one or the other of them. Moreover, how we, as anthropologists, might consume what they produced would likely depend on tastes arising from within our own (nationally distinct) discipline; and what we learn from one historian may enhance our own work, while the work of another may reveal the limitations of what we have learned.

In this chapter I will use an article by Hobsbawm alongside the interpretations I drew writing quite shortly after that article was published, to explore what can be learned from these intellectual reconstructions of past insurrections for potential current ones. But first I need to elaborate on what I mean by different ways of seeing history. So I begin by suggesting two positions on a spectrum. This helps to frame an initial distinction that becomes more complicated as the actual historical and ethnographic material is presented. There I seek first to see how the angle of our work differs, but I move on to intertwine our respective conclusions with a view to assessing the strengths and limitations of the two similar but distinct perspectives.

Scales and Perspectives in Anthropology and History

To a generation of Left anthropologists attracted to historical ethnography in the 1970s and 1980s, three key figures were Eric Hobsbawm, Eric Wolf and Edward Thompson. In each case the value of their work arose from their own dissatisfaction with existing currents of thought. Hobsbawm's background in the communist party meant that a strong element of orthodoxy lay with the role of industrial labour in revolutionary struggle. His early interest in other kinds of livelihood, especially, though not uniquely, rural workers, can be seen as a move to explore the edges of an older orthodoxy. Eric Wolf's work was always strongly historical, and as early as the Puerto Rico Project (Steward 1956) showed a concern to understand local 'cultures' in terms of the historical forces of a larger social setting. Yet his decision to write a book about the role of peasants in revolutionary struggles of the twentieth century, driven as it was by his own involvement in opposition to the American war on South East Asia, represented a radical move outside anthropological orthodoxy. Both mobilization and peasants had been of interest to anthropologists, but Wolf brought the two together and addressed the issue of how the objects of anthropological study – in this case, peasants – might become a force in history.

Thompson's work arose among a generation of dissident historians who were directing attention away from the great events and the powerful people that mostly preoccupied the guild, and were focusing on 'the social' and especially the often hidden world of working people and the poor. The particular feature of his work that had such a strong impact on a later generation of anthropologists was the way he understood culture. In proposing as he did that the collective culture of the English working class was formed precisely in the mould of people's struggle for expression and material well-being against class forces intent on diminishing them, Thompson introduced a way of understanding the production of culture that drew on the collective politics of his time but which was foreign to contemporaneous anthropological orthodoxy when it was published in 1963.

The point then is that there is nothing unique about current dissidents' attempts to move out of the straitjacket that went before. I want to suggest here though that, even as dissident historians and dissident anthropologists become intertwined as the latter try to make their own work as intellectuals useful for their politics, the tensions within each discipline are likely to affect the way they 'do history'.

For example Holmes and Marcus (2005), in a provocative article that pushes at the edges of what ethnographic enquiry might be, speak of two distinct methodological approaches in anthropology, the one prioritizing 'the architecture of social relations', the other 'the understanding of the natives' point-of-view'. An analogous, but not quite identical, tension runs through engaged social history – what Raphael Samuel (1992) called 'history as fact grubbing versus history as mind reading'.

This seems to suggest that, even taking similar political projects into account, the way people do history or historical anthropology may differ. In a conversation between two labour historians of France, for example, Louise Tilly was critical of a kind of historian who claimed to produce people's histories by endorsing personal accounts of experience at the expense of 'sources ... compared systematically, and frequently quantitatively analysed' (Tilly 1985: 16). While agreeing that such history always has its place, Isabelle Bertaux-Wiame responded by suggesting that for some historians equally concerned about people's history but focusing on 'mentalities, consciousness and the like ... the literal accuracy of accounts is not their chief interest' (Bertaux-Wiame 1985: 25).

In many cases this can be read in terms of scale, both temporal and spatial, as though the further away the past is from us, the more we must rely on bits of hard data since we have so little access to 'experience', especially for those whose experience cannot be recorded through the written word (Hobsbawm 1959. But see Ladurie 1978; Ginzberg 1982). More recent history, on the other hand, and especially the oral history recorded in ethnography does allow for possible access to what the subjects of our study mean. And of course we develop techniques for interpreting that meaning, often at a more intimate scale. We see this conjuncture of scale and historical genre if we contrast two historians of everyday life: Fernand Braudel, a master historian of continental Europe, and Alessandro Portelli, whose histories seek to get at the fine grain of people's lives.

Fernand Braudel writes of a kind of balance sheet:

> Historical reconstruction [can] perfectly well take micro-history as it's starting point ... [But] history is the keyboard on which these individual notes are sounded ... I would conclude with the paradox that *the true man of action is he who can measure most nearly the constraints upon him* ... All efforts against the tide of history – which is not always obvious – are doomed to failure. (Quoted by Richard Mayne, in Braudel 1995: xxiii. Italics mine)

While not denigrating the agency of historical actors, Braudel then is arguing for the importance of a history which needs to be studied across a broader scale – temporally and spatially. He contrasts this with 'a history of brief, rapid, nervous fluctuations, by definition ultrasensitive; the least tremor sets all its antennae quivering. But as such, it is the most exciting of all [kinds of history], the richest in human interest, and also the most dangerous. We must learn to distrust this history with its still-burning passions (Braudel 1995: 87–88).

So here is the verdict of the master of big history. And yet the first volume of his study of capitalism bears the title *The Structures of Everyday Life* – surely a level of reality we tend to associate with a smaller scale. Interestingly, Alessandro Portelli invokes the same contrasts but seems to reverse the order, when he explains the principles that guide his work:

> the dramatic distance and indissoluble bond between 'history' and personal experience, between the *private unique* and solitary spores of sorrow in houses, kitchens, and anguished memories, *and the historian's perception and reconstruction of broad, public historical events* ... The task and theme of oral history ... is to explore this distance and this bond – without violating that space, without cracking the uniqueness of each spore ... – *to connect them with 'history' and in turn force history to listen to them.* (Portelli 1997: viii. Italics added)

The history that matters to Portelli then is an instance of the kind of history that Braudel describes as 'lived by contemporaries whose lives were as short and as short-sighted as ours' (ibid.).

So here then are two quite different versions of the historian's job. Which we choose will obviously depend on our purpose at hand, and that is as likely to be a function of the intellectual task we set ourselves within the academy as it is to result from our political inclinations – how we would like to see the world and what we see our contribution to that world being. And this need not be an entirely personal matter. Even if the person in question is committed to making some kind of political contribution with their intellectual work, how they assess what that might be will depend on prevailing political conditions – or at least on what they see those conditions to be.

Braudel would be justly surprised if he were told that he was not interested in meanings or *mentalités* but, writing when he did, it was from the *structures* of everyday life that we might get at such issues. Writing some decades later it is unlikely that Portelli was not influenced by his predecessor – but, especially concerned about his political contribution, he was describing his projects in terms of 'the text and the voice', 'oral history and the art of dialogue' and 'the biography of a city'. These are clearly different entry points into historical reality and I tend to think that they do not reflect just the relationship between the politics of these people's times and the writing of history, but also the tensions arising in a particular discipline and at a particular time and place (Bourdieu 1990b, 2003).

What is most striking in the dialogue I have forced on these two authors is the different perspective they have on the thing they are studying. The older historian seems to stand back and assess the *structure* of the building from the outside, pointing up relationships among its parts but is unwilling to thrust open the door and invade the intimacy of those within. What matters – or what matters more – is the external structure revealed by historical enquiry. By contrast, Portelli advocates a kind of enquiry in which (in the words of Sherry Ortner 1995: 173) the practitioner tries to 'enter the space of the world the researcher seeks to understand'. And yet it would be a mistake to suggest that this is *all* Portelli is doing. He says the task is to explore 'the distance between the uniqueness of the kind of history he acquires in this way and the broader kind of history' of society available to him as a professional historian. Nonetheless there is no doubt that his priority lies with the former as I suspect it does for me, the anthropologist; just as the latter I think is what motivates Hobsbawm the historian to look at a particular case, as we will see below (see Hobsbawm 2005).

The three books that were of especial influence on me by older authors[2] were all written with an agenda aimed at enhancing the agency of working people as a positive force in history. In writing against the current of orthodoxy, a generation of anthropologists interested in historical ethnography followed their lead, among them Gerald Sider (1986, 2003), William Roseberry (1983, 1989), Donald Donham (1999), Don Kalb (1997) and Michel-Rolph Trouillot (1997).[3] These were people for whom some kind of intellectual partiality in respect to the politics of the subaltern were quite evident. And yet the achievement of becoming a positive force in history relies on two pivotal but distinct elements: the ability to mobilize people and the assessment of strategic action; what Gramsci called the forging of multiple dispersed wills into a material force, on the one hand, and what Braudel called the assessment of the conditions of the possible, on the other. It is possible to read the different perspectives of fact-grubbing historians versus mind-reading historians through these crucially interconnected political imperatives. But disciplines themselves serve to assign priorities here too. While anthropologists performing ethnography can be the envy of historians because they have access to a small number of people through long-term fieldwork, this disciplinary tradition has implications for both the timescale and the social-scale that their history is inclined to embrace. And, as we saw in the exchange I imposed on Braudel and Portelli, this too can have implications for the prioritizing of intimate constructions in a search more for meanings on the one hand and the prioritizing of 'the architecture of social relations' on the other. The relative usefulness of what arises therefrom has implications for our contribution to facilitating popular mobilization versus assessing the possibilities for strategic action.

Strongly influenced by these authors and motivated no doubt as much by the desire to emulate as by the spirit of critique, I formulated a research project that focused on rural mobilization and that took me to central Peru just as Hobsbawm was writing an article on the same subject.[4] In the remainder of this chapter I juxtapose Hobsbawm's work alongside my own with a view to assessing the effect of differences in perspective and scale as I have so far discussed them. I conclude by trying to weigh up the limitations and strengths of each for counter-politics understood in terms of 'popular mobilization' and 'strategic action'.

What makes a comparison of these studies relevant to movements today, despite being made at an earlier time and with a different focus, is that they are slightly different histories of a political mobilization with many points of similarity with current movements. No outside political party or leader played a significant role, for example, nor were decisions made by a clearly designated cohort of leaders but rather 'by a sense of the meeting'. Orthodox politics were treated with scepticism. The evidence is drawn from just one case but the different genres of history that we find being produced here might nonetheless provide resources for contemporary movements – not to mention the kinds of histories we write about them.

'The Question of Peasant Revolutionary Activity'

On the suggestion of Eric Hobsbawm I did fieldwork in the central Peruvian Andes (and in the inner-city slums and *barriadas* of Lima) in 1972–73. While I was there Hobsbawm wrote an article that was published in *Past and Present* the following year. The purpose of the paper, he said, 'is to throw light on the question of peasant revolutionary activity' (Hobsbawm 1974: 120) and for the most part it focused on the history of the people with whom I spent those two years. Some forty years later I found myself sharing some old photos with people I knew in Huasicancha. One of them shows a bold man in his early twenties on a spectacular black horse which is *bailando* (lit. dancing). I was particularly proud of this photo, taken in 1980, since I knew it was of Samuel the son of Martin Ramos, one of the key figures in all three of Huasicancha's successful *reivindicaciones* of the last century. Now Pedro, who had helped me with my fieldwork in the 1970s, takes the photo from me and says, 'Samuel! He is selling fruit in Lima'.[5]

I was especially excited by this news because I had been told that fewer and fewer huasicanchino migrants in Lima were still doing this, and I was despairing of the possibility of meeting anybody on my return to Lima. 'I can tell you where he is', said Pedro giving me the exact corner on two Lima streets that I knew well. And he turned the photo over and wrote, 'Samuel Ramos, taken in Huasicancha 1980 by my compadre Gavin Smith. Saludos de Pedro Cano'. 'Go and talk to him and take this for him.'

So now we are drinking beer in the evening, near Samuel's tricycle, and he is telling my companions a story about his father Martin and the part he played at a key moment in the struggle back in the 1930s. It is a story I had heard a number of times forty years ago and once from Martin himself. As a young man he had faced up to the powerful *hacienda* administrator, Manuel Pielago, in court. But Pielago told the judge, 'He can't speak for the people of Huasicancha. He's from Yauyos, he's too young and anyway he can't be a *comunero* because he's not married.'[6]

As Samuel tells us the story I interject an inflection here or there, as I remember his father's version. On returning disheartened to the community, Martin was met by the older villagers who resolved to answer each of the *hacendado*'s objections. A community authority was brought in who made out a birth certificate bringing Martin to an age of majority.[7] Then he was presented with a number of single young women from among whom he was to choose a wife. He was duly married and returned to the court to pursue the case. But Samuel says, 'No, no. It wasn't like that. Martin came back. He had a friend, Victor, and it was *his* sister Martin wanted to marry. But there was a problem. Her aunt was the hacendada, Maria Luisa Chavez. How could he become a comunero by marrying a relative of the hacendada?' In Samuel's account, they married anyway and, perhaps to counter any objections, Martin then turned the tables on Pielago, arguing that his claim to be married to the owner was false. He was merely a 'servant' of Maria Luisa, who did in fact have two legitimate sons as well as other relatives more legitimate than him. These are the stories Samuel and Martin told.

In his article Hobsbawm provides an outline of the various *reivindaciones* – he calls them invasions or land occupations – in which the huasicanchinos were involved, beginning as follows:

> To understand the nature of such invasions and the role they play in peasant actions, it may be convenient to follow one particular such movement through at least some of its ramifications: that of the community of Huasicancha, a small and overwhelmingly pastoral Indian settlement in the central highlands of Peru ... We are fortunately able to trace the struggle of this community ... back to the sixteenth century. (Hobsbawm 1974: 131)

After noting the importance for the huasicanchinos' struggles of being recognized by the government as a comunidad indigena in 1930, he lays out the older historical evidence succinctly:[8]

> Somewhere on the high *puna* – at and above four thousand metres – Huasicancha had always possessed a large tract of communal pastures 'belonging to the Inca king', which were apparently usurped by one Juan Iparraguirre, against whom they obtained an *expediente* in the year 1607 from an authority described by the represenatives of the community in the 1960s as 'el Virrey de la Republica residente en Lima'; from which we may infer that litigation had begun some decades earlier.[9] The boundaries of this tract are defined in this document, and remained those which the community claimed in the 1960s, being verified at that date by ocular inspection, toponymy and other suitable methods by an inspecting judge. The dispute, which dragged along the centuries, settled down into a dispute with the Hacienda Tucle, which appears to have been formed towards the end of the sixteenth century and expanded over the centuries into a vast livestock ranch. Like most such haciendas, Tucle lived in a relation of conflict and symbiosis with its surrounding communities, whose lands it had taken and whose members supplied it with labour. (Hobsbawm 1974: 132–33)

Hobsbawm then takes us through what he calls the long-standing 'campaign' of the huasicanchinos, describing one insurrectionary outbreak after another and the downtime in between. In each case he describes both the broader national and sometimes international conjuncture that provided the 'conditions of possibility' as well as the local political mobilization, the evidence providing progressively more detail as he gets closer to the present, as one would expect.

At the point during the early 1880s when Chilean troops drove the defeated Peruvian army back into the central highlands in the War of the Pacific (1879–84), General Caceres, at the head of the Peruvian resistance, recruited *guerrilleros* from the highland communities surrounding the haciendas of which Tucle was a part. One Tomas Laimes, an erstwhile corporal in an earlier campaign, was especially active in and around Huasicancha and took the opportunity to overrun the haciendas and carry off livestock to the point that the owner, Bernarda Pielago, claimed in 1887 that Tucle had been reduced from forty thousand to three thousand head of sheep. 'What had happened was that … the Indians had been armed as guerrillas against the victorious Chileans, and had immediately entered upon the only war that made any sense to them, occupying their alienated lands' (ibid.: 133). Caceres so entirely lost control of the highland fighters that eventually he had to entice Laimes into the Mantaro Valley, where the regular troops were, and have him and four of his aids executed. 'Local legend, in the usual syncretic fashion, confuses him with the great Indian rebel Tupac Amaru and claims that he was drawn and quartered in Huancayo' (ibid.).

Hobsbawm then shifts scale to account for a downtime: the Civilista decades after the 1880s evidenced a political current unfavourable to the Indian communities, while the growing European market for wool encouraged the haciendas to concentrate on sheep and to tighten control on pasturage.

Then moving to the 1930s Hobsbawm notes that, following recognition as an official *comunidad*, Huasicancha 'began the process of formally reclaiming all its lost heritage, asking for what amounted to half of Tucle, all of [Hacienda] Rio de la Virgen, a large part of [Hacienda] Antapongo, possibly even some of [Hacienda] Laive' (ibid.: 137). The 'taking possession' of the haciendas during the war with Chile had been a momentary massive success, and an experience from which something had been learned, but no spoils were left with the vanquished. The settlement of 1937, on the other hand, though small, turned out in retrospect to be the beginning of a succession of 'stages' [his term] in Huasicancha's campaign. At this point Hobsbawm notes a 'settlement' supposedly between Huasicancha and a neighbouring *caserío* (annex). What appears thus in the Property Registry however, was the form the settlement made between Huasicancha and Hacienda Tucle took to grant the pasture associated with this so-called *caserío* to the community. Some third of the comuneros had moved onto this land to assert their claim to it, and it was the litigation component of this combined strategy that Martin had described to me in 1973 and that his son had repeated forty years later.

Again apprising us of the political setting, Hobsbawm then brings us to '[t]he great rural awakening of 1945–48, no less significant for being virtually unrecorded by historians'. And he then turns to the local situation:

> On Christmas Day [1946] a mass of men, women and children from Huasicancha invaded Tucle with all their livestock, destroyed boundary walls and refused to evacuate part of the land. The rest of the communities soon followed, until on 23rd January a number of peasants were massacred by the 43rd Infantry Battalion, after which the invasions subsided.
>
> Huasicancha, which incidentally seems to have avoided the massacre by a timely withdrawal, gained a large part of the Pampa de Tucle by this invasion, for the owners sold it to the community under the mistaken impression that by doing so the community forewent its claims, the sale price consisting of the construction of a boundary wall.[10]

Again this moment of initiative and success is followed by a downtime with the coming of the Odria dictatorship (1948–56) which used massive repression to stamp out the Left populist party of APRA (see Note 10) and kept a tight lid on rural political expression too. Hobsbawm picks up the story again in 1963 when agrarian unrest in Peru was reaching tsunami proportions – 'Huasicancha was again ready' (ibid.: 141), beginning by lodging a claim against Tucle:

> When the law appeared to fail them yet again, they invaded some three thousand hectares with four thousand beasts, eventually occupying some fifteen thousand hectares … They finally received a judgement in favour of their historic claims in 1970 … Indeed in the summer of 1971 they were still invading, this time the lands of the new cooperative [formed out of the neighbouring, now ex-, haciendas].[11] (ibid.: 141)

By laying out Hobsbawm's account in this way I am able to provide a straightforward narrative of events and their setting as things unfolded. At the same time we get a sense of the form his narrative takes: the past centuries of Huasicancha's claims to land are seen as an important backdrop to the present, and especially the experience of the guerrillero expropriation during the war with Chile. But it is the three 'stages' in a drawn out 'campaign', both terms Hobsbawm uses – of 1937–38, 1946–48 and 1964–72 – that most concern him in exploring the history of the peasantry to learn something about the way collective mobilization was organized and strategic action pursued.

Here I want to align the unfolding stages of my research, arising from the scale of fieldwork-based ethnography, with those of Hobsbawm. Strongly influenced by the work of people like Wolf (op. cit.) not to mention Hobsbawm himself, the monograph I eventually wrote embraced a quite broad historical and social scale. But I think its horizons remained strongly influenced by the concentric vision arising in the interpersonal encounters of my various field sites in the original period and on subsequent visits. And it is the differing insights and limitations arising respectively from Hobsbawm's and from my own vantage points that I want to explore here. For example, if we are to speak of scale then obviously the story Samuel told us over a beer, clutching an old photo nostalgically – and in fact the story his father told me many years ago, as we sat together in his house – these are of a much narrower scale than those accessible to Hobsbawm, and possibly even of interest to him. There is no doubt that they do effectively fine-tune what we learn from him, but the question remains as to what the price is for this kind of fine-tuning – in terms of its usefulness for mobilization and strategy. The question is whether they act as a sort of siren song pulling me away from the kind of scale of analysis (temporal and social) that Hobsbawm achieves as a function of the kind of problematic he had set out to address in the first place, or whether this kind of perspective helps to add something of importance.

'Habia diez anos – *tranquilo. Y entonces ya: otra invasion*' [There were ten years – *tranquilo.* And then ya: another invasion]

Perhaps Hobsbawm's article seems rather dated by its purpose: 'to throw light on the question of peasant revolutionary activity' (Hobsbawm 1974: 120). My own monograph (1989) is probably no less dated, having 'resistance' in the title. But terms like revolution and resistance are simply distracting here. The purpose is to examine how a historian of one generation on the one hand and an anthropologist of a subsequent generation on the other, faced with pretty much the same site and sharing a wish to learn about the political possibilities of popular collective struggle, 'do history'. In fact Hobsbawm (in the same paragraph) directs our attention to two interconnected foci which bring us back to the earlier discussion in this chapter: 'the actions of participants' [he says 'peasants'] and 'strategic thinking' – what I have called 'popular mobilization' and 'strategic action' respectively. These then are the litmus test: how do these different approaches help us to address what happens when people successfully mobilize collectively, and what problems have to be addressed in doing so? How are strategic points of leverage for their actions identified or misread?

It might be useful to begin by stating the obvious: where each of us started from. Hobsbawm makes clear that most of his information comes from the property registry in Huancayo and the archive being built up in Lima which was to house the records of all the haciendas being expropriated by Velasco's agrarian reform (1968–75). He also spoke to a local lawyer who had been employed by Huasicancha, a number of prominent historians (e.g. Pablo Macera, Juan Martinez Alier and Henri Favre) and the various young people working in the Lima archive. He subsequently told me that he actually visited the richest of the haciendas in the bloc of which Tucle was a part, Hacienda Laive. It is evident then that, equipped with the agenda described above, he gradually honed in on this one especially insurgent body of people.

Partly thanks to Hobsbawm and certainly due to the traditions of my discipline I moved in pretty much the opposite direction. After some difficulty being allowed by the huasicanchinos to live and work among them, it was agreed that I should write a history. At first I understood that the purpose of such a history was to offset the prevailing versions of what the huasicanchinos had done (destroyed a civilized way of life) and the kind of people they were (wily but savage *indios*). But with time and in the context of widespread *capacitación* (training) programmes on the part of the government, I was told that the purpose was also to provide an example for *la mobilación de los campesinos peruanos*.[12] Obviously, faced with this task, I knew that my job would include attending to the same kind of work we have seen Hobsbawm had done: working on records in Huancayo and the archives in Lima. And as time went by I knew that some hacienda records remained in Huancayo, still to be moved to the central archives. But the crucial period that formed my first encounter with Huasicancha's history and undoubtedly remained very sharply stamped on my mind came from speaking to people in the highland community itself. To give some sense of what this meant, here is part of a transcript recorded three weeks after I had arrived in the community, and this seventy-year-old man allowed me to live in the house he left empty during his stays in Huancayo:

> La invasion de la Hacienda Tucle. Este antes, ante-e-e-s, antes de mi abuelo. Peleaban. Le daban pedaso. Y asi el juicio. Ese a tiempo de mi mama. Animaban, animaban – pedaso le daban, pedaso le daban. Entraban asi adentro. Despues ya nosotros … Habia diez anos – tranquilo. Y entonces ya: otra invasion. Cuando yo estaba gobernador aca. Esta invasión vamos a hablar … [He then describes events beginning in 1964] (Don Angelino Cano, Field Notes Huasicancha, March 1972)

> The invasion of Hacienda Tucle. This before, befo-o-o-re (dragging out his voice), before my grandfather. They fought [*Peleaban* is more like fist fighting or hand-to-hand fighting]. They gave them a piece [of land]. And so the court

case [or judgement]. This was the time of my mother. Stirring up, stirring up [among the huasicanchinos] – they gave a piece, they gave a piece. Getting in [to the land of the *hacienda*] like this. Later, then us! There were ten years – *tranquilo*. And then ya: another invasion. When I was the *gobernador*[13] here. This is the invasion we are going to talk about …

Blurred Vision 1: Who Are these People?

From the outset I was concerned with how the people I had come to live with had mobilized themselves with such success. In the early weeks in Peru before getting to Huasicancha I had met quite a few anthropologists, Peruvian and foreign, who had worked in communities where no such mobilization had occurred. Perhaps then it is not surprising that, looking back at my field notes of 1972–73, I find that I was extremely concerned to come up with some kind of sense of who the people I was living with and trying to write about actually were. This was very far from being some kind of anthropologist's fixation on distinguishing the Nuer from the Dinka. Rather it was a question that anybody interested in issues of popular mobilization would find themselves asking.

In the early stages my confusion was mostly to do with my discovery of the extent of out-migration from this zone of rebels: were they also part of the people I was writing about, or were they other kinds of 'people'? And then my discovery that they were deeply involved in all of the various reivindicaciones from the outset: in what way then were they part of the rebellious huasicanchinos? How were they included? And so on. My confusion is interesting at least in part because at no point did I think, for one moment, that I was living with 'strange people', as would have been the case had I arrived with the strong prevailing view of 'the two Perus', the one *criollo* or *mestizo* and the other *cholo* or *indio* – *lo Andino* as Orin Starn (1991) subsequently accused many anthropologists of buying into, or indeed 'producing'. This was a view to be given a new lease of life by Mario Vargas Llosa in the 1980s, and one which prevailed through the twenty years of the last century when *Sendero Luminoso* was active (Vargas Llosa 1983; see Mayer 1991). While the people I was living with were openly hostile to any suggestion that they were *mestizo*, there was never a moment when they would allow me to see them as *cholos/indios* on one side of a clearly divided dual Peru. For better or worse, despite his quite frequent use of the term 'Indians', Hobsbawm too does not appear to frame his account around 'the cultural otherness' of the huasicanchinos.

So this early question – Who am I studying? – and the way I continually had to re-ask it, influenced the way I enquired about history and the way I recorded it. In other words, the mistake I avoided making (Starn notwithstanding), and the confusion I persisted in feeling, resulted from the way I began to learn and record things. Part of this was the result of what I was listening *for*, how I treated what I heard. And part of it came from the actual way in which things were told to me, sometimes simply fragments of information, sometimes ongoing accounts like that of Don Angelino, above, and sometimes accounts delivered by as many as six or seven speakers gathered together and addressing themselves as well as me. Once aware that I was to put together a history, I set about trying to accumulate facts – the dates of various encounters with the army and the *hacienda caporales* (guards), when the police outpost had finally been withdrawn from this remote community, and so on. Attuned to this task I became frustrated by the limitations of oral sources while filtering out what seemed to be the 'noise' of other material.

After a few months, I began to visit the Property Registry in Huancayo from time to time, and interview a lawyer who had taken on the community's case (the same one Hobsbawm interviewed in fact). As a result it gradually became clear to me that the 'structural' tension that arose between haciendas and the huasicanchinos was double-edged. The fact that they both employed and exploited huasicanchinos as workers impressed itself upon my emerging version of history. But at the same time tensions and disputes arose from the fact that these self same workers had land claims to possession of the pasture on which they worked. If the property regime pivotal to the capital–labour relation was what made it possible for workers to be exploited, this was severely complicated by the fact that the workers disputed this capitalist's ownership of property. The frustrations and contingencies of the actual collective struggles I was hearing about and actually witnessing resulted from the tensions arising from these structured relations.

The issue here of course is that, while much of the time the bedrock of historical reality that was beginning to come into shape for me reflects (with some exceptions) the evidence provided by Hobsbawm in his 1974 article, the colours and hues of my own account were quite different, as the oral accounts I was hearing set these tensions of complex belonging and contradictory expression into a world of geographical and familial proximity.

I have used Hobsbawm's article to establish a chronology. As one would expect, in my 1989 book the scale in terms of time and in terms of space allowed me to provide considerably more local detail and especially for the recent *revindicacion*. In many ways I stressed the same factors as we find Hobsbawm using too. In terms of the distinction Holmes and Marcus make, like Hobsbawm my inclination was to explore the architecture of social relations, and initially that might have made me a little impatient with the natives' point of view – with listening to how they told me what they told me. But given the setting in which I was working, that point of view was almost forced upon me, allowing me to tweak Hobsbawm's material with more details. The early migration of the 1940s, as he says, became much greater by the mid-1960s, but I suggest that it also changed in character. Hobsbawm speaks of increasing 'commercialization'. Coining the term *'confederations of households'*, I note an uneven shift towards simple commodity production and the implications this had for how units became enmeshed in social linkages as they sought to reproduce themselves (Smith 1989: 155–68). For example migrants establishing themselves in Lima in the 1940s began accumulating livestock back in the community through the 1950s. But it was only in the 1960s that the various migrant communities became sufficiently established that reciprocal obligations accumulated with village associates could now be redeemed through facilitating and hosting seasonal and longer term out-migration from the village. Migration became an institutionalized practice. Hence the question that initially troubled me turned out not to be some annoying early matter to be quickly cleared up. From a political point of view it is not as fruitful to speak of 'villagers' and 'the outside world' as Hobsbawm does, or even to speak in terms of the differing roles of 'migrants' and 'villagers', which may have been appropriate for the 1930s and 1940s – rather one should understand 'Huasicancha' as a dispersed community, albeit with heterogeneous membership.

Blurred Vision 2: Politics

The point is that the selected categories in this case appear to me to be misleading. And they are not just misleading because I see them close up – the wood for the trees; rather this information can have useful implications not just for organization in some settled sense, but for the *process* of organizing. And this complicating of the categories by the intricacies of the practices they are meant to capture begins to make many other colours start to run on a wider area of the canvass. A similar blurring of categories arises as we cross the line that distinguishes the down period drawing to an end in the early 1960s and the onset of vigorous confrontation as the decade unfolds. As Hobsbawm makes clear, 'down times' even during especially oppressive periods of which there were many did not stop the huasicanchinos from making persistent claims against the haciendas through the courts and the department of *Asuntos Indigenas*. But, beginning in the early 1960s, the idea that some kind of land reform through the reworking of property and rights to land became widespread through Andean South America. As Hobsbawm notes, the huasicanchinos, like so many other peasants, had always pressed hard on the legal apparatus to advance their cause; but under the Belaunde government (1963–68) a growing sense that legal documents and judiciary judgements would be the key to successful land settlements triggered a petition that was delivered to the presidential palace in November 1963.

It is at this moment that we come closest to being able to tie huasicanchino politics directly to established political parties, and this through the figure of Elias Tacunan, a native of the community whose inspirational role becomes increasingly ambivalent as the accounts I recorded approach the present (i.e. 1972–73). As Hobsbawm notes, Tacunan was a migrant who learned his politics in the mines and, with the support of APRA, became an energetic organizer of rural confederations in and around the province of Junin (of which Huasicancha is a part).[14] Breaking with the party in 1959 he founded a separate local peasant federation and political party, and endorsed Belaunde in the 1963 elections. He was, as Hobsbawm guesses, an office-holder in the community in the 1940s though at no point during a confrontation with the hacienda. Indeed in April 1963, as a major encounter was to be initiated, Tacunan was impeached in a communal assembly.

Seeing the way forward much more in terms of using his contacts for negotiating at the centre, he urged the various locales of huasicanchino migrants to petition to the president which they did later in that year. But my interviews and access to a key diary (see Smith 1989) suggest that at least part of other comuneros' initiative to go directly to the top was precisely to offset any suspicions that national authorities might have had that Huasicancha's split with Tacunan (a presidential ally after all) indicated their propensity for direct action.

This break (which proved final) between the one comunero who had achieved central regional political status not to say national recognition, and the bulk of the community itself, is revealing I think. Tacunan's career follows the classic path from indignation to negotiation. He sought to maximize his leverage at the upper levels of first regional and then national politics by using the weight of his popular support to barter for power – indeed to gain advances for supporters – only to find that the bartering at the top cast suspicions at the grass roots which led to reduced popular support. Seen from the local level, the huasicanchinos' fear was always of being forgotten: not of having one's voice enhanced by allegiance to one who could now be heard, but rather of having that voice drowned out by other demands from other followers with longer-standing familiarity with the byways of a politics of negotiation.[15] Hence Tacunan's break with APRA in 1959 greatly enhanced his legitimacy in Huasicancha as well as in a broad array of central Andean communities, while his bartering in 1963 lost him legitimacy in Huasicancha (though not in many of the other communities).[16]

As rumours of land reform increased and landlords and peasants alike became nervous about who 'possessed' what, so creeping land occupations began to spring up. Belaunde's attempt to regain control of affairs by announcing that peasants squatting on land would be eliminated from consideration for land reform resulted in widespread withdrawals. By contrast, not only did Huasicancha remain on occupied land, but advanced into the high *puna* hitherto never invaded before. Alarming headlines appeared in the Huancayo press warning of the impending terror.

At the point where Hobsbawm takes up this encounter Velasco had come to power (1968) and enacted the most radical land reform hitherto seen in South America, including the expropriation of the haciendas in the area, and replacing them with the massive production cooperative he speaks of. It is hard to speculate on the outcome of Huasicancha's rebelliousness had these conditions at the broader scale of national policy been less in concert with its goals. But by the time top-down land reform had reached the area, Huasicancha had been in a war of endurance with Tucle for four years and the hacienda buildings had already been massively destroyed and the administration driven out. Not only had Huasicancha, by the time I arrived, emphatically rejected the legitimacy of the new cooperative and refused membership therein; but soon after I left, the community actually began legal claims and physical incursions against it on the grounds that some of the so-called ex-hacienda land belonged in fact to the community.

Looking back it would be easy to see Elias Tacunan as precisely the kind of 'political leader' essential to peasant mobilization; and sentiment in the area to this day tends to reinforce this view, with a memorial day each year devoted to him and also a biography published in Huancayo by a migrant from the community (Anchimanya Flores 2010). But the relationship between the politics of Huasicancha's *reivindicación* and Elias Tacunan, the regional political organizer, are a great deal more complicated than such an image suggests. Indeed huasicanchinos' attitude toward the institution of 'politics' – one of suspicion not unlike today's street-level movements – was a significant component of what being *politico* among the huasicanchinos actually meant. This raises a difficult question, for the counter-nature of Huasicancha's politics was an immense part of the catalyst for action and what distinguished them from pretty much any of the other highland communities in the 1970s. But, as Hobsbawm notes, it also acted as a constraint in terms of the potential scale of insurgency.

This antipathy towards institutionalized politics will arise again in the next chapter as a result of an entirely different set of circumstances and with almost the opposite consequences. One possible reason for these different outcomes might lie with the relationship – or its absence – between the practices and organization necessary for the pursuit of livelihood and the practices and organization necessary for a politics that ensures the reproduction of the conditions necessary for that livelihood.

Blurred Vision 3: Livelihood and/or Resistance

We have already seen how the overall effect of out-migration, over time, was to increase investment in sheep. Many migrants of course left in distress and remained so, but some among them were able to accumulate occasionally and to use livestock to secure their savings. Others actually funded their initial migration through selling off some animals and, if then successful, reinvested. In their absence, flocks were cared for by kin and or neighbours (usually one and the same). While these arrangements achieved levels of complexity that puzzled even participants old and young, there was an underlying principle, captured in the term *huaccha*. In its narrowest sense the word means 'orphan' but, in so far as an orphan has no parents from whom to inherit livestock, *huaccha* can be used more generally to refer to a poor person (i.e. one without livestock). In employing a younger man or woman as herder one agreed to pass over fifteen or twenty animals at key moments in the life cycle – marriage, the birth of a child and so on – or in actual practice simply a number of animals for a given number of years of work. Through time, of course, the herd being guarded by the huacchero/a or his or her family would be made up of their own animals – themselves known as the huaccha or orphan animals – as well as the animals of their client or clients of whom there may be many and each with a different arrangement. As viewed by the comuneros then, physical flocks of animals had a mosaic-like quality in terms of ownership.

As the *hacienda* increasingly accumulated communal pastures through disposession, and then became ever more jealous in its exclusive use thereof, so two solutions offered themselves to shepherds. They could trespass or they could seek employment on the hacienda as shepherds. And yet even here the categories are misleading. The relationship between employer and employee on the hacienda was not very different from the arrangement among comuneros. In return for caring for say five hundred animals, employees were allowed to 'enter' the hacienda land with a designated number of the animals that they claimed as their own (but see above). These animals were referred to by the hacienda staff as the huacchas and in effect they constituted the wage, though with a built-in increment of course, in so far as the huaccha animals, obeying God's laws, went forth and multiplied. This fact (as well as many others, such as the intermingling of pure-bred hacienda sheep with unwashed *chuscos* [mongrels]) meant that there were endless disputes between shepherds and the hacienda.

While it is fairly obvious how trespassing with livestock works, there are a couple of features that need to be taken into account here. First, the vast stretches and hazardous landscape of the high *puna* make it extremely hard to control, to the point where the employment costs for the number of *caporales* (guards) to be effective offsets the benefits accruing from their work. Second, pastoral farming at these altitudes involves vast areas of rotation. Pastures have to be left idle to grow, but they cannot be so distant from one another that the animals 'walk off what they eat' just to get to them.

From a strictly functional point of view then, the huaccha beasts of an employee over and above those originally contracted for, and the flocks of trespassers large and small, presented much the same hazards to the hacendada. A further complication arose from the fact that an employee's animals were allowed to 'enter' hacienda property as payment for their services – animals the hacendada would call huacchas – but these were in fact made up of beasts belonging to migrants *and* those given to the shepherd over the years – as huacchas. Meanwhile the flock of a trespasser would be a mix of much the same kind; the more s/he wanted to earn sheep of his or her own by caring for those of others, the more urgently s/he had to trespass.

Nowhere then could the organization of livelihood and the threshold towards resistance (and the way it was organized) be more thoroughly entangled than here.

Blurred Vision 4: Kindred

There were then a number of important distinctions I had to sort out so as to move beyond the inevitable confusions of early fieldwork and get on with the task at hand. What I saw that task to be was at least partly a product of the work of the earlier writers discussed above. But the distinctions that motivated my early questions became blurred as my enquiries progressed. In my case, this did not mean throwing out the importance of these distinctions – figuring out who the people were that I was living with, working out the issues of their politics and so on – but rather forcing myself to see them in more processual terms than I had been prepared for. In coming to this understanding I was obliged to interweave the problems of one distinction with the problems of the other. This is nicely revealed by returning to my first question – who are these people? – which had not been satisfactorily answered by *criollo/cholo* or even by *hacienda/ comunidad* distinctions. In doing so I will speak of four people I knew from three generations of huasicanchinos.

I opened this section with a story about Martin Ramos who, as a young man, had been the catalyst that led to the initiation of Huasicancha's first successful encounter with the hacienda in 1937. The first time I heard a version of this story was during a rest we were taking at a community *faena* (collective work project). Primitivo Llacua, forty years old and an elected authority, was directing our work and interjecting occasionally with some aspect or other of the story of Martin. Primitivo himself was married to Mauricia Jacinto and for a moment I will turn to what her father Sabino Jacinto was doing at the time of the story of Martin's court-room manoeuvres. As that case was proceeding, Sabino Jacinto was heading a bridgehead of comuneros who ringed off some of the especially rich riverine land of the hacienda. (This is the *caserio* to which Hobsbawm refers earlier.) Just as with Martin, I had been told stories about Sabino too.

Indeed by the time I arrived in the area Sabino was a legendary figure, and I will return to his activities, looking at them from a different perspective, in Chapter 5.

Separated by over forty years in age and each apparently pursuing the two connected arms of an overall manoeuvre, Sabino and Martin had some striking features in common. Both had extensive experience as employees of haciendas. They were both familiar alike with what Martínez Alier (1973) calls *asedio interno* (bringing extra animals into the hacienda when being employed there) and *asedio externo* (trespassing their animals). In both cases there is evidence that the hacienda administration regarded them as especially problematic. Accounts suggest that this was because they combined intimate knowledge of the hacienda, its territory and its ways of operating, with the ability to mobilize significant numbers of families for their trespassing expeditions. In the case of Sabino, it is hard to assess when the tipping point was when the hacienda or the community realized that *entrando de ganado* in the form of trespassing for the purposes of livelihood had got to the point that it had to be treated as *entrando de la comunidad de Huasicancha* and hence a political challenge to hacienda control of land.

And then there are similarities too with Primitivo, my frequent interlocutor during fieldwork and member of a third generation. After early years living in a *choza* (hut) on the high puna, he had gone to Lima for his high-school education and returned to the community where he married Mauricia. They and their household and immediate kin had some seven hundred sheep and llamas which they grazed mostly in the high puna. Primitivo had been in prison some eight years before I knew him, at the height of the reivindicación, accused of being an 'agitator'. And yet his name rarely came up as one of the symbolic figures in accounts of the invasions. No doubt there are many reasons for this, but one of them could be that after some years as a hacienda shepherd he had become a caporal – that is one of the gamekeeper, guards – on Hacienda Tucle just as the confrontation got off to a start. As discussions in the community began to shift from the legal claims and formal petitions already in motion to more aggressive action, in May 1964 he was asked by the community authorities to act as a guide, first in locating key land marks for their claims and then in suggesting suitable spots for 'entering' the hacienda land. Shopped by other caporales, Primitivo was then removed by the hacienda to work in Huancayo. Once there he was approached with offers from the hacendado in return for ceasing his activities on behalf of the community. It was when he refused that he was imprisoned.

In Primitivo's case it looks as though the pressures arose from his excessive use of *asedio interno*, rising up through the ranks within the hacienda, insisting on more grazing rights as he did, to the point where in his case he flipped from being a guard to being a guide – to the invading community. But what happened next brings us back to the opening story, about Martin – for the initial reaction of the administration was not to fire Primitivo, but first to move him to a job away from the action, then to try to bribe him with offers (of money? of land?), and only as a last resort to have him arrested and accused of agitation. In some versions, Martin's story is continued from the 1937–38 encounter to the 1946–48 reivindicación when he too is taken aside and offered first some land in the Mantaro Valley which he refuses, then land in the jungle which he again refuses, and finally money – the stories tend to repeat each incident like the chorus in a song.

This addendum to the shorter story may allow us to rethink the problem of his marrying his best friend's sister who happened to be a blood relative of the owner of the hacienda. The story, after all, is told in retrospect. In the shorter version this appears to provide a pretext for the hacienda's representative to question Martin's role as a legitimate opponent of the hacendada. In the longer version the issue appears to be the reverse: the issue of marriage into the hacendada's family appears to expose Martin to the same temptations offered to Primitivo – to test his loyalties to the community. And we learn that he resisted them.

The issue of overlapping kinship returns again, this time in the case of Martin's brother-in-law and best friend, Victor, who turns out to be a key figure in accounts of the 1946–48 reivindicación. I was told that at an especially terrifying moment when invading members of the community were confronted by the 42nd Infantry and had heard the sound of the massacre that had just occurred in a nearby community to which Hobsbawm refers, Victor instructed everybody to sit down on the ground while he approached the officer-in-charge and engaged him in conversation (Smith 1977). He was subsequently captured, accused of being an APRA agitator, and imprisoned in *El Fronton*. And yet if Martin's wife was a blood relative of the hacendada then so must Victor have been, and indeed in one account the hacendada's mother, Anselma Garcia Espinoza, is said to have died in his arms.

At first it is striking that so many of these people are, one way or another, related to Maria Luisa Chavez,[17] the direct descendent of Bernarda Pielago who owned Tucle during the war with Chile. Certainly this works against the easy slotting of participants into

Kin Ties of Hacienda and Huasicancha Families

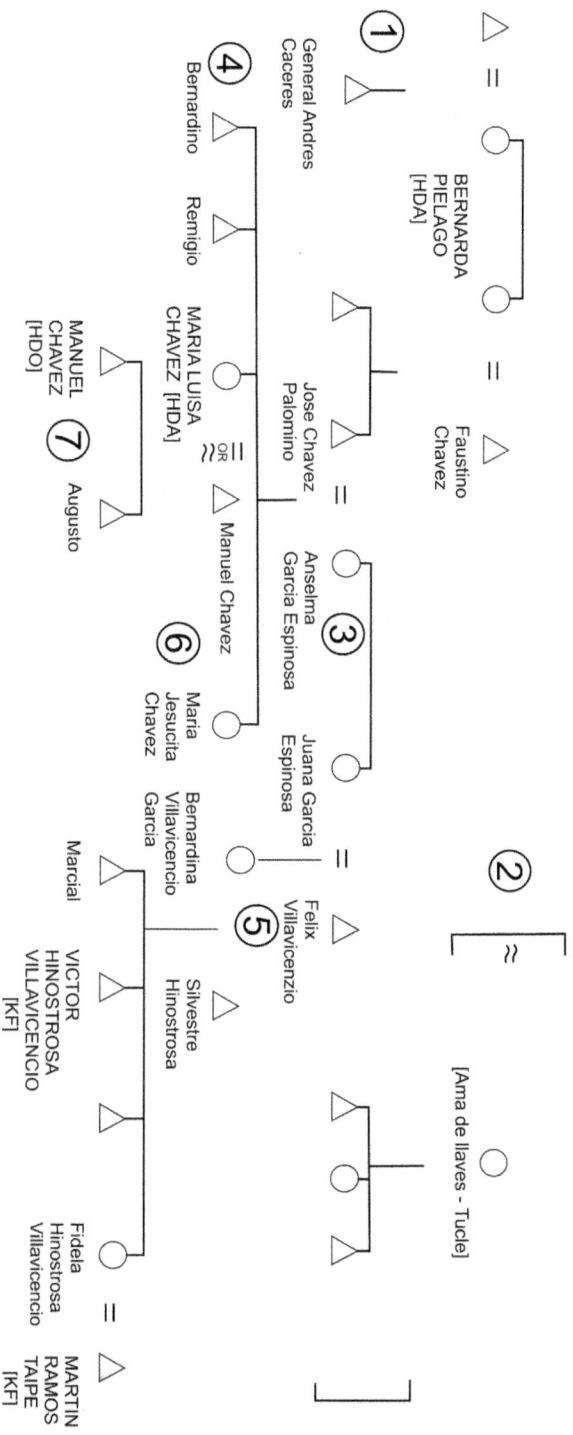

General Andres Caceres

BERNARDA PIELAGO [HDA]

Faustino Chavez

Bernardino

Remigio

Jose Chavez Palomino

Anselma Garcia Espinosa

Juana Garcia Espinosa

Felix Villavicenzio

[Ama de llaves - Tucle]

MARIA LUISA CHAVEZ [HDA]

Manuel Chavez

MANUEL CHAVEZ [HDO]

Augusto

Maria Jesucita Chavez

Bernardina Villavicencio Garcia

Marcial

VICTOR HINOSTROSA VILLAVICENCIO [KF]

Silvestre Hinostrosa

Fidela Hinostrosa Villavicencio

MARTIN RAMOS TAIPE [KF]

[Hda] or [Hdo] = Hacendada or Hacendado; [KF] = Key Figure in stories

1. Caceres, president of Peru 3 times in 1880s & 1890s. Nephew of Bernarda.
2. Faustino Chavez reputed to have died leaving three children of house mistress of Tucle.
3. Anselma, Maria Luisa's mother said to have died in the arms of Victor Hinostrosa, 'Maria Luisa's cousin'.
4. Bernardino died in childhood; Remigio is said to have died in his late teens. On a visit to Huasicancha he 'went into a trance' and was killed when his horse bolted through a low arch; Maria Luisa bought Maria Jesucita's share of Hacienda Tucle and died aged 103 in Huancayo in 1974.
5. Primitivo Llacua [KF] lived on the *estancia* of Bernadina Villavicencio & Silvestre Hinsotrosa until he was seven.
6. Manuel Pielago, the administrator of Hacienda Tucle, claimed to have married Maria Luisa and hence claimed to be the hacendado.
7. Manuel Chavez took over as hacendado from his elderly mother; Augusto was sometime administrator of the hacienda. The marriage was disputed by Martin Ramos [KF]

Author: Gavin Smith

Created by: Margarita Sandoval

one side or the other of the conventional image of the two Perus. But more interesting is the way these terms of proximity and gradations of distance sit within the tensions and bucklings of associated yet contradictory reproductive logics of different livelihoods. What made possible the migrants' accumulation of livestock as a hedge against the hazards of urban petty trades was the fact that the care of their flocks did not require cash outgoings. This was made possible by the perpetual actualizing of sets of intricate and intimate relations – or, in their absence, as an exclusion – being an orphan, a huaccha. Built into the huacchero relationship among the cumuneros however was the possibility of accumulating livestock on the part of the worker – to the point where sufficient animals were acquired that the orphan could break away and become an independent shepherd.

The hacienda used the same terminology for analogous institutions that were used in the community – and by extension the family. But if there was an ideological or mystifying feature to such usage it was not at the level of 'superstructure' but rather was as embedded in the social relations of production, as fetishism is embedded within the commodity. In the case of the institution of the *huacchilla* for example, the principle remained but the practice was reversed. It was not the heritage of animals that was missing and had to be made good, but the heritage of pasture which was missing and had to be made good.

The stories are about these tensions of intimacy played out across a growing set of material conditions ripe for class conflict. So, having found that one element of their role as key figures in the narratives of resistance is that both Martin and Victor could have chosen a kin allegiance and yet expressed their political agency by refusing it, what of Primitivo? At first it seems surprising that Tucle's administration gave him the job of guard, knowing as they surely did that he was married to the daughter of their most aggressive adversary. And then first they treat him with kid gloves when he misbehaves trying the same game of bribes on him as Martin was worried they may try on him (as in fact they subsequently did). And yet it seems that Primitivo had been as much a part of the hacienda as he had been a part of the community. Indeed until a few years before I knew him he had spent by far the greater part of his life either as a migrant or working for the hacienda. The first seven years of his life he lived and worked in the highland *estancia* of the parents of Victor: Silvestre Hinostrosa and Bernadina Villavicencio Garcia, the cousin of the owner of Tucle, Maria Luisa Chavez (see kin diagram above). In a sense Primitivo Llacua and his wife Mauricia Jacinto condense the issues at stake here – the former as soon as he could contribute his labour earning livestock through *huacchilla*, the latter born into an extended kindred that had long owned livestock and then regained pasture.

And if seeing the processes that produce the intricacies of relationship in this sphere complicates the picture, then so too for the categories we associate with politics. As I have argued elsewhere (Smith 1999: 53–87), personalities do not emerge in these narratives in the form of assertive or charismatic 'leaders' but rather as figures that condense in their actions the tensions of struggle within and by an apparently knowable community. Martin Ramos was by no means the leader of the 1937–38 encounter. He was scarcely old enough. He was simply a key figure in a variety of narratives. As we have seen for example, the legalistic role he played offset the confrontational role played by Sabino.[18] But the point is that all the accounts in their different ways have the effect of shifting decisive roles amongst a wide variety of people, old and young, villager and migrant, hacienda employee and comunero, comunero and comunera, and so on. The same goes for 1946–48, Victor Hinsostrosa is an emblematic figure but one among many with key positions. And from 1963–72 the number of people involved in the stories at one time or another is vast. The reason for focusing on accounts in which these people's roles arise is because they are difficult to fit into any one category – less so perhaps the kinds of categories that we might feel comfortable with: peasant, migrant and so on – but certainly any kind of categories that would be taken as final and frozen for the huasicanchinos themselves.

Most at issue here is the way in which we see community and the ways in which it takes form, whether we are speaking of a fairly non-affectual organic set of social relations that take form in a given space, or whether we are speaking of particularistic affectual ties.[19] At one point in his writings, Raymond Williams notes that the sense of a community as 'knowable' arose in rural England only with the expansion of the town lands; in other words, only at a moment when people who had shared a way of life, though by no means common conditions of living, were threatened – perhaps not threatened in identical ways but nonetheless one way or another threatened. Hobsbawm notes, as we have seen, that some form of organization is what gives collective action leverage and longevity, and he includes here traditional peasant community organization. In the down periods Huasicancha was a dispersed and often ephemeral community that became more 'knowable' when threatened in much the way Williams describes. But 'community', as we have seen, was perpetually problematic both in terms of the social relations in production practised by pastoralists and in terms of the ties of intimacy of key members. Community, then, neither pre-existed the politics of struggle nor did it emerge spontaneously in the face of opposition. It was nonetheless an essential component in the armoury of subaltern struggle.

Conclusion

There are then quite different political conclusions that arise from the two studies, but overall their different perspectives are complementary. Between 1963 and the Agrarian Reform that came into full force by 1970 the polarized social order of the countryside slipped out of control as a range of forms of insurrection spread through Peru (and other Andean countries too). These ranged from vanguardist guerrilla groups to peasant federations and agrarian labour unions, but most widespread in the case of Peru were a patchwork of land occupations of varying size, organization and effectiveness. In his article Hobsbawm sought to assess the political significance of these latter as distinct from the others. In doing so he tried to assess the kind of leverage that these scattered occupations, taken together, might have. And he used the evidence he had at his disposal to plumb the form that 'popular mobilization' in these cases took. In pursuing this project he used the especially rich archival material he found on Huasicancha and Hacienda Tucle. Seen in this light, his article is a contribution to the understanding of the effectiveness and possibilities for different kinds of rural mobilization at a time when such movements were having a powerful impact on the direction of Latin American politics and indeed politics further afield.

These same years also saw heightened collective struggle on the part of the huasicanchinos, a struggle that was still taking place as I began my fieldwork. Placed alongside other kinds of mobilization, the various Huasicancha uprisings could be seen as stages in a long-standing campaign in which different strategies served the interests of the various participants – residents and migrants, large herders and small, hacienda employees and comunero land-claimants, and so on. And Hobsbawm addresses all these issues making it possible to situate these kinds of political intervention alongside others. By contrast, while my own problematic was not dissimilar to his, for better or worse the intensity of my own research experience had the effect of placing those other forms of political organization and struggle on the horizon of my attention. Instead it inclined me towards the agenda Portelli (1997) speaks of, to explore 'the dramatic distance and indissoluble bond between "history" and personal experience, … and the historian's perception and reconstruction of broad, public historical events'.

Were we writing today it is doubtful that we would be assessing the strengths and limitations of peasant movements in revolutionary activity. We would be inclined to interrogate a variety of political movements rather than single out those of 'peasants'. And people identified as 'peasants' may not figure in any of those movements. Revolutionary activity too may be regarded as an unnecessary extreme for subaltern politics (though, see N. Smith 2010; Zizek 2011). But these differences do not change the spirit of the exercise. So what can we learn from the way we studied subaltern resistance and the different assessments that could thereby be made of the strengths and limitations of these kinds of movements? Perhaps by juxtaposing the figures of Braudel and Portelli we can then explore the interweaving of two somewhat different genres of history with a view to assessing what we can learn about the lynch pin that articulates popular mobilization with the leverage potential of strategic actions: what we can learn, that is, both from the movement itself – a movement that took place in the middle of the last century in highland Peru – and from the two differing accounts of that movement that I have presented here.

In the case of Braudel and Portelli there were differences both in scale and in a focus on what we might call 'conditions of possibility' versus a focus on 'structures of feeling'. Yet neither author dismissed the relevance the other's priorities. Likewise when Holmes and Marcus distinguished styles of ethnography, they were not speaking of one perspective to the exclusion of the other, but rather of a question of priorities, or angles of perception, rather than willed occlusions. It was important to set out the case in this way, so as to make clear how these differing forms of attention make differing kinds of contributions to the issue of popular mobilization and to the issue of strategic action (what I have been calling 'leverage') respectively.

First a rather basic point, and one that has nothing to do with 'fact grubbing versus mind reading' but is simply to do with how a professional historian works and how an anthropologist in the field works. In one sense they are quite similar. If read carefully, Hobsbawm, both in this article and elsewhere in his work, can be seen to be setting out a typology or a possible causal relationship and then subjecting it to attack from the evidence.[20] The historian organizes the desk by making sure the documents are consigned to useful categories before proceeding, and then substantially re-orders them after the evidence has been absorbed. The anthropologist arriving in the field tends to employ the same method, whether s/he admits it or not, but the result can be considerably more alarming not to say discomforting. I found myself perpetually faced with the confusion of my surroundings and found that attempts to order things into the categories I had at my disposal only produced further discomfort – a sense of lack of fit. And I tried to resolve this.

But what resulted did in fact push me towards a different understanding of what might be called the history of the present. As I hope I have shown, the priorities I set myself often drew me away from ways of seeing and listening that were crucial to the history I was supposed to be learning about. As it turned out, the prioritizing of 'the architecture of social relations' over 'the natives' point of view' was not sustainable. Fortunately for me the people of Huascancha were sufficiently forceful and excited about their current lives and their past history that they would not let me retreat to the comfort of my own categories. My 'desk' was perpetually being tossed into disorder. This in turned affected 'the way I did history' in a distinctive way from Hobsbawm and, if we are to take Cooper seriously, how I thought about politics too. Especially important was the way in which the categories that emerged were only useful tools (as opposed to obstacles) when the relationship among them was rendered in terms of their perpetual 'processual' interweaving.

This in turn meant that my interpretation of the tactics on the ground and their connection to the way people went about making a living did not so much differ from how Hobsbawm saw it but rather took on a more fluid character. It also meant that the crucial question of organization had to break out of a mechanistic imagery to include how what Raymond Williams calls 'changes of presence' were re-formed as the prevailing structure of feeling among huasicanchinos unfolded through history. Perhaps it is obvious that the culture of opposition that led the huasicanchinos to expropriate the livestock of the highland haciendas in the 1880s was not the same as the culture I found in the 1970s. But just how the transmission from the one to the other took place cannot be reduced to the presence or not of 'organization' unless we expand the use of that term. And as I have already said, using the word 'community' as a means of doing so simply adds to the mystification. Let me deal with each of these issues in turn.

In regard to the first, Hobsbawm (1974) notes as follows:

'A land invasion is normally a rather standardized affair, decided and carried out by the entire community as a collective entity.' (126)
'The intention to invade is therefore normally known to the landlords and the authorities, who are in a position to take countermeasures, if police, troops or their armed men can be got to the disputed area.' (126)
'The invasion itself is a major ceremonial affair.' (127)

It is of course when the community decides to turn trespassing by individual comuneros and their families into something to be done 'by the entire community as a collective entity' that the practical business of livelihood becomes the political business of resistance. Hobsbawm's reference to the calling in of troops reminds us that this can be a pivotal moment that could go one way or the other for the community. It may be that making the invasion a ceremonial (in contrast to a quotidian) affair is one of the means for announcing this transition, certainly to the hacienda but perhaps also to the participants. For one thing it invokes the idea that the collectivity of huasicanchinos is sufficiently a community to observe certain shared ceremonies. But the way Hobsbawm puts it here gives the impression that the choice of such a transition tends to lie with the invaders. Yet it may in fact be that the hacienda has called in the troops or been especially brutal in its use of its own guards that pushes the community to act collectively, employ ceremony, and hence inevitably raise the issue to one to be dealt with in the courts.

In other words there is a quite decisive moment when multiple practices of livelihood, albeit perpetual irritants to the hacienda, are turned into 'popular mobilization' precisely for the purposes of leverage. This makes it hard to agree with the distinction Hobsbawm makes between instrumental 'demonstrations', such as sit-ins that are used as 'a means to an end' and are to be found in 'modern' political negotiations, and what he calls 'traditional movements' in which squatting and occupations are 'not the means but the end in itself' (ibid.: 129). The distinction he appears to be making here – between a political move that is a cog in the machine of negotiation, and a political move that, taken as such, is a non-negotiable end in itself – is not I think one that distinguishes modern from traditional forms of resistance, nor a distinction that serves useful analytic purposes. But it *is* one that may play a very important role in strategic actions themselves, as Hobsbawm himself seems to suggest with this delightful remark: 'Not being either Western liberals or student insurrectionaries, the peasants quite failed to make a choice in principle between peaceful and violent, legal and non-legal methods, 'physical' and 'moral' force, using either or both as occasion appeared to demand' (ibid.: 142).

Secondly, in his discussion of Piven and Cloward, Hobsbawm argues that it is not protest per se that troubles the authorities; what worries them is when they see protest being organized in 'formalized collectivities, however structured' (as discussed earlier in this chapter). He also notes that it is through organization that protest at one time is recoverable for later moments. Of course I have been at pains to make clear to the reader that while there was certainly a great deal of organizing of protest going on while I did my fieldwork, I had some difficulty identifying the collectivity that was pertinent to my study – or at least where the edges of that collectivity might lie.

In the article Hobsbawm acknowledges the vital role of local people, especially those with large and influential families, but for him it is important that 'by their side as often as not were "instigators" or "agitators"' (ibid.: 146), and he speaks of communist and Aprista agitators. 'The role of the political movements – APRA until its transformation, and later the various Marxist movements – is plainly important, both as mobilizers of local cadres [and] as catalysts of peasant activity' (ibid.: 145–46). The transformation to which Hobsbawm refers occurred around the time that Tacunan left the party in 1959, and yet he himself quotes at some length from hacienda correspondence of 1945 – just as renewed confrontations were on the horizon – in which the chief regional figure in APRA 'has offered [us, i.e. the hacendados] all support within his power', while the Aprista mayor of Huancayo is lauded for warning at public meetings that 'the Party of the People would [not] support any movement of the communities to the detriment of the haciendas' (Laive Papers 16 Oct 1945. Ibid.: 139).

As in the previous issue, here too the different positionalities we occupied as we 'did' our history generate different kinds of historical narrative. Given the nature of the sources, mostly the hacienda administration and the regional press located at some distance from the pampa and quite aware that fear sells papers, the written information itself is hard to assess. Hobsbawm's astute remark about Tacunan seems to me to catch much better the relationship between established parties and their officers on the one hand and the *reivindicación* struggles in the highlands on the other. 'His career and their struggle were not the same' (ibid.: 142). And it is noteworthy that while there were a number of people in Huasicancha who had been figures of authority and who openly declared themselves to be Apristas – in all cases through their ties to Tacunan – all those I spoke to who had actually been imprisoned denied any party interest, let alone formal linkage.[21]

If we are to get at the texture of a mobilization like that of the huasicanchinos we will need to remain on the threshold between publicly acknowledged institutional political organization and the kinds of fluid and elusive forms of organized collectivity that I found among the huasicanchinos. This in turn raises the question of how different forms of organization and formalized collectivity transmit the experience of protest from one period to another. So how moments of the past were accessed and the form of their transmission necessarily became a focus of interest. Not just the expropriation of the 1880s but the reivindicación of 1937, and again in the late 1940s, were crucially important for participants in actions in the 1970s, even if in many cases the present actors were not alive when those things happened. This current access to past historical experience could not be taken for granted but the role of organization alone does not seem a sufficient explanation. Instead we need to note that the forms of transmission changed as did the character of what was being transmitted. It is not that the terminology of 'stages' in a 'campaign' are wrong but rather that, given the perspective I was increasingly taking, what I was seeing was an unfolding culture of opposition whose shape-changing arose in and around the different conditions of possibility and resulting potentialities from one conjuncture to another.

The awkward moment of resting on the threshold between the institutional organization of 'negotiated politics' and a pervasive culture of opposition that arises from a history of 'a politics of refusal' means that we need to be careful about how we assess interests and goals. It would be absurd to speak of any kind of politics without reference to goals of course. But given the unfolding of a collective culture of opposition – whose character itself included shifts in the communicative techniques for its transmission – we cannot impute the interests of one category or group across historical periods. Anyway a reading of any of my instances of blurred vision reveals how unhelpful both the categories and the imputing of interests are for trying to get at the kind of history – or better put, histories – I was recording.

* * * * *

As I hope I have shown, finding myself among a group of people engaged in a resistance campaign, features that seem fundamental to such struggles like collectivity and solidarity were very hard to grasp. The kinds of conflicts that arose in the era of industrial mass production in which the lock-out or strike had the effect of drawing clear lines of conflict between the 'us' and 'them' are frequently contrasted with the multiple lines of connection and conflict of current movements. The lines of dependency on the one hand and conflict on the other shifted wildly across the Tucle-huasicanchino complex in a way not entirely dissimilar to current movements. Moments of heightened interdependency induced tensions that led to conflict. And the same went for the differing trajectories of the figures themselves. There may have been moments when the curtain went up and the spotlights flashed on and actors froze in unison: no one could be seen to budge. There were other times that involved winding through the jagged terrain of negotiation – for individuals, families and groups. Nor should we forget what those on the other side of this picture were doing: the instances of actual and physical repression were useful not just in and of themselves, but acted as well as perpetual threatening and potential off-stage reminders that repression by force was always possible. The way history was recounted by huasicanchinos was not just *about* these things; it was against them too.

My purpose has been less to suggest that any kind of history is as good as another, but rather that it is important to take into account the purpose that an author sees his or her intellectual intervention to be serving. Given a shared Left political project, different inflections of historical interpretation may be more useful when combined than when held apart. In the case of Huasicancha as an instance of 'peasant land occupations', I would say that their perpetual view that the current institutional reality is not as it should be and that it can and should be opposed has become synonymous with the huasicanchinos' collective sense of what it is to be huasicanchino – what might be called their culture.[22] This seems to draw together the work of Hobsbawm on the role of organization and the work of Thompson on the role of a culture of opposition in the constitution of subaltern refusal.

Notes

1. In 2012 alone, three anthropology journals devoted special issues to anthropology and anarchy, the stamp of approval coming perhaps a little oddly but also revealingly from Mauss, the social democrat. They were joined by two non-anthropologists with a special knack for catching the mood of the moment: Jared Diamond (2012) who offers us *The World until Yesterday: What We Can Learn from Traditional Societies?*, and James Scott (2012) who published a paean to anarchism.

2. *Primitive Rebels* (Hobsbawm 1959), *The Making of the English Working Class* (Thompson 1963) and *Peasant Wars of the Twentieth Century* (Wolf 1969).

3. Roseberry (2002) tackled paradigmatic shifts in anthropology by employing the notion of different generations of scholars; in doing so he was influenced by Abrams (1982). Although Hobsbawm's *Age of Extremes* (1994) is considered the most personal in his series, it is interesting to note that he begins on a very touching personal note in *Age of Empire* (1997) in order to then reflect on 'the twilight zone between memory and history' produced by transmission across generations when we move to a more recent historical period. The book begins:

   In the summer of 1913 a young lady graduated from secondary school in Vienna, capital of the empire of Austria-Hungary ... To celebrate the occasion, her parents decided to offer her a year abroad ... Uncle Albert was happy to welcome his young relative, who travelled to Egypt on a steamer ... The young lady was the present author's mother.

   [It goes on] Some years earlier a young man also travelled to Egypt ... That young man was the author's future father, who thus met his future wife where the economics and politics of the Age of Empire, not to mention its social history, brought them together. (Hobsbawm 1997: 1–2)

4. This was not a coincidence. I had written a critical assessment of *Primitive Rebels* in the early days of my graduate school. I argued that his stress on the role of outside leadership and party support for the 'success' of peasant rebellion, failed to take due regard of how they themselves might assess 'success'. Possibly a passing acquaintance of Hobsbawm, my supervisor sent the paper to him. Hobsbawm suggested a meeting in which he encouraged me to find a field site that would demonstrate my case. Some weeks later, after a visit to Peru, he suggested the site and provided me with the various contacts that got me to Peru. On my return (after he had written this article) he provided endless encouragement and critique, thereby providing a model for intellectual engagement that it would be hard to emulate.

5. I would like to thank Corin Sworn and Creative Scotland for making this trip possible.

6. A word on terms. *Hacienda, hacendado. Comunidad, comunero.* 'Hacienda' refers to a [usually quite large] farm originally in principle (though rarely in practice) granted to owners by the Spanish crown; 'hacendado/a' refers to the owner. After 1919 rural communities could make a claim for a collective legal identity based on their character as 'indigenous' people, hence 'comunidad indigena'. In the late 1960s the term 'indigena' was replaced by the term 'campesino' or peasant – 'comunidad campesina'. A person with a claim to membership in such a community is a 'comunero/a'.

   Much of the literature in English uses expressions like land 'invasion' or 'occupation'. In Spanish one finds the terms *entrar, entrando* meaning literally that the lands claimed by the *hacienda* were 'entered' by others – possibly as trespassers, possibly actually claiming the land. *Asedio* may also be used for these latter instances, meaning either 'harassment' or 'siege'. The term systematically used by huasicanchinos both during my fieldwork and today is *reivindición*. There is no proper translation for this term in English. 'Recuperation' fails to express the sense of redressment involved, and the latter word fails to include the sense of forceful and assertive politics implied. I therefore generally retain the Spanish word.

7. An interesting point here is that Martin's date of birth is still recorded as 1912 by a local historian. Since, if true, this would have made him 23 or 24 at the time, it seems that the records were indeed adjusted. The accusation of being from another community was patently false however, as indicated by the fact that no version of the story refers to community authorities responding to it. I suspect it was part of the common accusation made by the *haciendas* and the press that outside agitators were involved (see Hobsbawm, below).

8. He later suggests that the decision to apply for this kind of recognition 'evidently marks a stage in the development of communal political consciousness'. Among other things, it gave a formal standing to authorities hitherto of a merely de facto community, and 'it necessitated both the formation of a cadre of campaigning leadership (drawn from both resident and emigrant *comuneros*) and a mechanism for collecting funds (Hobsbawm 1974: 136–37).

9. In case the reader misses it, from the fact that there could not have been a Vice-Regent of a republic, Hobsbawm draws the conclusion that the original claim must have been made when Peru still recognized the Spanish crown. Faced with similar documents, others have often more cynically ascribed such phrases to the sheer ignorance of the peasants who were making up their claims as they went along.

10. Interestingly the people of Huasicancha take the opposite view to Hobsbawm's suggestion that Tucle was mistaken in using a deed of sale to settle the land issue. They feel that, because the settlement did not take the form of a court document, they could not begin the subsequent attack from the point they reached in 1948, but had to claim this earlier land in addition to that of the next stage. This supports Hobsbawm's observation that, while quick to engage in confrontational struggle, these peasants – like many others – placed very high regard on the legal recognition of their claims, if not over and above then certainly alongside their physical occupancy of territory. Payment took the form not of a wall but of the digging of a massive ditch (*sanja*), visible to this day.

11. Hobsbawm would no doubt be amused to know that currently (2013) Huasicancha has now gone through two successful court hearings in which it is claiming 40,000 hectares of land once run by Hacienda Antapongo. They are optimistic that the final hearing will meet with success.

12. *Capacitación* under Velasco involved more than is usually understood by the term 'training'. Formed in 1971 as a special government organization to work on the orientation and organization of the national population SINAMOS (Sistema Nacional de Apoyo a la Mobilización Social) – whose acronym, '*sin amos*', translates as 'without bosses' – became the focal point of public intellectuals with prior experience of a range of mobilization strategies. Headed by Carlos Delgado who had been an organizer of youth for APRA, among its figures was Hector Bejar released from prison by the regime after his capture as a guerrilla leader.

13. Formally recognized *comunidades indigenas* and later *campesinas* produced an extensive range of formal positions for village authorities to occupy – administrative president, vigilance president, mayor, governor, justice of the peace, and so on. There were sufficient for them to be circulated continuously around the elder male members of the community and, through the committees attached to them, to provide apprenticeships for younger men.

14. APRA (Alianza Popular Revolucionaria Americana), as the name suggests, was originally founded as an anti-imperialist, popular left nationalist party in 1924. After extended periods of frequent illegality in the years leading up to Belaunde's presidency the party had become increasingly centrist with a view to taking the ballot box, losing many of its rural radicals as a result.

15. While apparently aware of the differences between the significantly more internally commercialized (and hence differentiated) 'communities' of the Mantaro Valley (many of whom gave initial support to Tacunan and his movement) and highland communities

like Huasicancha, Hobsbawm often tends to lump them all together. The much larger and better-off towns of the valley had long-standing experience of negotiating with departmental, regional and national political entities (see Long and Roberts 1984, among others). It is in these more incorporated towns (not really peasant communities, since in many cases the legal *comuneros* were in fact the least powerful in the municipality) that the various regional and national political parties played an important role.

16. The heuristic and tactical value of thinking of subaltern politics along a spectrum between negotiation and refusal is developed at greater length in Chapter 6.

17. And perhaps even more remarkable when we note that Maria Luisa's grandmother, Bernarda Pielago, was the aunt of General Andres Caceres, twice President of the Republic. And it was through her that he managed to recruit *guerrilleros* in the highlands.

18. As Hobsbawm notes, 'The entrenched legalism of peasant land invasions is a fact which both the student and the agitator neglect at their peril' (1974: 124).

19. Excluded here is the legal fact of community as the *Comunidad Campesina* which was, as Hobsbawm notes, a crucial pre-condition to the land claims following 1919. Land claims and recognition of indigenous collective identity however were by no means as tightly connected as such claims often are today, especially in North and South America.

20. For example, in this article he begins by proposing three distinct bases for peasant land occupations. One of these is 'acquisition on principle': the principle that labour on land bestows ownership. But he then shows that this supposedly peasant principle turns out to be a principle of land ownership held by Spanish colonial law too. So in so far as the vast majority of *haciendas* based their ownership on deeds drawn up at that time, his other two bases for distinguishing among occupations have to be rethought.

21. At this point it will have dawned on the reader familiar with Latin America that I have studiously avoided any reference to the twenty-year period of *Sendero Luminoso* and army conflict that followed my last visit to Huasicancha in 1980. While I am aware that discussion of the role of vanguardist cadres in peasant communities is central to questions about this period, this paper is intentionally constrained by the limits of my own evidence and Hobsbawm's at the time he wrote. That said, however, I do think the evidence here is useful for understandings of the relationship between *Sendero* and the highland people of this region (see Mayer 2009).

22. When I visited huasicanchinos in Huancayo in 2013, forty years after I had begun fieldwork, I was given a fat dossier: the community's claim to a further 64,000 hectares of land. Migrant clubs there, as well as in Lima and in Italy, are actively involved in this campaign, not simply by organizing sporting and musical events to raise money, but also by engaging in animated discussions about strategy.

– Chapter 4 –

HISTORY'S ABSENT PRESENCE IN THE EVERYDAY POLITICS OF CONTEMPORARY RURAL SPAIN

[I]t is a fact about the modes of domination that they select from and consequently exclude the full range of human practice. What ... the dominant has effectively seized is indeed the ruling definition of the social ... It is this seizure that has especially to be resisted. For there is always, though in varying degrees, practical consciousness, in specific relationships, specific skills, specific perceptions, that is unquestionably social and that a specifically dominant social order neglects, excludes, represses, or simply fails to recognize. A distinctive and comparative feature of any dominant social order is how far it reaches in a whole range of [these] practices.

– Raymond Williams, *Marxism and Literature*

Introduction

In the last chapter I took a particular moment in the past and a particular place to explore the relationship between an instance of collective praxis and two slightly different intellectual projects that sought to understand it.[1] The hope is that despite the distance in time and place we can still learn something, both from that collective praxis and from the pluses and minuses of the respective interpretations. I now turn to a very different kind of political setting but I continue to reflect on the political implications of differing interpretations of what is happening here. We return again to Spain, and we begin with the moment I began my fieldwork in 1978 and then move on to subsequent periods.

There was a *Pacto de Silencio* (Pact of Silence) in Spain when I arrived in search of a field site. Franco had died in 1975, and in the period that followed the heads of the various political parties agreed that the transition to democracy could only be negotiated if there was an agreement to forget – known in Spain as the *Transición*, with a capital 'T'. The length of that Transition period is up for dispute. Indeed, in light of the high-handed conduct of Spain's Partido Popular after 2010, some may argue that there has been no transition from a dictatorial regime to a democratic one (Torres López 2013). Even so, once the Spanish Socialist Party (PSOE) became more established, following their election in 1982, what some would call 'the culture industry' went into high gear. A vast array of books, newspaper articles, and television documentaries began to appear, all in their various ways agonizing over the period since the Civil War (1936–39). As I will explain below, I refer to this kind of expression as the realm of 'formal culture'. As the years went by a kind of political discomfort about the past began to be heard throughout Spain from a different realm, a kind of culture that arises out of what I call 'practical sense'. By the turn of the century a number of (mostly) rural communities were taking the initiative of opening the mass graves in which the victims of Franco's repression had been buried. Expressions of this kind interrupted the hitherto rather compartmentalized realm of intellectual production of 'history' so that eventually, in 2007, the Socialist government passed a law generally referred to as 'The Law of Historical Memory'.[2] It would not be true to say that what was occurring here was a fruitful conversation between professionals in the business of producing formal culture and another kind of cultural production arising from ordinary people's practical sense – as though the matters of concern to people going about the business of making a livelihood in other occupations were given serious attention.

I will try to reproduce the unease this caused me in different settings and at different times by beginning with two stories that occurred over this period.

Salamis and Paellas

Some ten years after I finished doing fieldwork in the Bajo Segura I was travelling through Aragon with my son visiting some of the towns that had been caught along the front between the Nationalists and the Republicans. I had brought with me a novel that was set in the area near Girona at the end of the Civil War. One evening, as we drank on a patio in a small village, I found myself reading a review of the English translation which had just come out. Colm Toibin, a much respected Irish novelist, spoke of the book in glowing terms, remarking that apart from one or two local histories it was perhaps the first real confrontation with Spain's difficult past.[3] Later, when I saw the dust cover of the English version, I found that Mario Vargas Llosa spoke of it as one of the great Spanish novels of recent times.

The book, a huge popular success and made into an art-house film, was *Soldados de Salamina* by Javier Cercas (Cercas 2001; and trans. 2003 as Soldiers of Salamis). The story revolved around an incident that actually occurred. Through the ramblings of a picaresque journalist and failed novelist we learn a convoluted story as he lights upon provocative 'facts' – which he often doubts – and begins to realize that he might have the makings of a best-selling novel. I cite the dust jacket of the English translation:

> In the final months of the Spanish civil war, as the remnants of the Republican army retreat north into exile, fifty prominent Nationalist prisoners are taken out to be shot. Among them is Rafael Sánchez Mazas – writer, Fascist, and founder of the Spanish Falange.
>
> As the machine guns fire, Sánchez Mazas takes advantage of the commotion and escapes into the forest. When his hiding place is discovered by a militiaman, he faces death for the second time that day, but the unknown soldier merely looks him in the eye and turns away…

To continue, the book revolves around the story of Sánchez Mazas, a well-known story for many Spaniards since he himself spent much time publicizing it after the war. Short-sighted to the point of near blindness and having all but destroyed his glasses in his escape, Sánchez Mazas is hidden and fed by young deserters from the Republican army. Although later subject to trial for their Republican past, these men and their families avoided punishment and were even the recipients of the occasional food packages, all courtesy of the generosity of their Fascist benefactor – or so at least was Sánchez Mazas's story.

The rascally journalist, though by no means a Fascist sympathizer, is sufficiently cynical about politics generally and enough of an opportunist himself to recognize a kindred spirit in Sánchez Mazas. But as he tries to make a novel out of a story which inevitably has such a sleazy character at its centre, he soon begins to realize that, without finding the soldier who spared him, the story is dead in the water. In the last third of the book the figure of Miralles emerges. Although 'he knew nothing about politics' (Cercas 2003: 150) and was originally attracted to the Anarchists, he found himself, more or less through chance, in the Communist forces of General Líster[4] which 'liquidated the Aragonese anarchist collectives on Líster's orders' (ibid.: 151). Our author is frustrated by Miralles's refusal to come clean about whether or not he was the soldier in question, and indeed Cercas plays the same game on the reader; we never really know if this character in the book is, like Sánchez Mazas, a real life figure or not. In many ways though, he represents not just every Republican who fought – in so far as 'he fought in Belchite, in Teruel, at the Ebro…' and then retreated with the other 450,000 across the French border (ibid.: 151); and he represents not just every boot soldier who fought for the Republic – but every soldier: 'soldiers always fight for civilization'.

What seemed especially appealing to the reviewers I read was the poignant image of *individuals* caught up in the chaos of war and the corruption of political positions. Along with the picaresque author figure and the militiaman Miralles, a minor figure sets the mood for the book early on, saying to the author, 'I don't know what you think, sir, but to me a civilized country is one where people don't have to waste their time on politics' (ibid.: 16). That, then, is one story.

A second story takes us back to my early fieldwork in the late 1970s and early 1980s, and moves us from the world of novels, film renditions and reviewers to the more mundane world of making a livelihood by working in agriculture, the workshops and homework in the Bajo Segura region, south of Alicante. As we have seen in the previous chapter, the people in my Peruvian fieldwork would speak about the politics of their *reivindicaciones* almost to the exclusion of anything else. So it came as something of a surprise how apparently de-politicized talk about politics was in this new site. After all, the constituent elections were taking place during my first year, with local candidates running for all the major parties. And yet issues were of little social consequence. Instead the major debate was whether one or other candidate would have influence in the halls of power, tugging at the sleeve of a more powerful member of his party apparatus. Hardly surprisingly then the results saw a landslide victory for the incumbent party, the *Unión del Centro Democrático* (UCD), whose leader had been appointed by Franco to manage the Transition. Perhaps I should not have been surprised after so many years in which their political views were repressed and anyway irrelevant in the absence of elections. But I pressed on anyway. Although it was by no means central to my research project, occasionally I would mention to people that I was interested in the Civil War. One day, sitting outside his house, a friend my own age who was from the area joked about my persistence: 'You English have a fetish about the Civil War. We don't talk about it. Around here there is no politics; we're just not political.'

Most of the time my attention was drawn elsewhere for it to matter. The frustrations of trying to find people who would help me figure out questions of livelihood were far too frustrating to think about (historical) resistance as well. Apart from two factories with a couple of hundred workers each, work was either widely dispersed among homeworkers or took place in semi-legal workshops, many of them hidden behind esparto grass in the countryside. It was hot work for them; and frustrating work for me much of the time, seeking out one isolated informant or another and then urging them to give me time in the hot and sweaty setting of their workplace. Gradually, as the weeks turned into months and the spring turned to summer, my partner, who had just had our second child, and I, together with our eldest daughter, became part of a circle of friends.

During the hot Sundays of summer we would join these families and walk the four kilometres to a natural swimming hole. There the children swam while we drank the strong heavy local wine and set about preparing a large paella. These were relaxed and drawn-out afternoons of idle chatter and companionship. We talked about our families; my friends talked about their work, some stressing the many and varied jobs they had worked at, others taking pride in a small *choza* they had in the fields and the work they did there in the evenings. When that first year or so was over I looked back fondly at those momentary breaks when both my informants and I shared in a break from the very different stresses of our respective work. The watering hole at Albaterra was a time of spontaneous *communitas* when we could let our cares go and talk about whatever came to mind (Turner 1969: 132). Or so I thought.

It was some years after those pleasant moments by the waterhole that I was wandering through the stacks of the library at the University of Toronto and came across a directory of people killed by Franco after the end of the Civil War in 1939. About four inches thick across the spine, it was set out like an official gazetteer with the name, place of origin, sometimes a date of birth, and the date and place of death. As for the latter, I was so surprised to find 'Albaterra', the name of the few scruffy houses near our watering hole, referred to so frequently that I sought out a map of Spain to see if there were any other place with the same name. But no, this was Albaterra, Franco's concentration camp, which operated from the moment his troops reached the beleaguered Republicans on the docks of Alicante until the camp's closure in October 1939. And when I returned to look at the gazetteer a second time, I now found the various towns of my field site occurring with some frequency, as well as the family names of some of my drinking mates on those Sunday afternoons.

For me, I associated the watering hole with laughter. I had no other associations but those days with the kids splashing around, the wine, the food and the good company. Despite my professed interest in the Civil War, neither it nor the period that followed it were ever mentioned while we were there. And yet one historian of the period writes 'Albaterra was the camp which left the greatest memory and the biggest mark: a minimum of thirteen books tell us of the horrors that arose in the heat of the recent victory and the repressive urges of the troops and the Franco authorities' (Rodrigo 2005: 158). And a letter of one of the prisoners reads:

> Thirty kms from Alicante there was an extermination camp; every day in the mornings there were firing squad executions of all those who were officers or political commissars. I had to eat my commissar documents to save myself. Classifications took place, some were sent to jail, or others, officers and commissars, were shot; there were many beatings and minimally corporal punishments for the most minor of infractions and nothing to eat for two or three days. Pardons usually weren't worth anything [*no servían para nada*]: some who had them were simply passed on to face the firing squad ... When few of us were left, Franco had the place cleaned up; he didn't want anybody knowing that it had existed [*no quería que nadie supiera que había existido*]. (Written testimonial of Theo Francos, quoted in Rodrigo 2005: 158. My translation)

In those early months the man who had been mayor under Franco was still in office, but after the elections a new mayor arrived. One day, as I was trying to put some order into the jumbled papers thrown into an abandoned room in the municipal building, he poked his head round the door and said, 'I got a call the other day from a numismatist in Madrid. If you find any old coins in there, let me know'. It seemed an odd request, but the jumbled mess in the room was such that I thought he could equally well have asked for a horse and cart. Did he know, or was it just the Madrid coin collector who knew, that all the land of that municipality had been expropriated by an Anarchist (CNT) and Socialist (UGT) alliance. The greater part under the Anarchists had been collectivized and local currency printed. When my friend had dismissed politics did it mean what I had taken it to mean, or was he referring to the disdain Anarchists in the war had for the formal politics of the Republic? Did he even know?

Formal Culture and Practical Sense

In what follows I want to try to explore the relations – perhaps positive, perhaps negative – between neatly articulated accounts of the past produced in the present, and the past accessed in the present in more fractured, less formulaic ways. In doing so I run the risk of too neatly carving up the social space into two spheres. I acknowledge the dangers of such a Manichean formula – and especially the relatively short shrift I give to the first of these spheres; but even so I believe that, seen from this perspective, we do in fact learn something about the dead weight of current exercises in liberal or social democracy.[5]

I want to talk about the production of accounts of the past that have as their purpose the creating of a narrative of the past – like Cercas's novel, among other forms. And I want to talk too, about the sense of the past that arises perhaps almost tangentially as other purposes are being pursued – or perhaps not at all, as appears to have been the case at the swimming hole. Halbwachs (1980: 40) notably remarked that 'individuals always use social frameworks when they remember'. So what if those frameworks, those sites where the interactions to which Halbwachs is referring, are absent? After years of interviewing workers in the U.S. Studs Terkel bemoaned the fact that they had been 'conditioned not to have a sense of history. Experiences are perceived as individual, almost chance, not collective' (Terkel and Grele 1985: 43). Perhaps the same applied here.

These two spheres are profoundly interconnected: the one the everyday world of getting on with the practicalities of work and the daily affairs of life, and the other the kind of work whose purpose is to produce narratives of one sort or another – although the ways in which this occurs depend a great deal on the political setting from one time and place to another. There are many similarities between the evocations of the past in *Soldados de Salamina*, for example, and those of my informants in the Vega Baja. The book is indeed a compendium of the shattered fragments of privatized, isolated and disoriented memories that many ordinary people hold, and the fictitious author's sentiments are often close to their own, not least his ambivalence about the few facts that do emerge unsystematically out of his personal journey. But whether it is the way the book reflects this grass-roots feeling that accounts for its success, or whether it contributes to a broader process that has the effect of suggesting that these feelings are 'natural', legitimate, and if not the best way to be in this world then at least one that serves for the moment – these are issues I want to take up in this chapter.

It is of course quite evident that the politics of contemporary Spain cannot be set loose from the country's past. Whether we are speaking of the degree to which the political class are truly representative of the people they claim to speak for, as they claim, but as the *indignados* insist is not the case; or whether Spain is a fully paid-up member of 'Europe' or its victim: these issues are not just to do with how different people understand matters of the moment, but are how they locate this moment in their understandings of the past. And yet, even were we to stick with these pressing concerns of the day it only takes a little leap in the imagination to realize that were we to ask a professional politician or a national journalist for his or her view of events, not only would the content of what they told us be distinct from the response of a stevedore taken away for a moment from his work, or a woman homeworker stitching shoes, the *form* of their reply would differ strikingly too. Holmes and Marcus (2005) have spoken of the former interaction as a kind of meta-ethnography; it is as though, as a result of the work they do in producing accounts, the respondents already have a narrative to hand. My initial examples, however, of the novel and the watering hole are concerned with ways of articulating – or not – understandings of the past, and it is this that concerns me here.

Perhaps I am being too simplistic but the image I want to invoke is of two different realms of society in which culture is produced. To a certain extent this reproduces a very old distinction in the meaning of the word, one I associate with Matthew Arnold. Here culture is what is sought by those devoted to its production to ward off philistinism and anarchy: '[Culture] seeks ... to make the best that has been thought and known in the world current everywhere; to make all men [*sic*] live in an atmosphere of sweetness and light' (1994). And the other appears to be more like the multiple ways in which I learned about culture as an anthropology graduate student. Since that time, of course, anthropologists themselves have rendered the notion much more complex and controversial, while other disciplines have resorted to the term for a vast array of uses and hence meanings (Scott 2003), while Arnold's usage though continuing has become rather an embarrassment, an apologia for 'the canon'. Nevertheless, despite their differences, both these meanings persist as we see especially in the work of Bourdieu where the idea of culture as a means of distinction and also as a broad societal realm of what is taken for granted comes close to usages of hegemony by many anthropologists.

I do not depart in any significant way from Bourdieu's framework,[6] but I do think it is useful to distinguish between the culture that is made by those in the business of producing cultural artefacts and the atmosphere that results from the consumption of those artefacts taken as a whole.

> [C]ultural producers are important because they help to maintain or undermine belief in the legitimacy of the prevailing power arrangements. They help to set the boundaries of the thinkable. They confirm or change the stories through which we tell ourselves who we are. (Sinfield 2004: 308–9)

Likewise I think it is useful to distinguish this kind of atmosphere from the emergence of a taken-for-granted world that arises from ongoing activities that are less self-conscious about the business of producing 'culture'. I would say that *Soldados de Salamina*, for example, represents a quite self-conscious instance of the production of a cultural artefact, not quite in Arnold's sense, although the positive assessments of his writing colleagues does seem to put it in the realm of 'the best that has been thought and known'.[7] And I would say that the kind of sense that people held when I chatted with them during their work or even at the swimming hole did not represent such a self-conscious production of culture. To distinguish between these two I use the expression 'formal culture' to refer to the first of these as well as its intentionality vis-à-vis its effects. I use Gramsci's term 'practical sense'[8] to refer to the other, and what interests me is the way the two interact. I find Williams' notion of 'structures of feeling' helpful in exploring this problem.

History's Reach as Formal Culture

In mid-2006, a journalist writing a comment column in a Spanish national newspaper remarked, 'The [Civil] War continues and its conclusion is uncertain' (*El Pais*, 15 June 2006). From the moment the conservative Partido Popular (PP), which had governed since 1996, fell from power to be replaced by the Partido Socialista Obrero Español (PSOE) following the Madrid bombing of March 2004, disputes in the public arena over Spain's recent past became increasingly acrimonious. The new government's attempts to open up a dialogue with Basque nationalists were at first so promising that the PP could only respond by accusing the Prime Minister, Zapatero, of cowardice – for withdrawing from Iraq, and for talking to 'terrorists'.

The PP campaign found little public sympathy until the party turned to an entirely new strategy. They began to mobilize the 'victims of terrorism', largely the families of those killed by ETA (*Euskadi Ta Askatasuna* [Homeland and Freedom]). By suggesting that the PSOE were showing no respect for *victims*, the PP was attempting to turn the tables on the formula it had held while in power. Instead of the old narrative of victors and vanquished they now sought to invoke a balance between two sets of 'victims': 'ours', the Francoists who had 'died for God and country' and 'yours', the Republicans. It was in reference to these kinds of face-offs that the journalist remarked that the Civil War was not over.

A few years earlier, just after the Partido Popular had formed their first government, the Spanish anthropologist Susana Narotzky and I were talking with three women and a man in a day-labourer's house in a *barrio* in the Bajo Segura. All of them had been secret members of the Socialist Party throughout the Franco period. As we talked, each of us becoming more absorbed in the emotions stirred up by going back over life histories filled with the perpetual fear of the hunted, we all began to share a sense that we were doing something illicit. A silence suddenly fell, 'as though an angel had passed', as my mother would have said. We all looked at each other. Nobody quite knew how to move on. Then one woman shrugged and said, with a hesitant smile on her face, 'Ah well, we'll all be back in jail soon anyway', and the others laughed nervously. The man said, 'It's as though we have been out in the school yard. It won't be long now before they ring the bell and call us all back inside again'.

For me as I sat in that house with these old people, I think I interpreted their discomfort more as a sign of how deeply Franco's terror had affected their lives. I am not sure how much I felt that their fear – that they may find themselves back in jail – was a realistic assessment. But something else happens when we place it in the context not of the past but of the contemporary discourse of formal culture. Although the journalist's remark that the Civil War continues and its conclusion remains uncertain was no doubt meant flippantly and was made some years later, it is not hard to imagine that it takes on a much more ominous sense seen from the perspective of that barrio in south-eastern Spain. No doubt within the field of journalistic thrust and counter-thrust the remark was more of a rhetorical one than anything else. But seen from the perspective of the people who felt a silence pass, it is likely to induce quite different feelings and assessments of the present.

So before returning to the Bajo Segura I want to describe this broader setting – the discursive conduct of public politics whose effect is the constitution of a kind of emergent, taken-for-granted atmosphere within which political possibilities are discussed. This is one sense of the way in which Williams used the notion of a structure of feeling, the one that relates to what I am calling 'formal culture'. He was often urged to disaggregate what he meant, from the whole to its class differences. But he resisted this and insisted that, in given eras, there was a set of shared relevancies – albeit unevenly and in highly complex ways – across all members of a social formation in a given era.

> [W]hat we are defining is a particular quality of social experience and relationship, historically distinct from other particular qualities, which gives to the sense of a generation or a period. The relationship between this quality and the other specifying historical marks … [such as] the changing social and economic relations between and within classes, are an open question … At the same time [what we are referring to here is] taken as *social* experience, rather than as 'personal' experience. (Williams 1977: 131)

It is tempting to think of this as a kind of decentred or superorganic 'sprit of the age'.[9] But Williams was quite aware of the role of power in the forming of these sentiments, and spoke of how this felt for ordinary people.

> [We are speaking here of a] response to *a whole way of life largely determined elsewhere* … [This] unevenly shared consciousness of persistently external events … is then a specific form of consciousness which is inherent in the dominant mode of production, in which, in remarkably similar ways, our skills, our energies, our daily ordering of our lives, our perceptions of the shape of a lifetime, are to a critical extent defined and determined by external formulations of a necessary reality: that external, willed reality – *external because its means are in minority hands* – from which, in so much of our lives, we seem to have no option but to learn. (Williams 1973: 290, 295–96. Italics added)

We might think of the disputes at the national level over 'historical memory' as an (albeit perpetually failing) attempt to produce an integral 'spirit of the age', a broadly agreed-upon frame formed at the apex that would effectively configure the form *participation* of a very defined kind could take, given the history of Spain: something to be called 'democracy'.[10]

During the twelve years of PSOE government that followed our fraught discussion in the barrio, and on into the first years of the PP government that replaced it, debates in the realm of formal culture were framed by the pact of silence, up to the turn of the century in fact.

Then, on its return to power with an increased majority in 2000, the PP shifted away from its previous careful obtuseness about its links to the Franco regime and began increasingly to present itself as the party representing the values of integral Spain, a kind of nationalism that configured any variation on what the national (and class) project would be, not just as anti-Spanish, but as a threat to the very essence of the body of Spain – a discourse consistent with that of Franco's Movimiento.[11] This position in turn gave rise to a heterogeneous series of initiatives by small groups of people connected to those who had been victims of Franco's repression in the Civil War and afterwards to open up the mass graves of people summarily executed by the Movimiento. Starting in the small community of Vilafranca del Bierzo, within a couple of years these initiatives had become something the government could no longer control.[12]

They gave the lie to the prevailing expert opinions regarding Spain's peaceful transition from dictatorship to democracy. Political elites and scholars in Spain as well as public figures in the European community had made frequent pronouncements that the managed amnesia of the Transition engineered by Franco's technocrats had been a huge success, in so far as supposedly the entire Spanish population had signed a *pacto de silencio*. Yet now it was evidently falling apart. And newspapers, books, television and films soon took up the hue and cry.

This entry onto the public stage of historical memory exemplified by a media frenzy has been periodized by a number of 'historians of the present' (Aróstegui and Godicheau 2006), and strongly criticized for its sensationalism, inaccuracies and partisanship (Juliá 2006a, 2006b). But both the periodizations and the criticisms tend to discuss social memory since 1975 only within the realm of formal culture, suggesting that grass-roots experiences simply shadowed those developments. 'Spanish society embraced the new liberties and the experience of modernity without much interest in remembering the sordid past', says José Colmeiro. 'On the contrary it [*sic*] actively tried to dissociate from this past very rapidly' (Colmeiro 2011: 26).[13]

Hesitant Histories and Practical Sense

Santos Juliá (2006b: 68) describes the period when I had been going to the swimming hole and the next few years when I continued fieldwork in the following terms: 'The recent past was absolutely absent from Spanish public life during the Transition and in the 1980s'. And indeed I had been struck not just by this absence, but by a similar reluctance to engage with the past among the people with whom I was living. By contrast, one could hardly have said the same thing about the level of formal culture that followed, from 2000 to the fall of the government in 2004. Superficially, Sunday supplement magazine series, television documentaries and movie features all appeared to be debating Spain's recent history. Yet, like flies buzzing round a cowpat, every programme, photo series, and documentary refused to settle on anything decisive. The effect was not so much one of debate, but rather a noisy though well-packaged account, one which – albeit obscured by the talking heads who appeared to be opening up the closed doors of history – was notable for *not* significantly clashing with the account that had been surfacing in Franco's twilight years. The Republic and attempts to defend it during the Civil War were uniformly painted as Spain's inevitable and repeated descent into chaos and fratricidal killing, while the role of the army perpetuating the violence of the war years and of the Church in its enthusiastic and vicious destruction of the personas and families of Republican supporters were avoided as though circling dangerous bulls. And this very discourse seemed to belittle why on earth people would give their lives for such shallow matters. Nothing as fundamental as General Lister's explanation for why he fought was ever given an airing: 'We were waging an anti-Fascist war and a revolution at the same time: the peasants had their land, the workers ran the factories and the people had weapons' (*New York Times*, 10 Dec. 1994).

The point of relating the details of these events at the national level is to note the particular way in which they play upon and effectively produce a pervasive sense of unease and confusion, thereby confounding the emergence of a kind of political agency that would lead to even minimal democratic sovereignty. The political issues and personal ideals that might explain why one person was prepared to take a political position that led to the grave, while another was not, and still a third was the one with gun in hand, are given the Philistine term 'fratricidal war'. When I asked one informant in Barcelona whose grandparents had been anarcho-syndicalists whether he thought television treatment in this period of the Franco repression really affected people who had their own experiences to draw upon, he said, 'Two years ago my grandmother was quite clear about the ethical value of her people's action in the Civil War. Now she no longer talks about those people. She focuses instead on the dangers of Spain falling back into a Bosnia-like barbarism, bereft of political pattern or direction.'

It is important to recognize the effect of this perpetual chorus of threatened internal strife on the grass-roots interactions I want to talk about now. At the level of formal culture, during the Transition and in the years following it, a strange inversion took place. 'Democracy' was not associated with the open and often lively dialogue – on the streets and in the cafés – of fundamentally different political ideas, but rather with the necessary discretion of silence and compromise achieved by the Transition. And the alternative to ordered democracy was fratricidal chaos. Despite an attempted military coup to reinstall the military in 1981, the long shadows threatening Spain's voyage to civilization (called 'the European Union') were not those of a possible return to the likes of Franco's repression but a return to the likes of the Republic configured as a moment when real participation in government meant chaos. It is hardly surprising then that, among Spanish public figures, the refrain 'Franco's Spain, let us never go there again' was always drowned out by the refrain 'Let us forever be spared the experiment of Republican Spain'.

It is not my purpose to go beyond the moments leading up to the passing of the Law. Rather I want to use this period to turn now to the realm of cultural production that takes place within the everyday world of 'practical sense'. As I have said, a pervasive belief was that the order and amnesia that framed Spain's Transition arose from a general agreement among the Spanish *as a whole* not to revisit the past or to encourage a kind of civil society that would run the risk of chaos. This is the position for example of two of Spain's major writers on the period, Paloma Aguilar (1996) and Santos Juliá (1999). It is not a conclusion one would draw from living in the Bajo Segura over that period.

To address this I need first to turn to a methodological question – how we might seek to understand the insecurity and discomfort that arise from long experience of fear among an extremely fragmented group of people. To do this I will turn to a quite different element of Williams' notion of structures of feeling than the one I have so far discussed. First we need to accept two assumptions that he makes. The first is that all consciousness is social consciousness. Hence, 'its processes occur not only *between* but *within* the relationship and the related' [italics mine] (Williams 1977: 130). Second, we need to realize that, as students of social practice, we arrive on the scene after the event. We are rather like those who fetishize the finished product of the commodity, obscuring the labour process that produced it. But with us the fetish is the named social practice, rather than the experienced moment that we can only very roughly capture when we give it a name. For Williams this gap is not merely unfortunate or inconvenient; it misses out an absolutely vital element of the production of culture.

So I have already made a rudimentary distinction between formal culture and practical sense, and now we can make a further move. We are not making a distinction between a broad array of cultural forms shared in the public arena on the one hand, and on the other the intimate culture of the personal, somehow hidden away from society; rather we are assuming that practice is perforce social and then we are making distinctions with respect to the forms this takes. What I am calling practical sense is social in two ways which distinguish it from either formal culture or a categorizable social practice or relationship. These two characteristics Williams describes as 'changes of presence'. The first is that it is while these moments are being lived that they are experienced, and 'when they have been lived this is still their substantial characteristic' (Williams 1977: 132). And the second is that 'they do not have to await definition, classification ... before they exert palpable pressure ... on experience and action' (ibid.: 132). So I am concerned with these kinds of moments *and* their relations to formal culture – overt assent, private dissent, and more nuanced interaction with selective elements of formal culture.

Williams is talking in terms of a kind of unfolding through time. He is cautioning us in micro form against a kind of teleological history of action, in which all gestures move towards the result we find as we look back on them. We need to sense the initial contingency of a present moment while resisting anticipation of the outcome of a practice by naming it too early, and this is especially so in times of real change (hence his expression 'changes of presence'). Yet I do not think Williams can release himself entirely from a kind of teleology. Even as he keeps bringing us back to the lived moment, he is almost awaiting that next moment of culture when the lived becomes articulated, or perhaps it is better to say, when it becomes 'related'.

> [T]he peculiar location of a structure of feeling is the endless comparison that must occur ... between the articulated and the lived. The lived is only another word, if you like, for experience: but we have to find a word for that level. For all that is not articulated, all that comes through as disturbance, tension, blockage, emotional trouble ... If one immediately fills the gap with one of these great blockbuster words like experience it can have very unfortunate effects over the rest of the argument. (Williams 1979: 168)

What is being described here seems to me to address precisely the issue I am trying to deal with in the Bajo Segura – an acutely lived practical sense, and certainly one that is lived socially. It is not its private or non-social character that is at issue but its hesitance before the moment of being related, or articulated – 'tension, blockage, emotional trouble'. Williams actually refers here to 'comparison'. He talks of the endless comparison that must occur between something lived acutely and 'at this moment', and whatever vocabulary we have available to hang it on. Of course in a stable society formal culture provides such hooks.[14] As one Spanish historian working at the grass roots puts it, 'Any reading of an individual past is deeply conditioned by the prevailing framework because every person tries to make his/ her memories fit into it' (Cenarro 2002: 178). That Spanish formal culture following the Transition failed substantially if unevenly in this regard is evidenced by the movements to open up the mass graves.

While not necessarily thinking of unarticulated changes of presence in terms of a kind of delay in the progress of linguistic formation – and hence their eventual 'emergence' into language – Williams' injunction to seek a way of understanding in these terms can nonetheless be useful here. But instead of seeing this gap between present experience and the ability to articulate it in language, it might be heuristically helpful to see the gap rather as the result of the interface between formal culture and practical sense. And not just as they interact in the present but how they interacted in the past – and how the past history of that interaction provides the tools for the domination by formal culture of cultural meanings arising out of practical sense.

We need to know something about the peculiar nature of localized terror in Spain to understand this – how it was produced by Franco's Movimiento in the twenty years following the Civil War, and how it then became the foundation on which the Transition was built.[15] Put another way, we are speaking of a succession of regimes: a regime which destroyed the spaces of social interaction for selected enemies of the state thereby curtailing the social articulation of fear, and then a subsequent regime which relied absolutely on this failed articulation as the basis for the establishing of an especially tamed kind of liberal democracy.

As Susana Narotzky and I have written elsewhere (Narotzky and Smith, 2006), for many years it was really not possible to talk to people about the 1940s or 1950s. When one takes into account that I recorded eighty-seven life histories, it makes one realize the oddness of this statement. Of course the point is that lived moments and extended periods of fear do not get articulated, much less do they become related stories. Rather they crop up unexpectedly and unexplained like floating deadwood on a lake, ramming into your side, throwing you off the direction of your interview but – oddly I suppose – making both informant and enquirer conspire in heading back to the original direction. 'He came back sick.' 'I wish I could have spoken to her.' 'Yes, three daughters. Yes all married here. No. I've never seen the inside of the church, not since I was a girl of fifteen.' 'Yes Jesus was lucky. He originally had eleven siblings, but after the war there was just him, so he got the plot.' ... and so on.

Nonetheless as I met people over the years that I returned, this flotsam and jetsam did eventually begin to produce patterns that linked bits and pieces giving them an emergent coherence. Assurances by political elites and some scholars that nobody wanted to remember began to sound more like wishes than facts. In the years following Franco's death, evidence accumulated; it became increasingly obvious that the dominant classes were holding the reins of democracy very tight indeed. Especially for Socialist, Anarchist and broader Republican families this made them feel that, despite the end of the dictatorship, the sacrifices they and their elders had made had not given them the agency they had expected. They had expected their voices, their versions, to be heard, but instead found themselves asked to celebrate silence.

As our elderly interviewee's remark about the school yard suggests, nobody was so naive as to think that the old masters had gone; indeed from day to day one heard complaints about such local figures. But for those who had identified with the socialists during the Repression (and this had been the majority party in the town during the Republic), what was especially anesthetizing was the participation of the PSOE itself in this pact. Far from endorsing their sense of outrage the party de-legitimated it. Then, in 1996 when the conservative Partido Popular replaced the socialists, it was evident that the bad honeymoon was over. As frustrations grew and people heard of local initiatives elsewhere, narratives began hesitantly to emerge, handicapped by habits of fear and by public reminders that such narratives poisoned the present. Yet these emergent accounts put the lie to the new democracy by exposing the elite's suggestion that an unwakened memory meant a quiet sleep.

To the contrary, the effects first of political repression and then of the personal self-imposed repression that followed could be devastating as this case discussed by Angela Cenarro makes clear.

Elías Górriz's father and uncle were two victims of a vigilante mass execution. Elías's mother, however, never told him how or why his father had died. Elías in fact every Tuesday and Thursday evening went to a bar where he played cards with three other men. His mother was later to say that she said nothing to her son because she wanted him to lead a 'normal life'. The three other men were Franco supporters; two of them had held minor offices in the municipality.

As newspapers and television began to report sporadic actions around the mass graves and the destruction of memorials to Franco, Elías began to show some interest in a narrated past and indeed provided a rather awkward account of the immediate postwar period. He had a vague idea of the fact that his uncle had at one time been mayor, although he could not say exactly when. When I suggested that his uncle might have been mayor during the Popular Front government, he asked what the Popular Front was ... During the interview, he raised objections when I encouraged him to persevere in his efforts to discover information about his relatives' past. Although he expressed the need to know more about them, he explicitly declared his fear of discovering an uncomfortable truth ... The inability to create a coherent narrative about his genealogy resulted in a sense of guilt. After projecting [this] guilt onto his father's background ... [he had] fantasies about a presumed dishonest past and acceptance of his relatives' guilt.

Over the course of time, and partly at the urging of a young local historian, Elías raised the issue with his mother and discovered some of the details of his relatives political past. He is no longer welcome at the bi-weekly card games. (from Cenarro 2002: 174–76)

As I began to go over my field notes from the early days of the Transition and rehearse what I found in them back to people in the town, it began to emerge that personal accounts seemed either to recall survival through acceptance of an albeit humiliating hierarchical order, or to recall survival through short-term hazardous manoeuvre. The more integral stories served to stress membership in the local community, understood as a social order dominated by the local *patrones*.[16] As one woman put it, as she ended her description of the period, 'Todo en su sitio, todo en su sitio' with a certain gleam of satisfaction on her face – 'Everything in its place, everything in its place'. The year was 1979. She was almost perfectly repeating a famous phrase Franco had used in one of his last speeches to the nation, as he handed the reins to others, assuring the Spanish people, that 'all is lashed down and well lashed down' [todo ha quedado atado, y bien atado] (Preston 1993: 748).

But another kind of narrative made no reference at all to the social order and concentrated entirely on the hazards of the black market. The very haphazardness of the stories, often flying out of the blue, apparently from nowhere, not only recalled the structure of feeling felt at that time but reformulated it through the sense of the present they produced in their sporadic telling.

To understand the differences between these two emergent senses of the past we have to embed them in the different kinds of practical sense from which they arise. Franco's 'formal economy' was controlled through ration cards. For a town generally under suspicion for its Republican sympathies, not to say something much worse, many people were denied cards unless they could secure *un aval* (a letter of good character) from a member of the local hierarchy. For those who had been especially active in their support for the Republic these were very scarce indeed. 'When I came back', says Celestino, 'nobody would speak to me. It wasn't that you had no friends, but friends avoided one another. I got work in the next town.' To be deprived of a linkage to the community in terms of hierarchy, then, meant to be deprived of *un aval*; and being deprived of *un aval* meant being prevented from securing the ration card that gave at least minimal access to the formal economy. It was not economic hardship as such that pushed one into the *estraperlo* (the semi-legal market) but evidence of 'politics'. And this in turn formed the conditions of social practice and interaction: the essentials of what social membership there was available.

Fernando Arroyo had a similar background to Celestino. He had a reinforced bicycle on which he carried smuggled wheat. The people in his immediate world were so strapped for cash that no family alone could afford his supplies, so he went round accumulating small orders for each trip, and in this way gradually developed a network of people who shared in common their 'exile' from Franco's new society. 'Exile' has a special meaning for people who lived in Franco's Spain. For many years in approved dictionaries there was no ordinary entry for the word exiliado. It simply meant to have committed a crime against Spain, to be a traitor. The dictionary I have from 1960, republished in 1975, has only:

> **Exiliarse:** *vivir voluntariamente lejos de la patria* [to live voluntarily far from one's homeland]. (Alonso [1960] 1975)

Often I discovered that people who said that they had 'gone away' or 'had come back' had not in fact moved at all. Indeed that was the case for Celestino. He did not 'return' as he says; he had never been away. Rather he had been in hiding. Such people had been cast out.

On the other hand the narratives of order did not reflect directly the political sympathies of the narrator's family, so much as the social order that defined their means of livelihood in the early days after the war. As landlords and large tenants returned to the town, a kind of Machiavellian *modus vivendi* took shape. They were, after all, faced with the almost quintessential unreliable labour force. By using the *aval* and by bestowing tiny plots of land on selected families they were able to regenerate powerful vertical ties between themselves and what were known as *aniaga* families.[17] Again, the practical sense and the form and content of accounts of the past are inextricably bound together.

What is notable about these two kinds of memories of the twenty years after the Civil War is that one incorporates the person in what Williams would call a 'knowable community', one which is locally confined, hierarchical and above all ordered; while the other is about a kind of social exile and stresses in short sound bites quite intense 'changes of presence' for the person (see Chapter 5). As these bits and pieces accumulated over the years of my interaction with people, I felt that there was a threshold of articulation that could not be crossed. I think you see it in the story of Elías, above, in Carmen's problematic account of her father below, and in the small moments that Celestino and Fernando are able to throw into their discussions with me about quite other things.

But putting these two kinds of local accounts alongside the narratives of formal culture reveals something else. As I have said, during the Franco regime Republican democratic voice was configured as a chaotic fratricidal period that tore apart the body of Spain, while under Franco's Movimiento, because nobody spoke out of place, peace and order were brought to the sacred body of Spain. Then, with the Transition, the Republic is portrayed as a deficient kind of democracy that could return again to Spain; one which, left to the uneducated popular sentiment, risks the emergence of partisan hatreds that would threaten to tear apart the social fabric. By contrast the kind of democracy offered by the elite through the Transition ensures that nobody speaks without first exercising careful constraint – nobody 'speaks out of place' in other words. And the result will be peace and order. If we think of this in terms of violence, then an extraordinary inversion has taken place. The terror of Franco's repression is made to stand for order *against* violence, while the agency of the masses represented by Republican democracy is made to stand for the violent rending apart of the social body. This is asserted with a steel hand under Franco and repeated in a velvet glove through the Transition. And it finds its echo in my field site in southern Alicante – where order and hierarchy *can* be articulated by those absorbed into the integral community but the political agency of day-labourers is expressed only through fragmented allusions to picayune opportunities in the black economy.

It is not then simply that the repression silenced those who had sympathized with the Republic. It was that this repression made possible the ordered democracy of the Transition, which in turn then imposed guilt on anybody seeking to make sense of their own or their relatives' more agential democracy by trying to bridge the gap that Williams talks of between experience and articulation.[18]

We can sense the kind of personal anguish that can result in the case of the liminal figure of Carmen Gutierez who, as a schoolteacher, finds herself not just responsible for voicing the narrative of formal culture but herself confusingly embedded in it. Confusing because Carmen, as the daughter of a man who had been mayor for a short period when the Anarchists controlled the town, comes from the background of the exiles not the integrated. After Franco's victory, the Falangistas caught him and beat him so badly that the doctor could not get the threads of his shirt out of his flesh. He died two days later.

Carmen knows that I know about her father. We are sitting on her patio trying to talk about the past, when Carmen nervously remarks on the conditions of the roads in those days, and then, as we seem to approach somewhere near her father, she says 'It wasn't really political here. Things were just in turmoil. There was so much ignorance.' Carmen's mother comes out onto the patio. There seems to be a quiet anger in her voice. I am not sure if it is directed at the elisions of her daughter or simply at the facts of her past. 'He was a baker', she says. 'We had the bakery.' Then she shifts the time frame to the years following her husband's death. 'The people here would come in and buy bread. Everyday. And they wouldn't say a word. Some wouldn't even look at me. For twenty-five years it was like that. I had three daughters marry here. They wouldn't let me into the church. I stood in the *plaza* outside.' As the old lady told me this, Carmen was so profoundly shamed she showed every sign of wanting to leave the room. 'Yes,' she said, 'my father was an Anarchist. But even so he was a good father.'

Again, I need to stress: it is not the difficulty of accessing a traumatic and unhappy past in itself that is the only issue here. It is the role played by the multiple channels and artefacts of what I am calling formal culture that have the effect of denigrating not just Carmen's father – who managed to be a good one at that, despite being an Anarchist – but denigrating any kind of Left history she tries to access. Nor is it just that in all our many conversations Carmen omitted to speak of her mother's absence from the church at her wedding; she was actually ashamed of it.

The blockages and confusions that Williams speaks of are not just confined to the people of Carmen's generation who have found themselves caught up with the apparatus of state that produces formal culture. It can happen too across generations where the uncompromising nature of counter-politics in one generation gets passed on to the next, only to be caught up within the terms of negotiation of the new kind of 'democracy'. We see this especially clearly in the final case that I want to relate here, one where the main protagonist had for years insisted on expressing his socialist principles. For Juan Gil, socialism was not *unfortunately* about class conflict; it was *inherently* about an insistent struggle by manual workers against those who exploited them. This was a Left politics that could only succeed through collective solidarity and uncompromised confrontation with the class enemy. Moreover the need for 'no-compromise' was especially important in the Spanish case, as Juan saw it, because the structural antagonism built into the social relations of labourer and landlord was multiplied by the extreme political sympathies of the latter. As the possibilities for political organization began to open up with Franco's old age, Juan began gathering day-labourers together who insisted on a uniform daily wage and hours of work.[19] And by the time I arrived in the field he was recruiting people into the socialist union, the UGT [Unión General de Trabajadores].

Some years later Juan's son, Juan Jr, was urged by his neighbours to run for mayor on the Socialist platform. By now the father was an old man and his son had been encouraged to run in some respects as the symbolic representative of his father. In the event he did not get a clear majority and so had to negotiate with others as each issue arose. Yet every time he did this, his father flew into a rage. Here is the younger Juan's description:

> When Franco died, my greatest desire was to install a democracy, but to go from a dictatorship to a democracy without firing guns as we did here is very difficult … not so much for people my age [he was born in 1940] but for older people. On either side they still had open wounds … but we started to work in order to bring the rest of them over to our way … it was difficult but the fight for democracy was my job … We had this fight with older people … I had these terrible discussions with my father and often we didn't speak to each other for several days … I wanted them to see the way of realism … What we could not have is a situation where if twenty years ago you threw a stone at me, now I throw it back at you. I couldn't understand that … We had to think of a way … but it was very hard because [my father] had suffered and endured a lot in those years and he couldn't forget it … But nowadays things have changed a lot and one has to recognize it … one has to be democratic. (Field Notes 1995)

For the younger Juan, the compromises he had to make were temporary ones, made necessary by the tensions of the early years of the Transition. But increasingly the party office in Alicante insisted on further compromises, more discussions, and less and less on the substance of what Juan Jr felt had drawn him into politics. For Juan there finally came a point where he felt a choice had to be made between engaging in politics and his own self-respect among his colleagues, and he withdrew from all forms of political office. The last time I saw him he told me that he felt he had been broken by this journey away into the alien world of politics. He had, he said, sacrificed dignity and responsibility for a politics of convenience and compromise, and was threatened with the loss of the respect of his family and neighbours as a result.

Conclusion: Realms of History and Picaresque Politics

If, as one historian of Spain has noted, 'For the individual man or woman who does the act of remembering, memory is a kind of social inheritance … in which the individual is placed from birth' (Cenarro 2002: 178), then the younger Juan's entry into the political arena has caught him between the inheritance of his father's insistent memories and the demands of a formal culture of amnesia. But in this he was the exception that proves the rule. Unlike his peers, he had not entirely dismissed the path of politics. And his father had not taken the route, for example, of Elías's mother, who had sought to ensure her son's social integration through her own reticence.

The story of the two Juans, father and son, serves as a means for thinking how entry into the arena of political agency can begin to give fragmented accounts a potential coherence.[20] The character of the local accounts that stress order and integration is that they are reinforced by the narratives produced by formal culture; their coherence relies precisely on a kind of settlement, an emersion in residual structures of feeling. What we see, as fragmented accounts begin to emerge, is the hesitance and difficulty that arises from the failure of formal culture to provide links across intense experiences, as though what vocabularies do emerge do so without grammars, or are hung on what grammars seem available – in this case a kind of picaresque agency that arose within the semi-legal economy.

In Chapter 3 I asked how the questions of an older generation of Left scholars might be both critiqued and built upon by a subsequent generation. I illustrated this by juxtaposing an article by Eric Hobsbawm with my own work. I tried to show how the fieldwork I did at the time Hobsbawm was writing cast the mould that shaped later modifications. But inevitably the end period of that research allowed me reformulations. We were both concerned with conditions of the possible and with how people press up against those conditions. Hobsbawm perhaps leant towards prioritizing the first of these, while increasingly through the course of my work, urged on by the people of Huasicancha themselves, I leant towards the second: how they pressed up against those conditions.

The approach I have used here shows how I thought about such issues by the end of my fieldwork in the Bajo Segura of Spain. I suppose I have to acknowledge a tinge of disappointment, not to say pessimism, as the period of that research wound down. And I think it is precisely this kind of disappointment that attracts us to a certain kind of evocation of the past through literary techniques quite similar to those of the novel. A cynicism towards history as a wasted past leads to a pessimism towards history's possible openings into the future. And a kind of picaresque individual character emerges, savvy, amused, evasive, but always clothed in the respectable garments of 'good scholarship', 'good art' and 'good writing'. And there is no question that such writing, as I have shown for Javier Cercas, captures an element of the present – perhaps even serves to provide us with insight into the structure of feeling of the current epoch. But it should only provide a model for the way we write ethnography if we do so simply for the accolades earned in the realm of formal culture, but without social or political purpose.

In the chapter that follows I suggest that the small-scale interpersonal and vivid nature of encounters over the contained period of fieldwork, usually of not more than a year or so, make such a choice tempting. I try to show how we might instead inflect the lens of our vision in our ethnographic work so as to shine albeit momentary shafts of light on the potentialities we find for collective class praxis as we pursue our studies both on the ground and in the archive. Then, in Chapter 6 I combine the conditions of the possible with emergent possibilities for negotiated and for counter-politics.

Notes

1. An earlier version of this chapter was published as Smith 2009.
2. While generally referred to in these terms, the actual title of the law makes no reference to historical memory: *La Ley por la que se reconocen y amplían derechos y se establecen medidas en*

favor de quienes padecieron persecución o violencia durante la Guerra Civil y la Dictadura [Law for the recognition and expansion of the rights and to establish means in favour of those who suffered persecution or violence during the Civil War and the Dictatorship].

3. As I have noted above, far from there being one or two local histories available, by 2001 there was a flood of material. See also Rodrigo's 2005 (158) comment below.

4. A communist who later manned Castro's heavy artillery during the Bay of Pigs invasion, Lister was the most successful of the Republican generals.

5. Williams (1989b: 206) refers to 'a distinction which obviously comes to mind: between those intellectual and cultural processes which, as we have seen Marx arguing, are necessary elements of any form of truly human labour, and those other forms of intellectual and cultural production which are undertaken in their own terms … what Marx called … "ends in themselves"'. He then rejects such a distinction as a general rule, but argues that it does arise from features of modern capitalist society.

6. 'Cultural producers hold a specific power, the properly symbolic power of showing things and making people believe in them, of revealing, in an explicit, objectified way the more or less confused, vague, unformulated, even unformulatable experiences of the natural world, and of thereby bringing them into existence' (Bourdieu 1990a: 146).

7. Of course, Javier Cercas's book was just one element of formal culture as it was produced at a particular moment, and I will return to describe other elements as they were produced at other moments.

8. I do not want to go into the distinctions often made in English translations between *common sense, good sense* and *practical sense*. I find most attempts to explain Gramsci's supposed distinctions slippery to the point of confusion. Much of the problem lies with the fact that in English 'common sense' can be used to refer to a situationally intelligent way of dealing with a problem, as distinct from a rather theoretical and hence stupid way. *Senso comune* does not carry this positive connotation in Italian (Thomas 2009: 16 n. 61), hence Gramsci's distinction 'good sense', which he does use to mean the practical but not necessarily scientific application of intelligence to a task. Common sense, in English, can of course have *some* negative connotations allowing Crehan (2002: 114) to suggest that 'For those who are interested in radical social change, common sense, apart from its nucleus in good sense, is something to be opposed'. Such a conclusion only makes sense by retaining the Italian meaning. I use the term 'practical sense' to refer to the positive attributes of the English 'common sense'. See also Note 10.

9. See, for example, Fernández de Mata's (2007) use of the expression '*espíritu de la Transición*'.

10. Williams' use of 'structure of feeling' here comes remarkably close to the way in which the editors of *Selections from the Prison Notebooks* explain the Italian meaning of the term *common sense*: 'used by Gramsci to mean the uncritical and largely unconscious way of perceiving and understanding the world that has become "common" in any given epoch' (Hoare and Nowell-Smith 1971). On the other hand, Williams employs the same term, as I note below, to refer precisely to unarticulated (unarticulatable?) yet nonetheless *social* sentiments that arise as a result of blockages in this kind of 'common sense' – hence my own useage of 'practical sense'.

11. El Movimiento was the name given to the alliance of right-wing interests behind Franco.

12. Discomfort and discussion about mass graves and disappearances were increasingly voiced through the 1990s. But among the relatives of those in Vilafranca del Bierzo was a journalist who brought these initiatives to the level of formal culture, co-authoring a book (Silva and Macías 2003). Meanwhile at a grass roots level an umbrella organization to help coordinate actions around the *fozas comunes* (common graves) and other sites of memory was set up, *Asociación para la recuperación de la memoria historica*, ARMH (Association for the recovery of historical memory). See http://www.memoriahistorica.org/

13. Colmeiro, who sees the only breach in this solidarity to be the autonomous regions, confines debate to that between the political elite who supposedly maintained the pact of silence and a series of artists, novelists and film-makers, who did not – in other words, debates confined to the realm of the producers of formal culture.

14. If this were so then, where formal culture failed to provide any kind of appropriate vocabulary, two things might happen. One is that a lived experience consistently gets hung on an inappropriate cultural hook – your past heroism in fighting for democracy was a disgrace, the result of psychological deficiency and so on. The other is that it simply slips off the hook, finding no articulation at the level of formal culture – a radical dis-articulation between practical sense and formal culture. This is Ranciere's point in respect to the importance of language (Rancière 2004, 2005; Deranty 2003).

15. The Spanish Civil War was the result of a failed *coup d'état* by Franco's Nationalists against the democratic government of the Republic. After Franco's total victory, there followed twenty years during which it is estimated that in excess of one hundred thousand people were disappeared (Richards 1998; Preston 2012) in a crusade [lit.] that Franco described in terms of a redemptive cleansing of the body of Spain from the Red sickness. 'In all of Spain after the final victory of the rebels at the end of March 1939, approximately twenty thousand Republicans were executed. Many more died of disease and malnutrition in overcrowded, unhygienic prisons and concentration camps. Others died in the slave labour conditions of work battalions. More than half a million refugees were forced into exile and many were to die of disease in French concentration camps. Several thousand were worked to death in Nazi camps' (Preston 2011: 1). Although the last fifteen years of the dictator's rule saw a change in policy, the fact remains that the last anarchist was garrotted as late as 1974, a year before the Caudillo's death.

16. For a discussion of integralism, see Holmes 2000.

17. Plots were so meagre and the crops so insufficient, even for subsistence, that these land–labour relationships were emphatically not a form of share-cropping. This is taken up at greater length in Narotzky and Smith 2006.

18. In our book *Immediate Struggles*, Narotzky and I make clear that the prior repression also provided the conditions that made possible the precarious out-sourcing economy found in the area, much celebrated as the cultural capital of the local 'regional economy'.

19. Juan's hard line was consistent with that of the PSOE during this period. As antagonistic to the PCE as it was to Francoism, the PSOE refused any compromises with Franco sympathizers of whatever stripe, and avoided joining the Junta Democratica, a loose alliance of left and centrist parties brought together by the Communists. It was only by the mid-1950s that this line was to soften.

20. I discuss the emergence of organic ideology in the context of hegemonic fields in Smith 1999, 2004b, etc.

– Chapter 5 –

HISTORY AS POSSIBILITIES

On the Threshold between Everyday Practice and Historical Praxis

 ℮⟋

One can say that man [*sic*] changes himself, modifies himself, to the same extent that he changes and modifies the whole complex of relations of which he is the nexus ... Each individual is not only the synthesis of existing relations but also the history of these relations, the sum of all the past. It will be said that what each individual is able to change is very little indeed. But considering that each individual is able to associate himself with all others who desire the same changes as himself ... the single individual is able to multiply himself by an impressive number and can thus obtain a far more radical change than would first appear.

– Antonio Gramsci, *The Modern Prince and Other Writings*

For politics, the fact that the people are internally divided is not, actually, a scandal to be deplored. It is the primary condition of the exercise of politics.

– Jacques Rancière, *Disgreement: Politics and Philosophy*

Introduction

In this chapter I revisit some of the ethnography I have presented in the previous two chapters but from a different perspective, one arising from a different purpose-at-hand. In the last chapter I made a distinction between formal culture and practical sense, contrasting the latter with the production of culture by professionals. Of course the different approaches to the writing of history discussed in Chapter 3 were instances of formal culture. And I spoke of how different interpretations provide alternate tools for political practice. But there was another striking difference in the two chapters. In the earlier chapter the role of collective agency in political change was the focus of attention, while in the last chapter the political agency even of individuals was quite limited. It is tempting to suggest that in the former case there is some evidence of the role of class forces in shaping politics while this would not be so for the latter case. But in this chapter I reframe our ideas of class so as to help us, as intellectuals, to identify the class and class-like vectors that might translate into political agency.

When we do fieldwork with people who have little power, their lack of agency vis-à-vis the existential issues of their livelihood impresses itself on us. Many of the tensions and conflicts that arise do so as a result of the specific conditions, of limited resources and little power, these people find themselves in. Hence the conditions that generate the tensions and conflicts are not only the same ones that limit any possibility of agency; they are also the conditions that produce the conflicts in the first place. And yet I want to offer a methodological point of view in this chapter that would allow us to start our enquiries with a view to seeking out the niches of potential leverage against those very conditions.

Of course the conditions are themselves one dimension of class, the control of important resources, and in turn this control inevitably plays a role in the other dimension: people's practices. Because all practices take place among and across people, so they are always 'social' practices. In so far as we speak of 'individual' practices, expressions, beliefs and so on, we know that they are in fact socially embedded individual practices; and inter-communicative practices at that. So individuality, such as it is, arises out of particular kinds of collectivity, just as collectivity arises out of certain kinds of individuals. Even if we were uninterested in class, how would we take into account these two undeniable elements of the social world – the mechanics of resource -control and the embeddedness of social practice in some kind of collectivity?

A Class Act

Anthropologists have long been concerned with the relationship between themselves as enquiring intellectuals and the people they study. But this became something more than a charming academic debate when the people anthropologists studied increasingly (albeit unevenly) began to engage in the making of history – not just their own local history, but often their sense of being part of a broader current in which ordinary people became a force in history (Grimshaw and Hart 1994; Smith 1999). This shift from being the objects of the anthropological gaze to being the subjects of history introduced a tension in the conversation over the intimacy of ethnography versus the detachment of theory: the extent to which we might learn from the intricacy of situated descriptions and interpretations versus the extent to which our monographs should seek out forms, processes, and tendencies of use above and beyond the contingencies and specificities of a time and a place.

Of course the very scale at which anthropologists do their fieldwork mitigates against leaping to broad conclusions. But if political engagement becomes important for anthropologists, at least some stretching beyond the local, the contingent, or the specific seems called for. Yet, caught within that conversation between ethnography and theory, many anthropologists have been tempted to leave class aside. By contrast, I argue that, in so far as the Left's interest in class is always about praxis, about people becoming the subjects of their own history, and in so far as the 'autonomous practices of the self' (see below) are very much what ethnography can expose, then ethnographic study has much to offer to our understanding of class.

In contradistinction to a sociological understanding of class then, I will argue here for a political understanding. By the former I mean a project to understand the social world in terms of 'classing' the population objectively in terms of their relative control over valued resources (broadly or narrowly defined),[1] this supposedly implying a subjective element expressed through their elective affinity (e.g. Goldthorpe and Hope 1974). In distinguishing this from a political understanding I come close to Rancière's (1999) distinction between police and politics. The one refers to the normative arena of debates and negotiations around the exercise of authorized power: the ruse of reason that can justify inequality. The other refers to situations in which effective demands are made for the real practice of a principle of radical equality.

> Looking at the history of the twentieth century, we may well take the view that … 'ordinary' citizens, classes … have come together to force … the state and its institutions (schools, the legal and political systems) to civilize themselves – that is to say … to represent the world to themselves as a shared space in which they have their place. (Balibar 2002: 33)

Class in the first case is a way of describing social inequality as an existing (possibly unavoidable) state of being. But if we take this other, political, view then class is an emergent phenomenon arising from the refusal to accept this social order. Far from an understanding of the subject in terms of being, it implies recognition that, inseparable from social practice, subjectivity is inherently a process of becoming.[2]

We may witness many instances of this kind of practice that are individual and situationally specific, but I reserve the term 'praxis' for the emergence of a collective subject that has historical purchase – 'history' in the sense of the making of history. Here I am departing from Rancière (whose focus anyway is not on class). Balibar concludes the above observation by noting that the historical trajectory he is describing 'would never have got off the ground … without autonomous "practices of the self" being constantly invented by those making up [the] multitude' (Balibar 2002).

This is the dimension of 'class potential'. But to get at both the possible catalysts for praxis and also its effective outcome, we need to attend to the conjunctural features of the relevant social formation. We need to be able to trace the link between the contradictions that arise in the unfolding reproduction or transformation of different forms of capitalism on the one hand, and cooperative and conflictual forms and practices on the other. This allows us to explore the conditions of class that allow opportunities for praxis.

This conditionality of class has to do with the fact that class is about the simultaneous mutual dependence and conflict that are inherent in capitalist relations of production: first the separation of those who *control property* from those who have *labour power* and then their recombining at the site of productive work. The division of the proceeds from what is produced, between those who provide tools and those who provide energy, is arrived at through a process of struggle between the two. Over time, these proportions may attain a kind of habitual norm and even some kind of legal endorsement. But Marx's point was that underlying such a norm is the balance of forces. 'Hence, in the history of capitalist production, the establishment of a norm … presents itself as … a struggle between collective capital, i.e. the class of capitalists, and collective labour, i.e. the working class' (Marx [1867] 1976: 342–44).

As we do ethnographic work, the challenge for this political – as opposed to sociological – way of understanding capitalist society in class terms is to expose the transformation that could potentially occur from the autonomous practices of the self to the collective agency of historical praxis. And the situated descriptions and interpretations that result from ethnography are well suited to revealing these autonomous practices of the self. So, as in other chapters, there are in fact two kinds of transformation that we are trying to work with: the intellectual one from dense ethnographic narrative to the tendencies and processes of more broadly applicable theory; and the political transformation from the isolated and situated practices of the person towards the praxis of the collective subject.

Using Stories

As we have seen in Chapters 3 and 4, much of the information I acquire in my ethnographic work comes in the form of stories. Or perhaps 'stories' is too well formed a term; perhaps 'accounts' would be better. Rather like those accumulated by an accountant, they may come in bits and pieces, many of them only acquiring some kind of form retrospectively as they are aligned for the coherence of a balance sheet. In any event, taken together, they provide me with what I know. Faced with the density of information gathered in this form anthropologists have employed at least three ways of using stories to convey something to the reader.

Sometimes their role is to illustrate, and hence back up, an argument. And if then what wiles are involved in the process of selection? Or the stories may be a theatrical set-up. I remember a Tom Stoppard play that began with the juxtaposition of entirely unlikely figures, a person ironing with a dead body on the ironing table, a parrot ... I cannot remember the details. But, as the curtain went up, it was certainly an eye-catcher. Then, as the play unfolded, we ended up with the curtain falling on that same scene and it all seemed so satisfactorily explainable. The playwright had taken our hand and guided us through, and the loud applause at the end showed that we were charmed, delighted and full of gratitude to him when we reached the end. Many anthropologists use initial stories for this purpose. One of the best cases though is by a historian, Roger Darnton (1984), in *The Great Cat Massacre*. There we are told a most extraordinary tale, surely in the realm of fantasy, and then the charm of the subsequent exposition is that everything falls into place, and we find ourselves Darnton's ally in interpretation, happy to be (almost) as perspicacious as he. A third possibility is to have the stories more or less stand alone. Perhaps, for example, an especially interesting story told by one or more of the people who are the objects of the monograph.

Because for the ethnographer stories provide an almost infinite set of referents, reminders, emotions, and so on, their chaotic density seems to work against the temptations of any broad conclusions. Yet here I want to work against such temptations and use them to help me to challenge the way I think about class and praxis. I will begin with the stories...

Sabino 1930s [1972][3]

To convey why the image of Sabino Jacinto became so important to me as I tried to insert myself nervously among a group of people whose principal feature in my own mind was that they had a long history of rebellion, I need to begin with a back-story. It has to do with seeing, a year or so before leaving for fieldwork, a film by Francesco Rosi, *Salvatore Giuliano*, about the famous Sicilian bandit. The manner in which the film was made had fascinated me with its weird mix of actual newsreel, documentary and dramatized genres, and its almost aggressive neutrality. It had sunk into my mind as a problematic movie. I could see how the contradictory figure of 'Turi', as Giuliano was know, might be of interest to Italians for whom the name would be familiar; but as an obscure corner of Sicilian history, its message to me was puzzling. So I was especially interested when the name arose again, this time in *Primitive Rebels* (Hobsbawm 1959; see also *Bandits*, 1969), where Hobsbawm speaks of the role of 'social' bandits as locally and temporally limited expressions of rebellion but often as precursors of later insurgency.

So now, living as I was with impoverished rural people engaged in a vigorous and occasionally violent struggle against large landlords – and include in that the police and the military – I was naturally fascinated by stories I heard about a man who some time ago had a reputation as a roaming figure who struck fear into the hearts of travelling outsiders. At the time of my arrival in the community, Sabino was a wily old loner living in a *choza* (hut) to be found at the end of a canyon up in the mountains. A major figure in the first successful campaign to recuperate land from the *haciendas*, he was notorious then and in subsequent encounters for his uncompromising stance and his threatening outbursts when confronted by authorities.

Many times I tried to arrange a visit to his *choza*, but, true to his reputation, he remained elusive. It became a running joke among my neighbours. At one point, in an uncharacteristically bold initiative, I had set off down the opening of a deep valley that I was assured would take me to his dwelling, only to get thoroughly lost, returning late in the evening exhausted and unsettled. On another occasion, in the cemetery during *Todos Santos* (All Saints' Day), an old woman came up to me leading a younger woman by the hand. 'Here,' she said, 'this is Sabino's granddaughter. You should marry her. Then she would take you to him.' And the two women burst out laughing.[4] One dark and stormy night (literally) I was drinking with some friends when a young man came in drenched and apparently in some panic. 'Sabino is dying', he said. 'He wants to speak to you.' And I was taken by horse down the canyon to his home where between his gasps for breath, I recorded his gravelly voice.

In the article discussed in Chapter 4, Hobsbawm (1974: 137) refers to an administrator of Hacienda Laive who writes that one campaign 'has been thought up, they tell me, by one Sabino or Sabini Román,[5] who used to work on [Hacienda] Ingahuasi and who has recently been made *alcalde* [mayor]' (ibid.). In his teens Sabino had been involved in a violent incident with a hacienda employee, possibly resulting in death. As a result he lost himself in the mountains but was imprisoned for a while nonetheless. A skilled pastoralist with extensive knowledge of the *puna*, he had worked as a butter maker at Laive (famous for its cheese) and on and off as a shepherd on Tucle and on more remote haciendas in the neighbouring province of Huancavelica. In the late 1930s he spearheaded the invasion of land claimed by Haciendas Tucle and Rio de la Virgen. As a result of his exemplary boldness during that *reivindicación* the community agreed to him and his extended kin settling on part of the land gained. Even so, in the years following that settlement Sabino often worked for one or other of the neighbouring haciendas. The manipulations this allowed him are evidenced in incidents like the following. First there is the following statement to be found in the community records of 1937 when a *comunero* is recorded as complaining, 'One day he tells me he commands here; the next day he says to me, 'Uncle? Don't call me uncle. I am no uncle of yours' (ibid.: 180). And then during an ocular inspection of Huasicancha's next land claim in 1947 we find Sabino becoming so enraged by the judge who he was convinced was in the pay of the hacendada that in the argument that ensued he was arrested and imprisoned. As he told me on those last days of his life, he was then accused of being a Communist, imprisoned in Lima where he was beaten with a rubber hose, bribed to sign a statement that he refers to as *un canto*, and planted with political leaflets he could not himself read. He ended his account of this chapter of his life, '*He sido loco saliendo de la carcel*' [I left the prison crazy] (Smith 1989: 181).

Alicia 1978 [1978]

This story takes place some six years later and in a strikingly different setting: the Bajo Segura in southern Valencia, Spain. The outcome is quite different, perhaps as a result of what Bourdieu would call an entirely different 'habitus'. I was walking back from the *guardaría*, where I had dropped off my daughter for the day, with Alicia who was on her way home after chatting to her friend who ran the day care. I told her who I was, and she laughed and said, 'I know who you are. You're the guy who listens to my Dad talking about the old *fincas*, like a communicant listening to the priest. If you want to know about that stuff, you should be talking to Uncle Ciriaco.' In fact, I knew that Alicia spent the bulk of her day as a homeworker doing a variety of unskilled jobs which she got from her Uncle Fernando, a work distributor for the local shoe factories, and I was more interested in infiltrating myself into her work day and chatting to her while she worked than seeking out old Tio Ciriaco who would talk to me any time.

I spent a few hours with Alicia that day, and managed to drop by casually from time to time to carry on our conversations. As the various people in her domestic life passed through the setting of her homework – one or other of her younger brothers, her mother, her father and so on – so conversation would turn to them. One day it was her Uncle Fernando who came up for discussion: 'He says I'm lucky he lets me have the work [she said], he could be giving it to others. When I started out ... perhaps then he was right. But now he gives me the hardest jobs and comes by late in the week with extra work he hasn't managed to get others to do' [Field Notes 1978]. I had heard variations on this theme time and again from women involved in various kinds of homework, and the figure could have been an uncle, a father, an aunt or simply a close friend. The use of intimacy as the lever of exploitation in sweated labour is the way I thought of it.

I did not see Alicia for a while. The next time we met was at a local soccer game. She was with some friends, teasing one another, laughing and exchanging local gossip. I paused long enough to catch the brunt of one or two teasing comments and was about to move off, when Fernando walked past. The laughter stopped and Alicia clearly tried to turn away enough not to make eye contact but not enough to be openly rude. Fernando made a remark about her unreliability and walked on. I must have looked surprised at how this encounter had turned out, because Alicia waited for him to be a suitable distance away and then, turning away from her friends and dropping the lightness of tone suited to a leisurely afternoon, she put one hand on her hip and said to me, 'I told him I'd had enough. He said I could find work elsewhere, so that's what I'm doing.'

As with Sabino's case, there is a back-story here too. First of all, Alicia was the latest in a series of generations of her family for whom kin terms like 'uncle' ('Tio' Ciriaco was in fact her grandfather) were deeply embedded in the social economics of livelihood – commercialized or otherwise.[6] Second, though not herself a participant, Alicia had friends among a group of women who had helped me with a project. In vain I had been trying to administer a small questionnaire to homeworkers. Mostly addressing factual issues, such as their household composition and how long they had been taking work in, there were also some questions that sought to draw out people's ideas of what it meant to help somebody, what it meant to work with or for somebody, and so on. I had almost given up on this small project when a neighbour, who had responded to one of my first attempts, offered to help me out. My problem was twofold. Firstly, women tended to be far too busy during the daytime to attend to what seemed to them an irrelevant and indeed disconnected set of questions. And secondly, each individual success in my quest seemed to be my last one. Unlike a compact worksite, the dispersal of homeworkers made it hard to follow one interview with another. Returning home one evening with a bunch of empty pages in hand, I complained about this to my neighbour who responded with impatience about my ineptitude, grabbed the bunch of forms, and said she would pass them through a network to be self-administered.

A couple of weeks later I found myself in a heated encounter with two or three women. As the questionnaire rolled through the kitchens and patios, what started as small questions to one another about how to answer this or that question had mushroomed into a lively debate about where being helpful began and where being taken advantage of left off. This in turn flowed into the issue of what one might call work and what one might call, well, something else. Fortunately, by the time I was confronted with all this, things had gone from one state to its opposite. The women who had cornered me, now joined by my neighbour, described it like this. First neighbours and friends had become highly sensitized to what they were asking of each other and doing for each other. Then they had begun to talk about the same issues with respect to the work distributors and eventually a group of some eleven women had decided to meet with the three most relevant work distributors to discuss 'issues'.

All these women were married and had children so, since Alicia was only at the stage of saving for her marriage chest, she was not among them; but she was quite aware of them, and my guess is that when the hand went to her hip and she turned to me to tell me that she no longer took work from her uncle, she was not unaware of the discussions that had revolved around the rolling questionnaire.

Chongos Alto and SAIS Cahuide 1970s and 1980s [1996]

The third story takes us back to Peru and, apart from the fact that this one was recorded by Enrique Mayer and not me, it is also noteworthy that the time of its recording and the incidents to which it refers are much more contained within a specific time frame than the story of Sabino, and more remote in time than the story of Alicia. I will begin with the back-story. As we have seen in Chapter 3, by the mid-1970s the persistent series of *reivindicaciones* had resulted in the recuperation of the land of some of Hacienda Tucle and all of Hacienda Rio de la Virgen. As a result, the huasicanchinos chose not to join the large agrarian cooperative formed by the Agrarian Reform of 1968–75. This vast enterprise made up of expropriated haciendas was managed by *tecnicos* and was, in principle, owned by the twenty-nine communities adjoining the ex-haciendas plus one further unit made up of ex-employees and now permanent workers.

By contrast, Huasicancha's neighbouring community, Chongos Alto, did become a member of the cooperative. Enrique Mayer, an anthropologist and native of the central Andes, records the growing frustration of the people of Chongos Alto as the realities of this supposedly revolutionary enterprise – the *SAIS Cahuide*[7] – set in. During the radical reforms of the Velasco regime (1968–75) and the years immediately preceding them community members and ex-hacienda workers alike felt that the land and its products rightly belonged to them. The form of this huge SAIS (the size of Massachusetts)[8] was designed to address these issues while also retaining control over the productivity of ex-haciendas. To this end the proceeds of the SAIS were on the one hand to go towards advances in agricultural efficiency – breeding, irrigation, machinery and so on – and on the other towards 'social development' in the communities. In principle, community members and workers, through their representatives, like shareholders, could vote on policy issues pertaining to the SAIS, although the policy parameters were set within the original constitution of the SAIS and in practice *tecnicos* were inclined to prioritize production issues and themselves choose the appropriate social development projects.

We pick up the story from here. Juvenal Chanco, a leader of Chongos Alto in the 1980s, recalls some ten years later, 'They would say to us,

"You are the owners, the ones who give the orders to the *empresa*."
Well, we the *comuneros* called them the "tecnocrats", no?; "the sacred
cows [of the urban central office of the SAIS]".' The leaders of Chongos
Alto and their representatives became increasingly aggressive in
their dealings with management as development policies appeared
far removed from their own priorities and production decisions
questionable in an economic climate adverse to livestock farming. At
this point Enrique Mayer turns to the view a *tecnico*, Plinio Dionisio,
had of those the *tecnicos* thought of as 'troublemakers, terrorists and
comuneros' (Mayer 2009: 206):

> There were the people belonging to the organizations in the communities
> who would sneak up to Laive (one of the SAIS administrative units)
> to ask, how much is a shepherd earning? How many perks does an
> administrator have? Why is it that an administrator has to have a cook?
> Why does an administrator have to live in such luxurious housing? ...
> Delegates constantly harped on [about] notions of equality. They would
> say for example, 'Why doesn't a pregnant woman from Chongos get milk
> and meat? Why is it only the workers and employees of the SAIS who get
> meat and milk? Why is the milk being taken to Huancayo [the local market
> town]? Why is it not sold in Chongos Alto, in Huasicancha, and in other
> villages?' (ibid.: 206–7)

Interestingly, while from the *comuneros'* point of view the SAIS
proceedings were lost in obscurity, another *tecnico* attributed the
tension to the fact that everything he and his colleagues did was so
visible. The SAIS's trucks drove out of the Laive gates loaded with
cheese and milk, and *comuneros* saw all and got none.

The story, as Mayer records it, is being told in 1996. In 1988 the
people of Chongos Alto, together with other communities, destroyed
the administrative unit closest to them, the ex-hacienda Antapongo.
And, as we now know, in the immediate subsequent years the reign
of Sendero Luminoso and the army campaign against them laid
waste the highlands and terrorized the town of Huancayo. But I will
leave the story here.

What I especially want to think about here is the way in which we
can cross scales of social interaction and practice while still employing
the features of class analysis. So, I will begin by applying class analysis
to the stories and their settings at a rather broad scale, less directly
linked to the immediacy of fieldwork and experience; then I will try
to understand these stories in a more embedded ethnographic way.

The Framing of Class

To begin, a word about class. The zero-sum struggle of one interested party against another could apply to any number of kinds of conflict. What makes a struggle a class conflict is that it is simultaneously about mutual dependence on one hand and conflict on the other. As I said at the outset the two are inherent in capitalist relations of production: first the separation of those who *control property* from those who have *labour power* and then their recombining at the site of productive work.[9] How the proceeds are divided, as between those who provide tools and those who provide energy, is determined through a process of struggle between the two. Over time, these proportions may attain a kind of habitual norm and even some kind of legal endorsement, but underlying them is the balance of forces.

Most of my fieldwork has been done in Peru (1972–85) and in Spain (1978–96). The first seems more amenable to thinking in terms generally associated with class, while the second does not. But this is only a superficial interpretation. The first was chosen explicitly to study the history of a rural rebellion in Peru. The people of Huasicancha had been infamous for their rebelliousness for some time, and I expected to find a strong sense of localized solidarity. But the research revealed that their success was at least in part the result of participation by people interlinked across spaces well beyond the site of the struggle itself: by no means confined to 'peasants'.

I chose the second field site to see if this kind of collective praxis could be found elsewhere. The issue could be posed in terms of a question about class. What had surprised me in Peru was that people combined in a collective struggle to secure the crucial means of production (in this case, pasture). Yet they nonetheless saw themselves as being exploited through a variety of social relationships, something they actually spoke of in terms of different forms of exploitation. So what I was seeking for the second project was a situation where there was a fairly long history of working-class relations across town and country, and across sectors of the economy. I could then explore the nature of the links between heterogeneous working people, as I had seen in Peru. Supposedly a central feature of industrial capitalism was to separate rural from urban livelihoods and to produce ever-sharper distinctions between different sectors of the economy. Would my Peru material provide insights that would belie this supposition?

When I began fieldwork in the Bajo Segura, quite intensive agriculture shared the rural landscape with small manufacturing, and most households tended to have a foot in both kinds of occupations. So here was a litmus test for the problems that interested me. Yet coming into this setting as I did at the end of the 1970s, rendering the landscape in class terms was not as immediately obvious as it had been in Peru. In many ways this could be explained by reference to the class literature itself. If some element of class had to do with the experience of collective work and the clear distinction between the factory owner and disciplined workers, then neither of these features was obvious in the Bajo Segura. But I think it would be hard for any anthropologist to live in that area and not be aware of the central role in people's lives of class relations. The role played by the flow of the value of their work away from these people in a perpetual if complicated and shifting process was strikingly evident – in other words, some form or other of exploitation. It is true that the term 'exploitation' could be heard only in the talk of union organizers and social scientists, and then more in its general pejorative sense. But a vast spectrum of people's conversations revolved precisely around the winding and erratic paths taken by the flow of value – its escape from one site, its holing up in another for a time, its slippage away again – as well as the elusive mysteries of its accumulation elsewhere.

I want to focus on the way they draw us to two essential elements of class, the one conditional the other potential. The conditional element of class has to do with a particular kind of society, one in which various ways of laying claim to and controlling property is used as the means for directing the flow of value from the people who produce it to the people who accumulate it. This is the actual element of class relations that can be found in the everyday practices and relations of work. The potential element is political and refers to the possibility of people's collective agency in modifying the conditions of their lives: praxis. By praxis I mean willed intervention in the unfolding of history.

Because both elements of class require work on development and control – albeit of a different kind in each case – organization, and the institutions that go along with organization, plays a significant role in the shaping of class. Along one dimension value has to be developed, through rational organization of the labour process, for example, and the appropriate use of machines and skills; and then as this value is transferred from where it is produced at the site of labour this movement has to be controlled to ensure that value arrives in the hands of the owners of capital. Along an entirely different dimension organization plays its role in the building (development) and sustaining (control) of collective praxis into a material force under conditions where contrary class forces work against this potential. By seeing the tensions inherent in class relations in this way we can begin constructing a bridge between micro practices and macro praxis.

In the Peruvian case, the way in which the *hacendada* used control of land to extract value from local people who she employed as shepherds was quite clear, as was the way in which monopolization of this pasture restricted them from using their labour for their own benefit. And, in so far as migrants engaged in volatile livelihoods beyond the region and therefore used livestock as a form of security, so they too were related to the *hacendada* through this land. Moreover, initially at least, these micro practices of livelihood are closely tied to the praxis of resistance, as we saw in Chapter 3. Yet the contingency of this particular history sets the limits on just how macro things were. Though much talk in the region referred in general to *campesinos* versus landlords, this actual struggle pitted a quite clearly bounded group of campesinos against quite specific landlords. There are limits to referring to what is happening here as an expression of class then. It may be that the very intensity of the solidarity I witnessed worked against a broader kind of class collectivity. The situation approximates closely the one that concerned Raymond Williams (1989a: 115): 'That because it had begun as local and affirmative, assuming an unproblematic extension from its local and community experience to a much more general movement, it was always insufficiently aware of the quite systematic obstacles which stood in the way.'

The issue is one of scale in terms of the praxis element of class. Scale too becomes relevant in the Spanish case, but along a different element of class. As I said, at the level at which fieldwork was carried out, the first element of class relations appeared to be confusing and complex, while evidence for the potentiality of some kind of collective intervention that might shift the conditions of history were likewise obscure. But the scale at which exploitative relations frame class may be far broader than anything that can be captured in the daily practices we observe in fieldwork. The temporal scale of history too may easily slip past us in the immediacy of the field site. And yet obviously class relations have a history – along both the dimensions I am trying to work along here: the specificity of the everyday ways in which control of resources was used vis-à-vis labour, first to produce value and then to channel it; and also a parallel history having to do with the balance of class forces. In the case of the Bajo Segura, as we have seen in Chapters 2 and 4, the form that livelihood took was itself a product of the very specific ways that repression operated in the region, shaping the labour process at the micro level and curtailing potential praxis, be it relatively local or across a larger scale.

These rather analytic approaches to class help to point us to questions that need to be asked and hence provide a baseline for thinking class while doing ethnography. But there may be another way of setting out to think about class. Before one can decide how to frame a question about the world in terms of class, perhaps one needs to think about what one is trying to do with one's life, and what one is trying to avoid – physical labour perhaps, the hazards of uncertainty, the indignity of failure. And if this kind of reflection is, as Bourdieu (2000) insists, a baseline for 'doing' a sociology of ourselves, it might also be a similar baseline for understanding the practical activity of the people we study.

Praxis against History

If we go back to the distinction I made at the outset, between the ethnographic urge and the urge towards broader theory then, seen in terms of the more academic kind of analysis of class I have just done, these ethnographic stories seem to have obvious limitations. And yet as I have also said, class analysis implies a concern with praxis and history or, perhaps better put: praxis *against* history, and each of these stories shows evidence of people defying the present. Indeed participants wilfully bracket certain elements of what is happening, the better to get leverage on what they *can* make happen – Sabino's denial of a kin relation may be less clear in this respect, but not so Alicia's denial of her uncle's making visible such a tie. And then there is the odd juxtaposition in which local peasants complain about the obscure nature of the SAIS's operations while a *tecnico* explains their discomfort by suggesting that they see too much. Perhaps what worries them is the way in which the conversion of their labour into value is being mystified through the occlusions of the bureaucracy, while what worries him is that what they are seeing are the results of physical value they produce on the site being siphoned off elsewhere. So while the stories do disturb the tendency towards the ordered symmetry more often found in broader analyses, I propose that the understanding of what is happening in these three small items of 'evidence' would be severely limited by a failure to understand them through what for me are class principles.

It is often said, or at least it used often to be said, that class is all about relationships. A class does not sit alone; it is made by the force of its opposed class. This may or may not be so. But to think of class in this way we need to go back one step further. The unfolding of our potential, the development of what we might be against the reality of what we currently are, is a struggle against the conditions that exist in the present to make them into new possibilities. This is as true for personal subjectivity as it is for collective identity. Practical work is precisely about destroying what currently exists to make it what needs to exist. In this work, relations have to be entered into, other relations constrained or confronted, and through this process personal and/or collective forms 'develop' (in a Hegelian sense). Our understanding of ourselves as coherent actors with agency (as opposed to fragmented subjects with pathologies) emerges through what Mikhail Bakhtin (1981) called the dialogical interaction that occurs in these relations: *among* those with whom we identify towards our individual and collective subjectivity; and *against* the force of conditions that arise as a result of the practices of others.

I need to rehearse all this because the individual agency of the picaresque actor is often – especially in ethnographic narrative – set against the emergence of collective forms of struggle. But there is always a tension between the emergence of particularistic senses of personal individuality and the *doxa* of collective membership. And the reverse is also true, but often forgotten – that the development of the self is inconceivable without this process of the practical struggle to make one's agency affect the world, and the necessity, in doing so, of engaging in dialogical relationships with others that effectively develop the social person.

The puzzle then, when we try to understand the role of class at the level of what I am calling ethnography, is not addressed by contrasting moments when 'class' supposedly arises, and others when the people that interest us appear to be isolated as individuals. Rather, if we take as fundamental that social being is nothing but social practice and that social practice is inconceivable without social relations which themselves have a dialogical character, then it is surely clear that we must pursue that understanding differently. At the level of ethnography we need to attend to the differing potential inhering in apparently similar practices. On the one hand there are the elements of practical work that have the effect of consecrating what *is*. On the other hand there are moments of crisis, disturbance and the like in which practice can go forward only by destroying not just the immediacy of the present – the undernourished sheep that has to be pastured, the shoe that has to be soled – but also has to hack away at the very social configuration that is responsible for the conditions of that present – the conditions of pasturage or of shoe production.

Clearly this is an issue of scale – in a number of dimensions. Alicia's reconfiguration of the jobber–worker relation away from its kin framing is not the same as Sabino and his associates' occupation of property controlled by a legally recognized hacienda. And the *tecnico*'s characterization of those who 'saw' goods being taken away for consumption elsewhere as 'troublemakers' has to be understood in the time when it took place – after the ex-hacienda production unit, of which he was a manager, had been destroyed during the upheavals of *Sendero Luminoso*.

Class analysis necessarily involves the interweaving of various scales,[10] the various scales of interaction and practice that produce society as capitalist on the one hand, and the various scales of counterforces that arise within and beyond those relations. Class has to do with a dialectical tension arising from the contradictions inherent to the relations of capitalist reproduction and the way in which those tensions get transmitted into the forming of social persons – persons who themselves are engaged in creative practices within and against the conditions of their present. The challenge for analysis is to explore under historically specific conditions the way one of these dimensions gets translated into another.

Seen from this perspective, what can we learn from these stories? To begin with, we need to recognize that they are short, selective descriptions, mostly at the level of the kind of social interaction that I associate with fieldwork. They are not sweeping narratives of the decline and fall of the Roman Empire, and they are not, for example, discussions of the current financial crisis that seek to explain elements that are not understandable simply at the level of experience: of homeowner's loss, or of the dreamworld of derivatives traders. In noting this rather obvious fact, we acknowledge that social reality can be addressed both at different scales of time and space – Alicia's work and family relations in 1978 versus the long decline of an empire – and at different depths, from appearance and experience to the underlying tensions and logics of social forms.

Anthropologists are frequently frustrated by the grand conclusions social analysts draw, especially those associated with policy. Nevertheless what evidence anthropologists can draw from the contingencies and complexities encountered in their own long-term engagement with ground-level practices and relationships have their own constraints. This is still more the case for the stories I have presented here. And the problems do not get much the less when ethnographic evidence of this kind gets packaged together, with little else, to form an entire monograph. Even so, I have chosen to see what we can learn from applying the notion of class to stories of this kind, as well as seeing what we can learn about the way class works by testing it against these stories. The cases here are not especially exemplary. Nor, after a fine exercise in deconstruction, will they reveal some hidden secret. Still less are they simply accumulated stories 'from the native's point of view'.

Yet these stories about the engagement of an agent in a social-relational practice do expose the way in which both the agent and the practice are always incomplete, always at a moment of potentiality. If this is so, then any critical analysis or engagement with that moment must at least in part address the degree to which that incompleteness is simply *open-ended and contingent*, or is potentially a step towards *shifting the prevailing conditions of possibility*. Addressing this question means tracing the ways in which the autonomous practices of the self are articulated with other scales and levels of the social world: the interactions with those with whom we identify; the counterforce of those who restrict that possible identification; and the logics of reproduction and transformation specific to the kind of society in which they are embedded.

While it is no doubt true that my long-standing concern with class analysis configures, from the start, the way I have set these stories out here, I have intentionally written them down before thinking about how they might be viewed through the lens of class. As I said at the outset, my particular concern is to explore the territory between what Balibar calls 'the autonomous practices of the self' and the potential for collective praxis.[11] My purpose is only to propose possible openings where tensions in the relational practices of work may have potential for transmission into elements of historical praxis. But this is a tentative exercise in method in order to see how we might interpret this evidence in terms of class, and I shall not consider how those potentials may work themselves out in each of these cases. Nonetheless, we can make some observations.

There are two especially provocative thresholds in Sabino's story. I have already noted the possibility of instances of social banditry in crystallizing subaltern people's immanent critique of prevailing social conditions. But in this case the prior history of these people's resistance to the haciendas as far back as the war with Chile suggests that Sabino's confrontations were themselves a product of an already-existing collective refusal of the given-ness of existing conditions. Superficially Sabino's story can be seen as an explanation of the local people's ability to rebel in terms of this charismatic figure, and the fact that this was a story known by everybody from childhood supports this view. But Sabino was himself a product of the dialogical interactions that characterized the community he lived in. And his story is both a further moment of that dialogue (reproduced in this instance in 1972) and also a powerful, condensed message about the threshold between the personal and familial practice of making a living and, in this case, the accompanying need to catalyse a moment of collective praxis to press against the conditions that were making such a living increasingly impossible.

There is a second threshold along the lines of the simultaneity of conflict and dependency essential to a class relationship. We see this in the way that Sabino shifts in and out of relationships to the community and to the hacienda. We know that he was especially sought after by the hacienda for his skills, both before the initiative of the 1930s and afterwards. And we know too that he was identified as a troublemaker around the same time – no doubt, at least partly, precisely because of those skills (extensive knowledge of local topography, ability to shift herds of livestock quickly and strategically, control over family retainers and *huacchilleros* and so on).[12] It is almost as though the ability to produce value was precisely what put Sabino in demand as an employee *and also* made his potential to disrupt the production and flow of value so real. While, from the hacienda administration's point of view, this had largely to do with the person of Sabino as an individual, the evidence suggests otherwise. Not only was his ability to resist the hacienda dependent upon his position within the collective body of the community and his ability to mobilize it, but his value as an employee relied both on what he had learned through his life among these people and the extent to which he could mobilize household and extended family members to act as *huacchilleros* (and in other roles) on the hacienda.[13]

As with the accounts Enrique Mayer presents, there is a significant gap between the events of the story and its telling here. This makes its role as a story quite different from Alicia's, which contains her own story about how she discarded her uncle and which relies on the many narratives I gathered from her over time. It is then, after all, really my own story about Alicia, recorded pretty much over the time it was happening. There is quite a lot we learn about class praxis from the Huasicanchino story that we cannot, I think, relate to Alicia's story. That is because Sabino's story itself played a significant part in the constitution of individual and collective subjects; versions of Sabino's account, and many others in multiple variations, circulated among urban and rural participants throughout the political campaign that

I studied in the field (Smith 1991, 1997). In spite of these differences, however, we see a persistent worrying away at what previous moments of popular intervention in the making of history might uncover. This seems an important element of what we are trying to reveal about the potential for current collective praxis. As I have argued in this chapter, it is the absence of those previous moments in Alicia's story that account for that story's lack of politics, in Rancière's use of the term. This reflects his observation that '[t]here is … an essential link between memory, history and democracy. Democratic struggles always occur as reiterations of previous inscriptions of equality' (quoted in Deranty 2003: 153).

If he is right, then this may go some way to understanding why the versions of history produced by formal culture in Spain, as I discussed them in the last chapter, do so much work in configuring prior moments of democracy as instances of barbarism and violence. It is a narrative in which promised organic integralism can only be reached through discussions among those claiming to be *representatives* of only those who accept the present in these highly contained, closed-up terms. History understood thus removes the collective praxis of people as a force in its making. Yet it seems to me that, situationally specific and microscopic as Alicia's rejection of exploitation through kin ties was, it nevertheless was an instance of what Balibar is calling 'autonomous practices of the self'. Yet it takes place in real material conditions that will affect its longer-term possibilities. These material conditions should not be seen as given. Rather they are the current outcome of the balance of forces, and those forces have for some time been directed against class as a collective subject of history. But in this chapter I have insisted on *tying* that kind of social practice quite firmly to another, more individual and quotidian pushing of practices against what is given in the world. In other words the mundane practices of making a living are dialectically tied to collective praxis in the constitution of social subjects: the formation of collective groups and of personal self-consciousness are interrelated processes, so fragmented collectivities induce fragmented individual agents, subjects, or social persons – or, perhaps better put, 'asocial' persons. By subjecting relationships and practices to a kind of interpretation that relies on a dialectical understanding of tension-filled class or class-like relations across a range of scales in this way we are able to see them in terms of always incomplete force and counterforce rather than more or less satisfactory classifications of social position.

Conclusion

In most current writing that refers to class, there is rarely any clear sense of which of its multiple uses is being employed (see Carrier, forthcoming). Indeed, we usually find a kind of generic use in which the author assumes the reader will accept any of a bundle of possible meanings. In my case, taking class seriously requires accepting Marx's understanding of society as a historical process in which social forms emerge dialectically out of tensions and contradictions in the process of social reproduction. As a result I have argued that, when the problem of historical praxis is made the organizing principle for our enquiries into class, more 'sociological' understandings need not be dismissed but rather can be interpreted for useful ends. So I have discussed class along both these lines, employing a sociological perspective though turning the lens along a distinctly Marxist plane. The more 'sociological' part of the enquiry serves to unravel the complex structured relations between those who control resources and those who contribute labour power. The more 'political' part (at least in the case of this chapter) is designed to work across the threshold between 'the autonomous practices of the self' and the collective agency of historical praxis to explore the potentialities and limitations of specific situations.[14]

This employment of class as a means for achieving one's purpose as an ethnographer should not be confused with another use of class for different purposes, since the one is inconsistent with the other. The Marxist sociological understanding of class as I have described it here is not consistent with a view of class that refers to a static description of the empirical features of socio-economic categories of people. There is no point therefore in critiquing the former on the grounds that its application does not provide us with the neat categories required of the latter. Nonetheless, it goes without saying that if there were *no* social expression of the structural features described here (and throughout), the exercise would lose even its political value. But the connection cannot be made by an unreflective leap from the dialectical and historical production of social forms to the allotment of people into categories based on their social function. Rather the challenge is, now as it always has been, to try to explore the ways in which these material tensions over the historical course of social reproduction through generations of people are transmitted, via experience, to people's actual praxis as social agents.

For me, it is this social praxis that is the initial kernel of the possibility of class. Although Edward Thompson tended to use the word 'agency' rather than praxis, his understanding of class is close to what I am trying to get at with the use of the latter term. In fact, despite his disclaimers, all the elements I have brought together here are contained in Thompson's famous summary:

> By class I understand a historical phenomenon, unifying a number of disparate and seemingly unconnected events, both in the raw material of experience and in consciousness. I emphasize that this is a *historical* phenomenon. I do not see class as a 'structure', nor even as a category, but as something which in fact happens (and can be shown to have happened) in human relationships. (Thompson 1968: 9)

> In the years between 1780 and 1832 most English working people came to feel an identity of interests as between themselves, and as against their rulers and employers. (ibid.: 12)

Despite Thompson's dismissal of class as a 'structure', his final sentence suggests that his problematic was much as I have laid it out here: it was as people came 'to feel an identity' among themselves and against those who controlled them through the leverage of property that material features of the society became translated into social forms – institutional forms, forms of relationship in everyday practice, and emergent forms of collective political expression. Despite overly culturalist readings of Thompson, his 'history' refers both to a material history of structural tensions in the emerging English industrial society and to the accumulation of experienced history.

Yet I would not be the first to note Thompson's failure to explain to us how 'the raw material of experience' performs the politically vital role of 'unifying a number of disparate and seemingly unconnected events'. Does this just happen – as new and apparently contingent happenings start to become *habitual*? Or is it 'consciousness' that works on the raw material of disparate experience to bring all this about? And if so, why should consciousness at one moment perform this operation and at another do precisely the opposite, denying the commonality of experiences and celebrating the particularity of individual distinctions?

As a reading of Chapter 1 would make clear, I do not find 'consciousness' or 'agency' very helpful terms for understanding the way that class – or even the looser, social subjectivity – works in capitalist society. And this in fact is the epistemological basis for the enquiries in this paper. There is no such thing as an a-historical, a-social personal (or collective) consciousness constituting the essence of the subject that then engages in some kind of agency. Rather the subject is constituted *from the start* through practice – an ineluctably interactive and always historically and positionally specific social engagement. I entitled my first book *Livelihood and Resistance* to break down the rather easy distinction we are prone to make in ethnographic fieldwork between observable daily livelihood – apparently habitual and amenable to practical sense – and the broader scale of actions involved in destroying or defending the conditions of that possibility – what I call here 'historical praxis' and what I called then 'resistance'.

From no insight of my own, but rather as a result of the acute and distressing struggles I was observing in my field site, the methodological challenge (at least from a political point of view) was to break down the line between the practical work of everyday practice and the historically fragile business of protecting or securing the conditions that make that livelihood possible, that is to say 'praxis'.[15] Seen in this way, there is no reason why we cannot explore quite microscopic inter-relational practices through this kind of lens. Moreover, by doing so, we might find a means of finding politically useful moments when daily practice seeds historical praxis, and would thus return some of the debt we owe to those whose prior historical praxis provided the bedrock for the struggles we face today.

Notes

1. For example, Marx's understanding of 'capital' refers to a quite specific form of value, while Bourdieu's (1990a) relies on a variety of forms.
2. I am not referring here to the much-cited distinction between 'a class in itself' and 'a class for itself'. Following Edward Thompson (1978), I find it hard to see how a class can be for itself in some *a posteriori* version of a hitherto inarticulate 'thing'.
3. The first date refers to the events recounted in the story, the second to the time when it was recorded.
4. Over the three days of *Todos Santos* the graves of those who had been interred, at a time when their families could not afford an appropriate burial, were opened and the deceased re-buried in better conditions. During the preparations for these ceremonies it was a custom for older women to tease young girls by proposing their hand in marriage to the bachelors working on the graves.
5. 'Román' is almost certainly a confusion with [Martin] Ramos. See Chapter 3.
6. Her grandfather, Tio Ciriaco, found his work through his father who, in turn, had found his job as a coach driver for a local landlord through his mother, the wet nurse for one of the landlord's children.
7. *Sociedad Agricola de Interés Social* [Agricultural Company (or Society) for Social Interests].
8. This account is taken from Mayer's extraordinary book, *Ugly stories of the Peruvian agrarian reform* (2009).

9. It will become clear that the particular way in which I understand class analysis makes many of the principles of class relations applicable to a range of social interactions – among kin, community and so on: adapting Marx's (1976: 1019–38) distinction, we might distinguish these in terms of formal exploitation and the real exploitation of capitalism. (For a contrary position – one which argues that class relations only occur under strictly capitalist relations – see Postone 1996).
10. Not the topological positioning of one scale to another, large and small, but precisely the 'interweaving' of scales.
11. In a chapter on individual *ladino* acts of dissent, Charles Hale writes, 'As individual acts, these sensibilities have important contextual and aggregate effects, *but they generally lack the transformative power achieved through organized collective action* [what I would call 'praxis']' (Hale 2006b: 170. Italics added). His exploration of this issue throughout *Más que un indio*, while pre-eminently about what he calls 'racial ambivalence', parallels my own discussion here.
12. The term *huacchillero* derives from the Quechua word *huacchilla* meaning to be an orphan or to be poor. It reflects well the interweaving of labour relations in the community with those on the hacienda. To become an orphan effectively meant to be deprived of an inheritance which in a pastoral community meant livestock. Such people could be taken in by a household (usually lacking labour) and given a start-up supply of animals in return for shepherding some of the household's animals. The progeny of the original animals were themselves referred to as *huacchos* and, in principle, were to be distinguished from the rest of the herd which had a household (i.e. unlike an orphan, belonged to a household). The hacienda extended this longstanding practice as a means for employing their own shepherds. But now the hacienda became the putative household and all its shepherds were treated as 'orphans' and the animals they were permitted to bring onto hacienda pasture, *huacchos*. As in its traditional form, so here too, *huacchos* were in principle to be kept distinct from hacienda animals. In both cases, one form of 'invading' property was to manipulate the balance of this relationship: be it actual orphans vis-à-vis the 'property' of their adopted household, or hacienda shepherds increasing the proportion of their *huacchos* to the hacienda's pure-bred animals, thereby 'eating' increasing amounts of hacienda pasture. The proportions of highland livestock then at any given moment were a reflection of the 'balance of forces' to which we have seen Marx refer.
13. *Huacchilleros* are discussed at greater length in Chapter 4.
14. My argument here suggests that Balibar's 'autonomous' in this expression would need to be qualified in the context of the dialogism of social relations.
15. Gramsci seems to work precisely across this divide. Unlike Thompson, for him the line between daily practice/practical sense and historical praxis/organic ideology is thoroughly problemetized. A perpetual challenge for Gramsci was to make possible the bridge between apparently contingent and localized experiences so as to 'unify a number of disparate and seemingly unconnected events'. The intellectual played a crucial role in this task, together with the dogged work of organization (see Gramsci 2000; Smith 1999, 2004).

PART III

POLITICS' EDGE

– Chapter 6 –

CONDITIONS OF POSSIBILITY
Dominant Blocs and Changing
Contours of the Hegemonic Field

Marxism is not a political philosophy but rather an economic one. It is not a political radicalism but an economic radicalism. It incites us, not to contest or reform political power, but rather to change and transform capitalism …

[T]here can never be satisfactory political solutions or systems: but there can be better economic ones, and Marxists and Leftists need to concentrate on those … I am led to affirm that the Utopian impulse … is profoundly economic and that everything in it, from the transformation of personal relations to that of production, of possession, of life itself, constitutes the attempt to imagine the life of a different mode of production, that is to say of a different economic system.

– Fredric Jameson, 'Represemting Capital'

Enumeration demands kinds of … people to count. Counting is hungry for categories.

– Ian Hacking, *The Emergence of Probability*

In fact, the mid-nineteenth-century liberals' suspicion that democracy would prove incompatible with a market economy may well prove … justified.

– E.J. Hobsbawm, *The Worlds of Labour*

In this chapter I move away from the ethnographic gaze and reverse the priority of the chapters in Part II. There I focused more on social practices and historical praxis. At various places I suggested that praxis has to arise out of a combination of popular mobilization and strategic action. Faced with the iniquities of capitalism and the complacent indifference to democracy of established politicians, we may deplore the relative lack of really mass demonstrations. Or, conversely, we may note how contemporary media channels make it hard for the establishment to remain silent when popular mobilization does occur. But in the pursuit of really effective praxis, popular mobilization needs to include assessments of where real leverage is possible: how actions can be strategic. So I turn now to my own rather particular characterization of the present conjuncture so as to begin an assessment of conditions of possibility for subaltern praxis. I compare these conditions to an earlier period, and then do little more than speculate on what such an assessment might mean for real counter-politics.

Such an exercise is of course a step, albeit shuffling, towards intellectual praxis. Both the scholarship on politics and the politics of scholarship are usually addressed from two possibly intertwined directions. They can be summed up by words scarcely to be avoided in current texts: 'governmentality' and 'multitude'. While studies from the perspective of governmentality have indeed become fascinated by neoliberalism they nonetheless have tended to so prioritize the effect of forms of governance on the constitution of the subject that both governance and subjectivities appear to have no relevant connection with the specifically capitalist nature of society. Perhaps once there were awful days when in such scholarship the economy trumped all; now it would seem it is the forms of government that trump all.

Many have remarked that the view from the perspective of governmentality was so pervasive that little was said either about how governmental programmes turn into a witches' brew when they hit the ground as one writer put it (Li 2007: 29), or how there might be forces moving in the opposite direction. It could be said that the work of Hardt and Negri (2000) was an answer to this criticism: Foucault trumped by Deleuze and Guattari. For others, acknowledgement of capitalism, the state, formal knowledge and so on were all to be dismissed as epistemological hubris rather than studied (de la Cadena and Starn 2007; Escobar 2008). Yet, gazing in the opposite viewpoint from their governmentality colleagues, those taking a perspective from the viewpoint of multitudes, variously conceived, gazed into a mist of decentred, unpopulated opposition – what Tim Brennan (2006: 182) calls the mystery of 'the disappeared antagonist' (see also Footnote 28). On the one side subaltern subjectivities were doggedly put down to 'state effects' (see Smith 2010b); on the other side, dominant blocs were simply the incidental personnel of runaway systems of domination, of which they were as much the spectators as the multitudes themselves.

So here then are two foci of intellectual political practice. There is a third body of literature concerned with that part of the multitude that lies beyond governmentality, what the Victorians called 'the residuum'.[1] Like the other two, this literature starts from the assumption that people are embedded in the social world in *multiple ways*; here authors are concerned with the juridical and ethical dilemmas that multiple forms of citizenship produce and especially the exclusions therefrom. Analogous concerns have taken up intellectual practice in the past: the particular nature of the dominant social formation; the various means, subjectivities and organizational forms that are its counterpoint; as well as what to do about what Marx called 'the ghostly figures' or *la racaille*. Frequently, then as now, each concern was dealt with apart from the others; and frequently, then as now, the issues were seen in ethical terms and their resolution therefore lay in the application of appropriate ethics: better governance, appropriate dissidence, deserving outcasts (or not). Anthropologists however have tended to be nervous about ethics applied in these ways because they smack of ethnocentrism. Instead they have tended to feel more comfortable with the infinite variabilities of culture[s] about which they once held a near monopoly of intellectual insight. This too may account for the sparsity of those moments when anthropologists have engaged with the peculiar nature of the societies most people live in, that is to say the particular reproductive logics of capitalism. One such moment was a brief period around the 1970s (Polier and Roseberry 1989; Roseberry 1996) Subsequently it has become commonplace to hear as taken for granted among socio-cultural anthropologists that their particular concern is to view phenomena from the perspective of the people being studied, be it sexuality, violence or perhaps even capitalism itself. This has made the profession quite comfortable with the dreams of commodity traders or refusals of the epistemic hubris of Western science, but less able to provide those they study with a critically incisive understanding of the social order within which, perforce, they live.

And yet, as I have shown in Chapter 1, this carving off of cognition from practice, and practice from relationship, and relationship from reproduction, is simultaneously a function of the 'appearance' of capitalism – its economic and political society – and, at the same time, its essential mystification. The task therefore for a historical realist anthropology is to comprehend the interrelationship between forms of domination (through governance, markets, violence, what have you), revindicative struggle, and the rendering of people as residual. These were precisely the concerns of Marx, who withdrew from the pressing concerns of political journalism and organization for the ten years following 1850. This episode of reflection began with an analysis of the heterogeneous actors in the 'political society' of Bonapartist France in the *Eighteenth Brumaire* (1913) as well as the ghostly figures beyond it. And it shifted through the lengthy period in which he made the notes for his *Grundrisse* that were to form the basis of his examination of 'economic society' in *Capital*. Marx used this especially intellectual moment in his life to assess the conditions of possibility that might contribute to the success of revindicative politics. And as his analyses of conditions changed, so too did his political interventions.

The foci here then remain the same as the three literatures I have mentioned – the forms of dominance (governmentality), the potentialities of subaltern agency (multitudes etc.), and the constitution of surplus populations (wasted lives) – but the task is to connect them up and to do so by embedding them in the shifting forms of the political economy. This is what Gramsci (1991: 178) meant in speaking of one task of the intellectual being the assessment of the conditions at stake for political intervention: 'to find the correct relation between what is organic and what is conjunctural'. This means respecting both the essential continuities of a kind of society ordered for the pursuit of profit through the garnering of surplus value, as well as the re-shaping of its form that invokes changes in possible political interventions: political interventions by fluid dominant blocs and political interventions by the variously constituted groups so dominated.

To do this I need to begin by setting out a framework for thinking about modern capitalist states and summarizing the argument that follows. I can then characterize the problematic to be addressed: alterations in the interplay between *the form of the capitalist economy* – its production, reproduction and regulation – and *the projects of dominant class blocs*. Moves by reconstituted dominant blocs to enhance the conditions for their own reproduction invoke changes in the principles of regulation. And these in turn provoke the readjustments they have to make once those new conditions take hold.

These sections take the form of an immanent critique, 'how and why capitalism's internal contradictoriness gives rise to oppositional demands and struggles which cannot be satisfied by the system as it is at present'[2] (Benhabib 1986: 109; Postone 1996: 87–90). The notion 'hegemony' addresses the fact that what emerges from the immanence of a dominant social formation is both an extension of its politics in the form of the collusion of those to be brought into its orbit and also, at least potentially, the dialectical production of a counter-politics outside that orbit. The one produces a politics negotiated within the framework of legitimacy of the hegemonic order; the other stands against that hegemonic order. I refer to the first of these as 'the politics of negotiation' and the second as 'counter-politics'. The two are not mutually exclusive but I will argue that the degree to which they overlap is a function of the form the hegemonic field takes from one social formation to another. Specifically I make a distinction between 'expansive hegemony', which configures the population as homogeneous and which, in theory though not in practice, could eventually include all within the orbit of hegemony; and 'selective hegemony', in which the population is configured in terms of heterogeneity – classifying populations in terms of the distinctions among them, no claim being made either in theory or in practice that populations beyond the orbit of this field can eventually be included. In a final brief and inconclusive section I make tentative suggestions about the implications for the political contribution of intellectuals.

Initial Point of Departure[3]

A state that combines a capitalist mode of production with a liberal democratic political system can be seen as a condensation of two forces.[4] These can be configured in a number of different ways. One might be in class terms: 'class' forces, one of which prioritizes the enhancement of the value of property, the other the enhancement of popular participation. Another might be in terms of metaphors of social space: economic society on the one hand and political society on the other. In a recent article (Smith 2011) I have suggested that the modern state at any given moment might be understood as the outcome of the working out of a tension between the drive towards the enhancement of the sovereignty of populations and another the drive towards the enhancement of the sovereign territory, 'the wealth of the nation'. I will use shorthand terms to capture these two moments: *demos* and *tecnos*.[5]

Lefebvre suggests that there is a tension of this kind between the building of a late modern state on the basis of the national-popular, in which the state becomes the condensation of popular sovereignty and the expanding interconnections of scale in the realm of production, such that 'the spatial arrangement of a city, a region, a nation or a continent increases productive forces, just as do the equipment and machines in a factory' (Lefebvre 2009: 188). This enveloping of space into the logics of production relies increasingly on coordination at the level of the state: '*Les gens de l'Etat* invent new instruments, for example, a space which is at one and the same time quantified, homogenized and controlled' (Lefebvre 2001: 774–75; also 1977). Less the teleology frequently alluded to in which people's politics are supposedly succeeded by the rule of experts, in this reading the modern state emerges out of the perpetual working out of this tension. While it is true for example that in Europe from 1789 to the Paris Commune of 1871 there were a series of attempts to insist that the state should be a condensation of the community understood as the people, this was not just *subsequently* replaced by the use of experts in the pursuit of national productivity. Well before that the absolute monarchy had been interested in enhancing productivity in a line from Colbert directly to Napoleon.[6] What followed the Revolution was a perpetual tension between concern with securitizing the economy – expressed, for example, in the legalization of joint stock companies (which increased 'security' by spreading investor risk through shares or 'securities') – and popular demands for the right to property, the right to 'representation' and subsequently the right to security of society (i.e. social security)[7] (Marshall 1963). In Lefebvre's words: 'The activity of the base, discontinuous, multiple, soon proposes a return to pre-capitalist space. Sometimes proposing a counter-space, it pushes toward the explosion of all spaces organized by the state bureaucratic rationality' (Lefebvre 2009: 189).

I will return to this counterforce at the end, but the point here is not to focus exclusively on a line from participation to expertise, nor to resort to a cynical argument for some kind of functional link between expansions of liberal democracy solely for the 'purposes' of enhancing national productivity. Rather we need to note the tensions that arise as the power of these two forces play off one another at the level of society as a whole. This is nicely illustrated in Marx's discussion of the passing of the Factory Acts of the 1840s and the response of industrialists. He argued that the acts were a government intervention to limit child labour and increases in the length of the working day, since they were a danger to the reproduction of the working class – taken as a whole, that is, in contrast to the specific labour forces in individual factories. The effect was to reduce labour's contribution to production, to which factory owners responded by increasing productivity through one version of what I am calling *tecnos* (efficiency of instruments, rationalization of the labour process, etc.) so as to produce *relative* surplus value (Marx 1973). Here then is an instance of what is in essence a perpetual dialectical interplay between people and production in terms of an ongoing struggle emanating from a contradiction which becomes a perpetual preoccupation for the state, not just in terms of struggles for the salience of one expert's programme over another, but more importantly struggles among power blocs, and between them and popular masses, as the form of capitalism changes, resulting in different state forms.

For Lefebvre (2001), the Keynesian national welfare state (KNWS) (Jessop 2006) was in many ways the perfect resolution of the *demos/tecnos* tension. It invested in that part of the population that enhanced national productivity. And while the Westphalian state was protected through frontiers and tariffs, advances in *tecnos* could always be enclosed and channelled. But by speaking of enclosure and channelling we are referring to a submerged element of the way in which the tension between *demos* and *tecnos* can be worked out.

If we take *tecnos* to refer to a set of strategies to increase productivity broadly conceived – bringing human energy to bear on ever more efficient instruments, enhancing skills and increasing the speed and quality of information flow and such like, under capitalism this produces a second tension. As Foucault noted for modern forms of power, so too with modern forms of productivity: the impetus to increase productivity relies in part on the enhancement of the creative potential of people. People acting 'freely' are inclined to be more fruitful than people locked in chains (Bourdieu 2000).[8] Toyota-ism and quality teams, for example, were attempts to stimulate creativity by playing on feelings of a certain freedom in the realms of both immaterial and material labour. Too much discipline works against productivity.

But the fruits of that labour are of no use to the capitalist unless their flow can be channelled. It is a principle of capitalism that capture of the flow of value so that it can be used to enhance the productivity of capital authorizes this capture. Freedom is only useful as long as the value of its products flows back to the capitalist: whether the enclosure be the factory's walls or the channelling techniques of production chains. So, beginning with the tensions between skilled craftsmen and early factory owners, there has always been a tension in capitalism between creativity and productivity on the one hand and enclosure and channelling on the other. But changes in the influence of one fraction of capital over others have resulted in the surfacing of this latter hitherto subsidiary element to a place of prominence.

In so far as the projects of the class of finance capital have been able increasingly to reformulate the role of the state and its various offshoot institutions, so tecnos has been redefined – the enhancement of productivity and its attendant instruments being replaced by the *channelling* of existing productive value and the instruments and institutions that serve the purposes of this channelling.[9] There has been a reconfiguration of the *productivity* and its *capture* pair and the *movement* and its *channelling* pair. This gives rise to entirely different kinds of tensions. Both *demos* and *tecnos* are redefined. As *tecnos* is increasingly associated with capture rather than production, so wealth is no longer measured in terms of (national) productivity but rather in terms of the market price of assets and the garnering of profits through their trading. The enhancement of the *demos* to increase the contribution they make to production capital now shifts towards the enhancement of the subject for the purposes of finance capital – not so much in terms of 'human capital' as the neoliberals argued (Foucault 2008), but rather in terms of their qualities seen as tradable assets. This in turn modifies the relationship of the state to national territory. A coherent and contained national polity whose coordination through planning served the purposes of national production capital now becomes a barrier to the movement necessary for financial profits. Regulation through planning via the state declines in the face of regulation – securitization – through market instruments.

Despite the variations among them (Smith 1999), postwar welfare states witnessed quite comprehensive state-planned interventions. National economic well-being was associated with social integration, to be achieved by offsetting tendencies inherent in capitalist reproduction. A large part of the state's role in regulation took the form of planning to coordinate national redistribution as against the acknowledged tendency of capitalism towards polarization (social and spatial). While the so-called triple alliance of capital, state and labour were to secure these goals *within* the productive economy, further integration was to be achieved through '*social* security' for that part of the *demos* who were not directly embedded in the capitalist economy, referred to variously as 'the excluded', 'the dependent', 'the underclass', and so on.[10]

The shift away from this formula has come to be known as 'neoliberalism'.[11] The term however is misleading. The dominant economic and political classes reversed their understanding of the relationship between the economy and the state. Those actions of the state that were once taken to offset the tendencies of the economy were now seen as a handicap to the free development of the economy (now differently understood). The function of the state (and institutions functioning to the same ends internationally) was therefore reversed; it was now to facilitate the use of market mechanisms as a means for value-assessment and hence distribution. The driving force here is not a doctrine – neoliberalism – but a class bloc. As Ben Fine notes, 'Where we see "markets", we should read "capital in general", and where we see "capital in general" we should read "finance in particular"' (Fine 2010a: 10).

A distinct feature of this emerging regime was its departure from planning as a process attending to the interlinkages between elements of a coherent, bounded polity (Guyer 2007). State interventions to coordinate relations between specific sub-national regions, populations or sectors, limited the transactional opportunities for trading across these differences and had to be replaced by uncoordinated 'local' initiatives to maximize comparative advantage – and hence transactional opportunities.[12] Neoliberalism was the discursive regime that facilitated this transition but its pervasiveness was a result of a successful series of interlinked projects directed at society via the state by specific class fractions.

Evidently this kind of framing allows us to see alterations in the way the threefold issues I have identified initially are reciprocally constituted – systemic domination, political responses and surplus populations. Finance capital ultimately relies on the surplus values made available through production (industrial capital) as well as the scarcity rents resulting from the latter's rapacious need for raw materials (resource capital).[13] But in and of itself it relies on movement, channelling and capture for the garnering of profits – and it does this through *transactions*.

This means the ideal ground for its operation has three features. As we have already seen, 'transactions' mean trading across differences. Little money is to be made from offering a merchant's (or a banker's) services for the exchange of identical pots between two people (see Chapter 1). Second, the fewer constraints there are on the movement (and speed) of trade, the greater the number of transactions that can be made. And third, advances in technology that increase movement and information for trade enhance the ability to channel and capture wealth, but they do no increase it. As the logic of finance capital begins to take hold of the reproductive logics of other branches of capital (often to the extent that these branches themselves morph into a version of finance) the pursuit of these three conditions becomes the political project of dominant class blocs: (1) these require recognition of effective difference (and ideally its multiplication); (2) by reducing constraints on movement they must invoke other forms of regulation; and (3) as the expanded reproduction of production capital gives way to channelling and capture, the way in which populations become surplus to capital's needs changes. I discuss these changes in the following sections in terms of changing forms of hegemony (see also Smith 1999, 2004, 2006, 2011).

Forms of Accumulation and Surplus Populations

As I have noted, bodies of literature I have glossed under the rubrics 'governmentality', 'multitude' and 'wasted lives' have all sought to address the issues both of heterogeneous citizenship and of 'surplus population' today. But none of these approaches seeks to understand the way in which such populations are *generated* by the specificities of the kind of political economy we live in. This allows those concerned with governance or ethics, but not especially with capitalism, to propose that it is programmes of rule or juridical regimes, and not the economy, that distinguishes some people while making others surplus. It is of course all of these.

The best way to begin a discussion of the ways in which a society dominated by the need to reproduce capital generates surplus people is to note how Marx saw this happening at the time he wrote. We can distinguish two distinct ways in which he dealt with the question of people being thrown out of the social economy. One had to do with the early days when there was a shift from a largely agricultural labour force to an industrial one, and the other had to do with the increasingly intense features of capital reinvestment in a much later period. Dispossession could and did occur at the initial stages of capitalism, not of work as such but of the means to make a livelihood. Once capitalism became established a cycle could arise that threw people out of their work producing what Marx called a relative surplus population. Though these are usually seen in terms of a before and an after, it is helpful to understand the distinct nature of the process in each case.

In the early years of the nineteenth century it was commonly understood that the primary point at which a small amount of surplus money left over after all other costs had been taken care of in one round of production was the result of the scrupulous saving and astute reinvestment of a rising entrepreneurial class. This was the fount of the primary moment of accumulation that kick-started the expanded reproduction of capital. Marx disagreed. He sought to point out that this primary moment had less to do with the economic wisdom of the new bourgeoisie and more to do with the violence of dispossession directed at smallholders, tenants and plebs by a new kind of landowning class aided by a new swathe of laws enacted by their political officers. This dispossession served a twofold purpose: it freed up the resources these populations had been sitting on or using for the use of the new agricultural and industrial capitalist class, and it freed up people too – now bereft of their means of subsistence and thus thrown onto the labour market with nothing of value but their own labour power. This was not to be the only time when capital's rapacious need to free up resources for its furnaces was to occur, nor would it put paid to processes that would make labour 'free' (Marx was especially attracted to irony). But it was an important primary or – to reflect its violence – primitive moment.[14]

There was however another kind of ejection resulting from a different logic, what Marx called 'the law of population peculiar to the capitalist mode of production' (Marx 1973: 630). (1) Because in a capitalist society labour capacity can attain its value only when its surplus labour adds value to capital, that is when it is saleable labour *power*; so when it is not adding value to capital it appears to be of no use (i.e. surplus, with surplus referring here to 'marketable' labour capacities). Put another way, if the only part of a person being valued is his/her marketable capacities, then value can be measured as a ratio of marketable to non-marketable capacities. And if this is so for a person then it is also so for entire groups of people, to the extent that if they cannot realize these capacities they will appear to be a surplus population.[15] (2) The accumulation of this population is inherent to the moment when capital uses instruments (machines) to increase the surplus it extracts from labour.[16] (3) The maintenance of these populations (either in their temporary 'down time' or over a longer term) must accrue to 'society' which, 'in its fractional parts undertakes for Mr Capitalist the business of keeping his virtual instrument of labour … intact as reserve for later use' (ibid.: 609–10).[17]

There is no need to doggedly superimpose the forms of capitalism that interested Marx on the present. But it *is* important to understand the distinct principles that he was identifying.

The Twilight of Production Capital and Expansive Hegemony in the North

By turning to Gramsci we are able to align some of the features of capitalist production with issues of political power. Just as we need to go to quite different parts of Marx's writing to note the two processes of ejection I have just identified, so too we need to bring Gramsci's reflections of hegemony together with what he had to say about Fordism. The way in which he thought about the notion of hegemony helped him to explore the political implications of the tension between the dual drive for *control over popular will and the pursuit of profit through the harnessing of labour* – or, better put, the growing realization that increases in productivity could be made by expanding the arena of influence over popular will: 'an intensification of exploitation achieved through new forms of management and corporatist strategies, and expansion of state intervention in the economy and society' (Forgacs 2000: 223). Here Gramsci is talking about how the state and capitalist enterprises in the form of a shape-changing dominant bloc imbricate persuasion with material power. These hegemonic projects can be seen as successive attempts to secure the future by percolating into civil society and thereby reformulating what it is.

He was of course developing these ideas in the 1920s and 1930s, whereas I am interested in the postwar period. Following the Bretton Woods Agreement, the core states pursued a broadly corporatist agenda, seeking to enhance productivity and reduce conflict through making alliances with the leaders of key 'stakeholders'. Initial pacts among the leaders of capital and labour were then expanded to a wider hegemonic field resulting in a regime of rule which I refer to as 'hegemonic expansion'. The best resolution of the tension between *demos* and *tecnos* was some distribution of the social good to the population. And the best vehicle for this project was the bounded national state, within which claims and rights were made in the language of citizenship. The universality of citizenship on which the authority of expansive hegemony relied required that the medium for claims on the state – citizenship – recognize only a homogeneous, uniform population.[18]

As the declining productivity of industrial capital set in at home, and the favourable terms of colonial trade with the periphery declined, some of the mystifications on which the welfare regime relied became exposed. Primary among them was the assumption that the contribution of labour to overall national productivity came via the formal economy in the shape of wage work – of any kind. This fixation on the equation of formal employment with participation in the economy, and hence society, led to stimulation of what came to be known as 'the service sector industry' since this produced good employment figures. Yet expansion of the proportion of the economy devoted to services reduced the average rate of national productivity since, unlike manufacturing industry, the addition of workers did not result in a geometric increase in the average productivity of each worker, but the reverse.[19] Meanwhile the place of last resort for personal welfare beyond the state – 'informal economy', 'black economy', 'getting by' and so on – became increasingly commodified and unavoidably obvious sources of national productivity.[20] These factors alone changed the character of the state and its relationship to its clients. But still more important was the fact that the declining-productivity pinch meant that the costs of the tripartite pact were outstripping states' means for garnering income from national taxation and domestic bond sources.

This in turn reconfigured the state itself as the condensation of popular sovereignty and national productivity. The welfare state was the last moment at which the tension between these two was resolved with any kind of balance, such that the forces of *demos* could be aligned with those of *tecnos*.[21] The tripartite alliance in which the political representatives of selected parts of the working class made deals with capital mediated by the state relied on a shared understanding of the relationship between the value of the present and what value the future should hold. It was faith in this promise that legitimated controlled (and then uncontrolled) inflation. The agreement not to bring out the cudgels today was delayed by the promise of higher profits and better wages tomorrow. Faith in continued productivity legitimated such a promise. With the shifts spoken of above, however, the smile remained but the cat had disappeared. Inflation relied on an increasingly false promise and, with the shrinking of national surpluses for financing public debt (through taxes etc.) other sources had to be found.[22] Two solutions brought us from the KNWS to its successor. One was to increasingly finance state expenditures through international finance markets: 'Instead of inflating the currency, governments began to borrow on an increasing scale to accommodate demands for benefits and services as a citizen's right' (Streeck 2011: 16). The other was to facilitate the instruments and institutions that would make possible increases in private debt. In both cases this shifted the terms of the relationship between the *demos* and the *tecnos* functions of the state (ibid.: 24).[23]

None of this is controversial. But the pervasive narrative has been that the moving force here was a shift in ideas – from welfare-ism to neoliberalism, from Keynes to the Chicago boys (Postone 2012: 229). The effect is to neuter politics because it takes class out of the equation. What we need to discover is what is happening to the relative importance of different forms of capital and hence the power of declining and emerging dominant blocs. If it is true that the productivity of industrial capital in Europe and North America was on the decline,[24] then it would not be a great leap to conclude that so too was the influence of production capitalists, so long as they remained just that. If both states and citizens were turning to financial markets to address the new conjuncture that arose as a result of the changing shape of the economy, it would not be unreasonable to conclude that this enhanced the influence of finance capitalists within dominant blocs. We have now learned so much about how the rule of experts through a form of rule called governmentality produces subjectivities whose principal characteristic is that they are self-managing, that there surely can be little more to learn along these lines. It has become such a truism throughout the academy that we might refer to it as *la vie en Rose* (see, inter alia: Rose 2000; Rose 2007). So pervasive an interpretation cannot be wrong but it must take some responsibility for the almost complete disappearance of enquiries into the class forces that underlie the so-called neoliberalism.

It is surely politically more useful to point out, for example, that as finance capital became more influential, inflationary currencies were not to their benefit, since they needed above all to control the money supply and reduce inflation to ensure the value of their money in the future. As Rolph Trouillot put it so clearly, 'Inflation ranks highest among a creditor's fears … As the value of money decreases, time works against the creditor who collects payments of decreasing worth. The domination of creditors means increasing pressure against economic recovery programs that risk provoking inflation within a currency sphere, from raises in the minimum wage to massive government projects' (Trouillot 2003: 52). Inflation was therefore attacked as an element for negotiating the *demos–tecnos* tension so, faced with the need to continue to provide public services in order to satisfy the 'democratic' imperative, governments increased public debt via the financial markets by floating bonds whose value was based on anticipated future national productivity. Then, as the productivity declined in real terms, so the role of finance increased still further: both its role in 'civil society' (private debts) and its role in 'political society' (public and sovereign debt) thereby driving on further modifications in policy. This in turn means that not only was 'the wealth of the nation' (*tecnos*) vastly outweighing 'the health of the nation' (*demos*), but the way in which *tecnos* was conceived and the degree to which it penetrated the operations of the state would reflect this shift in the balance of power within the dominant bloc.[25]

What I have argued then is that different forms of the KNWS reflected the hegemonic projects that arose from the variously composed dominant blocs from one state to another. As the productivity of industrial capitalism was increasingly seen to be achieved through mass production, the hegemonic field was configured around the central figure of the homogeneous citizen/ worker. Increases in the production of relative surplus value in industry effectively expelled workers who, although they could sometimes be reabsorbed, in various ways ultimately had to be provided with the means of survival, either temporarily or possibly permanently (social welfare). Meanwhile as it became ever more obvious that capitalism itself could not address the social and economic polarization built into the logic of its reproduction, so the state became a means for intervening in this process through planning. While there were of course many varieties (Smith 1999), the overall effect was to produce a hegemonic field imagined in terms of expansion to include in principle the national population.

Yet as with all hegemonic constructions, this involved a series of occlusions. On the one hand, while it linked the ordinary citizen to some form of formal employment and claimed to service 'the excluded', a wide variety of forms of complexly commodified forms of livelihood arose, both to service capitalism and to provision people in various forms of informal economy. And on the other hand, while it highlighted state expenditures towards the enhancement of the *demos* – social security, and so on – it obscured the extent to which the state was paying out to capital. As crises arose in the productivity of industrial capital, so these features began to rise out of obscurity.

Meanwhile large integrated oligopolistic corporations became increasingly global, reconfiguring the organization of production capital (through supply chains, outsourcing, and various forms of contractual integration among firms). This simultaneously reconfigured the relationship between large-scale production capitalists and the populations of specific states, while also requiring coordination provided through financial services.

The Dominance of Finance Capital and Selective Hegemony

Tensions that arose in the reproduction of capitalism then, and the management of that reproduction, gave rise to the increasing role of finance vis-à-vis both the state and large corporations embedded in the international economy. Essential features for the reproduction of this form of capitalism were secured and maintained through political means that gave shape to various forms of the welfare state. But we can see now that, in the course of these 'achievements', features of the relationship between the state and capital on the one hand and working people on the other were obscured. In this section I will follow the same agenda, suggesting that the transitional period that I have just discussed increasingly allowed finance capital to secure the technical conditions required for its reproduction. In so far as the ways in which such a form of capitalism garners surplus value now through flow and capture, so the character of the hegemonic field shifted: hegemony became selective and hence limited, and did so by largely replacing planning with the principles of risk as the basis for the management of political society. José Gabriel Palma describes this class driven shift in the following terms:

> A crucial mechanism for setting in motion this transformation was rather ingenious: the reintroduction of risk and the heightened uncertainty at the heart of a by then too self-confident 'welfarised' population and a (supposedly) too autonomous state ... A deliberate attempt ... to try to develop an environment in which capital could exercise both a more effective politics of dispossession and a more rent-seeking form for accumulation ... Capital should gain the upper hand via an economic environment that was permanently unstable and highly insecure for the majority of the population and the state ... In this kind of environment a highly mobile and malleable factor of production (especially finance capital) would have an unrivalled power to thrive. (Palma 2009: 844–45. See also Ivanova 2011)

This changed the immanent potential of the 'politics of negotiation' within the hegemonic field, as well as the form of counter-politics beyond it.[26]

Just as I prefaced the previous section with a discussion of key features of production capital, so here I discuss those features of finance capital that effectively reconfigure the nature of politics understood here in Rancière's term 'police'. While he would quarrel with my concern with different forms of political economy, I find his perceptions here useful:

> The police is thus first an order of bodies that defines the allocation of ways of doing, ways of being, and ways of saying, and sees that those bodies are as- signed by name to a particular place and task; it is an order of the visible and the sayable that sees a particular activity as visible and another as not, that this speech is understood as discourse and another as noise. (Rancière 1999: 29)

This in turn will allow us in the next section to explore how these politics invoke negotiated complicity among some, and revindicative counter-politics among others. In Rancière's terms, respectively, 'those who play the game of forms (the vindication of rights, the battle for representation, etc.) and those who direct the action designed to eradicate this play of forms' (ibid.: 86).

Finance capital generates profits through the speed and extent of its movement. Like the current in a river, the flow itself is not as important as the moment when dams and retainers can be built to channel and hold on to value for release at a later moment or in a different place – or, in terms of another metaphor, 'the power to liquefy and freeze relations' (Cooper 2010: 181). A series of political manoeuvres by the class of finance capitalists put in place the ideological and juridical conditions that would free up the movement necessary for this kind of economy. The first was to provide a rationale for a shift in the notion of 'good value' from the use of capital for deriving profits from productivity to a use of capital to garner profits through flow and capture. The second was to bring pressure on individual states, especially through international institutions like the IMF and the WTO, to enact a package of programmes that facilitated international capital flows through internal 'restructuring' and the selective dismantling of national (i.e. national popular) protections (tariffs, 'subsidies' in the form of social programmes that reduced the wage cost, and so on).

Peck and Tickell (2002) refer to these moves as the 'roll back' stage of neoliberalism. But this was a class project made possible (and even 'rational') by the financial undergirding of the state that had arisen out of the earlier tripartite pact. The securing of these conditions can be seen in terms of a series of hegemonic moves in which the securing of one set of institutions enhanced the securing of another set.

One of these was the state itself, as its own viability became increasingly tied to financial markets, producing a strangely distorting mirror effect. In order to become attractive as investment vehicles for financial operators, key components of the *tecnos* element of the state needed to be kept in splendid isolation from the blustery winds of liberal democratic politics. While a moat was built around central banks to protect them from the interference of ministers pursuing the 'social' policies of their governments, these same policies were themselves recast in terms of their economic viability, via 'the devolution to executive agencies of what used to be political functions' (Radice 2010: 36). The older compartmentalization into what Bourdieu (1998) called 'the left hand and the right hand of the state' now became obsolete. As dominant figures of the financial class became embedded in the highest executive functions of the state, they built a one-way bridge from the requirements of finance to state policies.[27]

Meanwhile a second bridgehead was achieved through enhancing the hegemony of finance over other capitalist fractions *within* dominant blocs, most importantly by reconfiguring the logic of the manufacturing firm. Michael Hudson (2011: 3) describes the process as follows:

> [The manufacturing firm's] objective is less and less to produce goods and services, except as a way to generate revenue that can be pledged as interest to obtain more credit from bankers and bond investors. These borrowings can be used to take over companies ('mergers and acquisitions') or to defend against such raids by loading themselves down with debt ('taking poison pills)'. Other firms indulge in 'wealth creation' simply by buying back their own shares on the stock exchange ... (IBM has spent about $10 billion annually in recent years to support its stock price in this way).[28] (Hudson 2011: 3)

The redirecting of the goals and hence the rationality of components of both the state and the large integrated corporation obviously shaped the everyday life of a broad array of the population. The principles of expansion built into the high point of production capital in North America and Europe could not be repeated in an era of finance capital. Instead the principles for establishing hegemony became selective. Gleaning profits through the transactions occurring through flow and capture inherently concentrates wealth. As a result allegiances have to be sought with selected targets. Selection of course relies on and produces distinctions, while concentration configures surplus populations along analogous lines.

Again the atmosphere, to appropriate Alfred Marshall's (1890) suitably amorphous but all-embracing notion is what we know as neoliberalism but, as can be seen from the above, the *relationship* between capital and a broad array of the working population had been modified. Two features were especially decisive. One has to do with the specific problems that arise from attempts to regulate the reconfigured space on which finance capital depends. The instruments used to do this at a global level have a knock-on effect at lower levels and more local scales. The other has to do with the way in which financial securitization relies first on the distinctions among social phenomena and then on the means for establishing equivalents among them. These two features – diversification and compartmentalization – are connected in multiple ways. And it is these interconnections that modify the architectural design for the building of hegemony.[29]

As the ability to make profits from capital mobility increased through the 1970s and 1980s – not just through the speed and ease of flow (movement), but through interrupting and channelling flows (capture) – so it created its own opportunities and its own problems.[30] A global problem had to do with money itself. A service provided by the state had long been the provision of a uniform currency across the polity and, for a while, its relative stability over time had been extended internationally through the gold standard. With the new order, changes in the exchange rate between, say Japanese and German currency, could not just become problematic for management issues across global production and supply chains but could spell doom for international contracts between firms. Arbitraging across 'spreads' of this kind had long been both the solution to the problem and the source of wealth for those so engaged, but as the sheer number and speed of such transactions increased, problems of flow arose.[31] We need to note too that a feature of transactions relies on there being an identifiable difference between albeit the same asset – in this case currency rates.

But the problem of trading across difference to hedge against such shifts has increasingly included transactions across qualitatively different 'assets', often with ever greater degrees of abstraction (Cooper 2010: 178). With vastly more movements of capital to secure the future of rainfall in a wheat-belt on the one hand and the cost of raw iron on the other, there was a need for instruments that could assess equivalents across phenomena with qualitatively different kinds of market value.

A variety of financial instruments arose to address these issues.[32] These instruments for achieving a kind of regulation now through risk management ('securitization') either replaced regulatory institutions for forward planning or reconstituted the principles of planning along analogous lines. Dealing in the present with a variety of expectations for possibilities in the future through financial instruments like derivatives (forwards, futures, options, etc.) means hedging in terms of risk, rather than envisioning some of the interconnected elements of a controllable space as predictable and hence susceptible to planning (Cooper 2010).[33] And this in turn changes the way in which the social is envisaged.[34] The pursuit of security through economic *diversification* requires envisioning the world in terms of *diversity*. 'The key to this imagination is that things that we have formerly thought of as singular, total entities can be decomposed into constituent dimensions, with each dimension then conceived as a discrete risk, and hence a discrete risk-based commodity'[35] (Bryan and Rafferty 2010: 203. See also their 2006).

Once the broad sphere of global flows was harnessed through these means diversification based on the break down of reality into ever more intricate, but necessarily discrete, units reconstituted the configuration of everyday life. This in turn changed the balance in the way surplus transfers took place – from exploitation in the capital–labour relationship of production capital towards expropriation through rents and interest on loans.[36] Increasing the terrain across which the latter could occur required the rethinking of ever more elements of the social world in terms of property that could be bought and sold, and hence given an asset value. At least in the economic sphere, a precondition for dispossession was the rendering of ever wider swathes of the social world in terms of the possession of assets. We see this in social theory in terms of notions like 'social capital' (Fine 2001a) and 'human capital' (Feher 2009).

There is nothing new in making profits by taking rents from working people and selling them access to credit. Indeed this is, and long has been, a means for extracting surpluses. Nor is there anything new in the way these kinds of extraction have a polarizing effect, impoverishing some households (or specific members thereof) while pushing others towards the extension of their working day or working life to meet these demands (for a detailed case, see Sider 2003). But 'decomposing loans into commodified risk attributes is a new invention. Moreover, what can be done for loans can be done for many facets of … social life' (Bryan and Rafferty 2010: 203). Recognition of changes in the political economy such as these do seem more useful than the singular use of governmentality. To speak of neoliberalism and the figure of the self-regulating individual out of such a context puts too much explanatory power on 'techniques of rule' beyond a context such as this:

> In the last twenty years or so we have seen labour being treated like capital, the household being treated like a small business … taking positions about an unknowable future. It comes back to the issue of the state withdrawing from guaranteeing the future. And it's not just decisions about interest payments. It's about deciding whether or not and how to 'invest' in a range of things. Education … my telephone and electricity … Which superannuation fund or pension fund? … The list is long, and you don't really have the choice of not playing. So being working class now means engaging in competitively driven risk calculation and management. (Bryan 2008: 7)

The ensuring of people's lives against the hazards of the future is called social security; the securing of the economy by using the hazards of people's futures as assets to be traded through a variety of synthetic instruments is called 'securitization'. In financial terms, 'security' is what you need in return for advancing a loan to somebody to offset the risk you take in making the loan. It is an asset which that party (a person, a company, a municipality and so on) owns that can be possessed if they 'default'. What is put up in this way is referred to as 'collateral'. This is one way of acquiring some assurance that what has been advanced will not be lost: assurance is tied to the exchange value of that one asset.

But the risk inherent in that one asset can be offset by *dispersing* these kinds of obligations, so that if one of them loses its asset value, another may gain. Again, securitization refers to the bundling together of multiple credit and debt contracts – from home mortgages and student loans, to corporate and government bonds. It is true then at an initial 'take' that securitization depends on a primary step – to induce rents or interest in credits (usually through extra-economic means) – but it is a mistake to get stuck at this level.[37] Securitization detaches the rent that can be derived from specific ownership – of a house, or a factory – or the interest that can be derived from making advances that allow people specific ownership – of their health care or their car – and thereby attains a new market value from the synthetic nature of the package that results. When this synthetic package is traded, the complexity of what actually makes it up means that it acquires a price that is less from these bits and pieces taken separately and more from the market sentiment that attaches to the value of their spread.

The instruments used by finance capital then to secure surplus-value while diversifying the risks thereby involved, brings the everyday world of the slum dweller in Bombay, the student in Santiago, and the ex-homeowner in Philadelphia into its orbit. We can see this as a generalized process like the spread of a disease, and this is consistent with thinking of hegemony in purely cultural terms – an effect of power that produces what is 'taken for granted'. The causes of the disease rest with ideas and the mystery of their spread. Speaking of the Janus-face of hegemony, I have referred to this as the consumption or reception dimension of hegemony. It focuses on the perspective from the subaltern end of class relations (Smith 1999). I have sought in this chapter to remind us of the other end too: the production end.

The idea that the legitimacy of the state had something to do with the amount of leverage the *demos* had on its operation was rendered increasingly irrelevant as the result of a class project. This meant reconfiguring the viability of the *tecnos* component of the state in terms of financial definitions of wealth – that is to say the ability to channel surplus value rather than produce it. As a result the logic that drove the state and its personnel, the rationale of its programme and policies, changed their relationship to the voting population on the one hand and capital on the other. We have seen this especially clearly in the crises of Portugal, Greece and Spain, and quite bare-facedly in the figure of Mario Monti who became the unelected prime minister of Italy in November 2011.[38]

Likewise the goals of manufacturing corporations were increasingly shifted towards feeding the needs of investment banks, hedge funds, and insurance and pension schemes. This reduced the value of ordinary people as potential sources for the extraction of surplus value through labour power. With off-loading through outsourcing and its inherent legitimizing (though not legalizing) of hitherto informal economic units, it turned workers into risk-managers and a sphere of the social world into what Andrés Guerrero (2012) calls 'the private administration of populations'. And then the domestic debt and life-course risk management that resulted cannot be isolated from the entire reach of financial securitization when distinctions among categories of people become simultaneously the source for multiplying transactions and the means for diversification against risk. This means the carving up of values *within* units – the household, the firm, the household-as-firm and so on. Securitization depends, in the language of finance, on diversification. This translates, in the language of society, into diversity.[39]

Finance capital is a channelling operation that works by speculating among difference through time and space. Taken together, channelling and diversity have the effect of breaking up targeted populations along a variety of criteria and so extracting rents with no attendant increase in productivity. So political society must be used to direct goods to designated groups and thereby enhance existing differences. The highly charged effect of tying scarcity or 'limited good' to the turbulence of crisis effectively narrate the unfolding of the present into the future in such as way as to legitimate programmes that can thereby explicitly be directed towards designated spaces of the social, be they one region over another or one kind of person over another.

To be the recipient of such goods, in what Guerrero (ibid.) refers to as 'a *process of identification* ruled by the "common sense" of private citizens'. people engage in the business of distinction themselves – credit-worthy single mothers differentiating themselves from less worthy mothers, entrepreneurial workers in a regional economy distinguishing themselves from those not possessing that kind of 'culture', and so on. The politics of negotiation *within* the arena of selective hegemony is therefore expressed through the pursuit of recognition – at first by the state, then by NGOs, and then among the people themselves.

But, as we have seen, the reciprocal equation between governance and popular sovereignty that would give value to such recognition has been curtailed by the redirection of the resources of the state. The link between (national) economic resources and the sovereign population via the state has been interrupted by the ways in which the latter secures its viability – not through the resources of productive industry and productive workers, but through reliance on financial markets. This means that except for an ever smaller (and hence more selective) component of the population, pursuit of various kinds of cultural, political, even legal, recognition are increasingly divorced from economic benefits. As a result, the processes of distinction that serve to manage the negotiated politics within the arena of selective hegemony, by rendering the population ever more heterogeneous, serves also to position that population vis-à-vis populations made permanently surplus by the concentrating features of channelling and capture.

Immanent Features of the Politics of Negotiation and Revindicative Politics

As I noted at the outset, concerned scholars have focused on such issues as techniques of rule, the more equitable distribution of resources, the ethics of wasted lives and so on, to which I have added my own perspective here. Out of any one or a combination of these formulations, possible progressive agendas arise for debate among responsible scholars and public figures with a view to producing more sophisticated agendas. The problem is that the more radical the agenda, the more the possibility that its realization comes up against the prevailing dominant bloc in the relevant social formation (from region to state, to supra-state, to international order). Then, even assuming some niche or other of enlightened response from insightful political elites and corporate management, they also come up against the current form society takes as a result of the reproductive/transformational logics of prevailing capital. Since these constraints, drawbacks, distortions and so on are then built in to the next round of debates, it is not hard to see that the overall effect is circular: what the initial problematic is to be (forms of government, ethics of citizenship, and so on) arises for the purpose of an acknowledged or unspoken political agenda whose purchase on reality relies on its acknowledgement of reality's limits. The question then arises: *how would the formulation of a problematic be shaped were it entered into from the outset in terms of the leverage it might provide for effective popular mobilization for albeit differently placed subaltern political actors?*

What if we *started* our studies by asking questions about the potential for popular praxis rather than the various alternatives for better or worse governance, or ethics, or distributional justice within the current society of capital? The immanence of Marx's analysis led him to the conclusion that the form of capital he studied gave rise to certain kinds of working people, and praxis for him arose from the counter-politics they might engage in. A similar analysis of a social formation dominated by finance capital would need to reformulate the conclusion he draws. But the question is what conclusions *can* we draw? Obviously in seeking the immanent features that give rise to potential counter forces in a particular conjuncture we would need to study a vast array of variables. Even if we put aside for the moment the vast array of historically embedded social, cultural and political forces *not* arising from the class contouring of capital, we would still need to know about the specificity of the relationship between finance capital and other forms of capital. We would need to know about the very particular ways and means in which these class blocs used techniques to shape a particular state form (or larger formation, like the European Union). All that can be done here is to propose possible steps that we might make as intellectuals assessing the conditions of possibility with the initial purpose of exposing the points of leverage for effective popular mobilization and strategic action.

For Fraser (2005) the problem of political representation is how to extend representation to those under-represented or entirely excluded from the democratic process. Transformative action involves what she calls 're-framing' by extending representation to a wide range of institutions not hitherto in any way democratic. But the limits to the effectiveness of such an argument are twofold. First, in my terms of reference she has pre-emptively compartmentalized the *demos* from *tecnos*, which enables her to imagine a relatively utopian democratic solution that takes no account of the fact that the vast array of institutions in our society are pre-eminently in the business of, well business, i.e. *tecnos*. And there is absolutely no incentive for these institutions to become more 'democratic' in even the widest meaning of that word – quite the contrary as I have shown. And second, even were we to focus entirely on the effective input of a wider array of the *demos*, this only addresses the popular mobilization question, not the strategic action one. Any number of hitherto disenfranchised people may be given 'voice', but unless it comes with some kind of *real politique* leverage, it will serve no greater purpose than providing inconvenient noise.

Instead I argue that two features of the technical project of finance capital have their extensions into political society. The first of these features is the reliance on credits and rents to channel wealth (rather than the extraction of surplus value in the process of production), and its own characteristic form of regulation – securitization – which relies on diversification of risk. This is extended into political society through the fetishization of a wide variety of social relations in terms of property, thereby reconstituting what the meaning of 'property' is (Maurer 1999). A prior condition for accumulation by dispossession (Harvey 2005) is the rendering of the social field in terms of possession – assets and property. As I have said, in the realm of the constitution of population the search for risk management through real and effective diversification translates into diversity and its proper assessment in ways that really count. One way to make it count is to target specific classifications of people for selected benefits, thereby reinforcing expressive distinction through material difference. Another way is for those being classified to get into the business of classification themselves: targeted groups collude in the selection process while the promise of possible selection combined with the fears that come with precarity make those on the edge of the field of selection especially vicious vis-à-vis the current residuum.

The first feature then has to do with selection within the field of hegemony. The second feature results from the fact that the *tecnos* of finance capital is enclosing and channelling. Because, as I have noted, current forms of investment are directed pre-eminently towards already existing assets rather the advancement of credit for future production, so its modus operandi is to concentrate wealth, not to expand it through production, cultivation and so on. As a result the relation between its operational logic and surplus populations is quite different from the process that produced Marx's relative surplus population. Because it does not expand overall wealth but only concentrates it, the residual population becomes a persistent problem.

And as a problem it is not confined to its habitual denizens. Those on the periphery of the field of selective hegemony are made vulnerable by both the fluctuating contingencies inherent to speculation capital and to its general trend towards concentration. The overall effect is that distinct groups become ephemeral – competing for example to be the single mothers of choice, or the most authentic of native people – while within the groups themselves individuals are targeted to be potentially expelled. Made up of human capital the household, now understood as a differentiated enterprise either for gain or for survival, identifies individuals with 'negative social capital'. The old, the sick and others metaphorically characterized as such become analogous to the highest risk tranches in a packaged debt obligation:

the bottom tranches slip from the privilege of selection to become the neophites among the residuum.

Left intellectuals need to think about the multiple forms of politics for those people who are slipping off the edge of the field of selective hegemony to become surplus populations, as well as the politics of those already part of this residuum. We may need to think of two entirely different kinds of popular praxis: an issue-sensitive politics of negotiation and a kind of social and political identity that arises as a result; and then a kind of politics that rejects the current principles of political economy itself, producing a different kind of political actor. Mimmo Porcaro puts it thus: 'two modalities of popular and class struggle: one that remains with the logic of the reproduction of capital and the other which builds the organizational, cultural and political conditions to get out of it' (Porcaro 2012: 93). Social analysis has not been very good at providing the conceptual tools for this latter kind of politics – except to use terms like terrorism, fundamentalism and violence.

One possibility may be to work quite carefully with the principles that drove Gramsci's enquiries in the 1920s and 1930s. As we have seen, for a long time populations were assessed on the valuation of labour in terms of its contribution to the production of surplus value through the labour process. Gramsci framed his argument in these terms. But the forms of capitalist socialization now dominant do not result in a form of hegemony which, in principle, might extend to 'the whole of society'. This means that the temporal dimension that links force to consent in Gramsci is broken.

Before bringing coercion and persuasion together under the rubric 'hegemony', Gramsci separates the two with numerical points:

> The functions in question are [those of] … social hegemony and political government. These comprise:
>
> 1. The 'spontaneous' consent given by the great masses of the population to the general direction imposed on social life by the dominant fundamental group …
> 2. The apparatus of state coercive power which 'legally' enforces discipline on those groups who do not 'consent' either actively or passively. (Gramsci 1971: 12–13)

So Gramsci refers to two processes directed at two distinct groups: those who consent to the project of the dominant bloc and those who do not.

The form of hegemony that provided the principles of the welfare pact is contained in the sentence that follows these numerical points.

'This apparatus [hegemony] is, however, constituted for the whole of society *in anticipation* of moments of crisis of command and direction when spontaneous consent has failed' (ibid. Italics added). Here persuasion and coercion are linked through time because hegemonic projects extend to 'the whole of society' in a context of cycles of capitalist expansion and contraction (just as had Marx's understanding of the function of the relative surplus population). So what allows this apparatus of hegemony to be expansive to 'the whole of society' is its sequential link.

Yet, when the temporal and spatial connections Gramsci (and Marx) envisaged are fractured, we are no longer talking of 'moments' when spontaneous consent fails, nor of expansive hegemonic projects potentially embracing the whole of society, but rather of hegemonic projects directed towards selective groups. The idea of the state as the condensation of universal popular sovereignty promised by expansive hegemony and sustained by the *tecnos* of increases in productivity cannot be sustained. Selective hegemonic projects work by being exclusive, thereby rendering obsolete the ideological power of universal popular sovereignty. Zizek speaks of this as 'post-politics', which 'mobilizes the vast apparatus of experts, social workers and so on, to reduce the overall demand of a particular group to just *this* demand, with its particular content' (Zizek 1999: 205. Italics added. See also Wang Hui 2006). Moreover, because selective hegemony reflects a form of capitalist socialization based on surplus extraction through *finance* capital, populations on the threshold of the hegemonic field do not perform the relative function of resolving the cycles in *production* capital in which their value is measured in terms of their potential for surplus extraction directly through the labour process.[40] Because they do not have this latent value, for these people coercion is not held off-stage as a threat for the future thereby giving power to persuasion; coercion is exercised in the present, unconnected to persuasion.

The temporal formulation that pushes people out of the social economy at one moment and unevenly pulls them back in at another now looks more like a permanent spatial metaphor on the social map: one space in which some are selected as part of a dominant bloc's pursuit of hegemonic strategies, and another metaphorical space occupied by an *absolute* surplus population subjected to an entirely different political agenda, but one that serves to reinforce the sentiments of selection produced within the hegemonic field. The coercion exercised with increasing openness on the residuum serves the function coercion served in Gramsci's original formulation, but now producing quite different social divisions and, I believe, quite distinct kinds of political responses: negotiated politics and counter-politics. Claims to various rights in terms of citizenship may effectively advance the conditions through which one is selected in civil society but they cannot be expected to ameliorate, still less resolve, those conditions of life that are made impossible by capitalist relations themselves. Such people are unlikely to accept either the principles of a liberal citizenship that is always grafted on to capitalism, or a kind of capitalist system that is no longer able to compensate for their exploitation through 'growth'. While obviously not addressing historical conditions of this kind, Gramsci does appear to see such a distinction in his own writing:

> These incessant and persistent efforts [of the dominant bloc to save the existing social relations] (since no social formation will ever admit that it has been superseded) form the terrain of the conjunctural, and it is upon this terrain that the forces of opposition organize. (Gramsci 2000: 201) …
>
> [As a result] Changes can come about either because a situation of well-being is threatened by the narrow self-interest of an opposing group [i.e. politics of negotiation], or because hardship has become intolerable, and no force is visible in the old society capable of mitigating it and of re-establishing normality by legal means [i.e counter-politics]. (ibid.: 209)

The concentrating properties of finance capital have an analogous effect on populations within the field of selective hegemony. That part of the population integrated into the principles of social relations in terms of assets is itself likely to become concentrated and defend its position as such. But because finance capital also derives speculative advantage from turbulence (Cooper 2010), attempts by the state to save finance capital by identifying the security of society itself with the security of finance have had the effect of pushing people – sometimes as individuals, sometimes as entire groups – out of the field of selective hegemony. They are obliged to abandon the siren song of participation through the value of their assets and the value of themselves as assets. The most interesting arena for exploring the potential for popular praxis directed at the overcoming of capitalism and the liberal democratic surveillance state might therefore lie in some kind of threshold between these two. Though not drawing this kind of conclusion, Bourdieu for example notes that discrepancies between promise and actuality

> and of occupation insecurity tend to multiply the situations of mismatch which generate tensions and frustrations. There will be no return to those social universes in which the quasi-perfect coincidence between objective

tendencies and subjective expectations made the experience of the world a continuous interlocking of confirmed expectations. The lack of a future, previously reserved for 'the wretched of the earth', is an increasingly widespread, even modal experience. (Bourdieu 2000: 234)

And Zizek continues his line of thought expressed above: 'no wonder this suffocating closure gives birth to "irrational" outbursts of violence as the only way to give expression to the dimension beyond particularity' (Zizek 1999: 205).

Gramsci of course spoke of a war of position and a war of manoeuvre in the context of mass mobilizations in which the labour–capital relation was strategically located in the industrial setting. In such a context, popular mobilization had an immediate potential as a strategic manoeuvre vis-à-vis prevailing power blocs. Yet the balance between such mass popular force was beginning to shift, even in his time, faced with the technology of oppression.[41] Today the techniques inducing collusion combined with the technology of surveillance, coercion and targeted 'pre-emptive' strikes, together with the changed forms of leverage arising from dispersed sites of production and services, force a reconsideration of what the role of popular mobilization might be and how it might relate to strategic action. It might therefore be useful to explore the conditions of possibility that arise in quite specific thresholds where it might be possible to identify points crucial to the relations between capitals and their sources of revenue.

- Because security for finance derives from diversification, so security and diversity might provide the contours for exploring these thresholds as potential bridgeheads for praxis. The thinking here is as follows.
- While the cycling in and out of the labour process must still provide some rationale for keeping capital's 'virtual instrument of labour … intact as reserve for later use [as direct wage labour]' (Marx, op. cit.) (especially where production capital is pervasive), the provision of social security by the state loses its rationale for at least two reasons. First because the effectiveness of liberal democracy in securing for the *demos* significant changes in state programmes is undermined by current state forms,[42] making the provision of social security unnecessary as a universal principle. And second, as I note below, because the generation of surplus value through precarious forms of labour is leveraged precisely through the passing of such security to 'the community', 'the family', 'the individual', and so on. Insecurity itself becomes a lever of exploitation.
- The bottom line is that it is the value generated through the wide variety of labour processes themselves that makes possible the rents and credits on which finance bases the value of those assets they derive from the *demos* (and hence their tradability) (Fine 2010b).

- Security and diversity at the other end of the social scale may be worth examining too. Reduction of security provided by the state, combined with increases in outsourced work to informal economic activity, obliges diverse kinds of workers to relocate security to intra- and inter-household relations. Yet we have seen how possession and dispossession have rendered these sites into forms of tradable commodities. This transfers the tension between 'society' and 'the economy' from a national scale to the intimate scale of complexly commodified social relations – i.e. the ever more entrepreneurial household.[43]
- Meanwhile the populations surplus to finance capital are those from whom no surpluses can be extracted through financial means. Hence few aspects of livelihood take the form of assets useful to the purposes of finance, making their 'resistance' to commodification systemic.[44]

If there is an immanent conclusion to be drawn from this, it may be that as for the dominant bloc, so for subaltern groups: not just security but response are to be achieved through diversification – through spread, not among assets but among people. This would mean, of course, not just the socialization of labour power but the socialization of property, which is the lynchpin that makes possible the valuation of life in terms of assets and thereby the extraction of rents. In so far as various forms of socialized property are crucial to their spheres of intimate relations in production, it may be that it is within the 'residuals' that the clue for the *resistants* will be found.

Recently Alberto Toscano has brought Ernst Bloch's discussion (1977) of the relationship between what he called synchronous and non-synchronous political expression together with Hobsbawm's discussion (1959) of millenarian politics. He argues that both were especially concerned with the possibility that the leverage of the organized Left to strategically disrupt capitalism might be grafted onto something else. Speaking of Hobsbawm, he writes: '[The] anachronism [of millenarian anarchism] is not gauged here by a fixed standard of development, but by the ability of the exploited to find suitable ways, not merely to "interrupt" the historical hegemony of capitalism but to shape it, and ultimately to undermine it' (Toscano 2010: 52).

Neither Bloch nor Hobsbawm were able to move beyond these kinds of speculations and it can easily be argued that the ambitions of revolutionary politics are now sufficiently buried to make them obsolete anyway. But this would be a rather dogmatic reading of their insights. What they suggest is that certain kinds of absolute refusal of capitalism and of liberal democracy – albeit necessary refusals in light of people's exclusion and their position as 'the risk populations' – should not be dismissed by the Left on the grounds of impracticality. Rather, we need to re-examine a kind of vision that arises in a context where the *demos* has been dismissed as relevant to the operations of the state and to significant sectors of capital too. This does not mean abandoning the idea of the state *tout court* but rather replacing the management of national resources (*tecnos*) that have become crucially delinked from the well-being of the population, whose labour once used to produce it within a thoroughly socialized state: what Lefebvre called 'autogestion'. Such a goal would change the terms of a politics of negotiation and make the threshold between this more instrumental kind of politics and the revindicative counter-politics of the residuum worthy of much greater attention.

The intellectual challenge will be to explore the lines of contradiction between the projects of specific capitals in political society and their constituents within the politics of negotiation; and then to explore the bridges that might link these participants disaffected by the politics of negotiation framed by selective hegemony to the complex of processes and ideas that transform surplus populations from being fragmented and divided into being collective subjects.

Notes

1. See, for example, Giorgio Agamben's *Homo Sacer* (1998), Zygmunt Bauman's *Wasted Lives: Modernity and its Outcasts* (2004), Mike Davis's *Planet of Slums* (2007), Mark Duffield's (2007) *Development, Security and Unending War*, a Foucauldian reading of 'development' as the liberal 'enlightened' form of eugenics, or Judith Butler's (2009) 'lives whose ending is ungrieved' in her *Frames of War*.
2. This is the precise opposite of Foucault who proposed its reverse: archaeology/genealogy – out of which came not immanence but assemblage, as though Henry Ford's empire strikes back!
3. Some of the argument that follows relies on the discussion of finance in Chapter 1. Readers who skipped that chapter may wish to check Part Three therein before proceeding.
4. In referring to the state as a kind of condensation of elements I am influenced by Sayer (1987) who notes that for Marx, with the withering away of the feudal community, the modern state arose as a kind of ersatz community in its place: a condensation of common people and common wealth.
5. I base the two terms on Canfora and Lefebvre respectively. Canfora 2006 (250): a 'form of relations between classes ... biased towards the "ascendancy of the demos"', quoted in Riley 2009 (48). Lefebvre 2001 (773): 'No one would deny that the relations between the economy and the State (*l'Etatique*) have changed during the course of the 20th century ... In Volume 4 of my book *De l'Etat* (1978), I have attempted to illuminate this general tendency in the contemporary world ... A qualitative transformation occurs from the moment in which the State takes charge of growth, whether directly or indirectly.' Wilhelm Streeck (2012: 14) makes a similar distinction to mine, though

avoiding the class implications: '[G]overnments are continually at risk of having to face a forced choice between two equally unpalatable options: sacrificing economic stability and performance to defend democratic legitimacy, and overruling popular claims for justice in the name of sound economic policy.'

6. The shift from measuring the worth of the nation in terms of the wealth of the citizens to measuring it in terms of their contribution to overall productivity was a slow and uneven emergence from mercantilism. Gregory King, who conducted the first sociological style survey of England in his *General Account* of the 1690s, divided the population into 500,586 nobles, merchants, lawyers, etc. who *increased* England's wealth, and 849,000 labouring people, seamen, servants, etc. who *decreased* it (cited in Mount 2004: 119–20).

7. From social security, to the securities and exchange commission, to national security, to neighbourhood security, to food security, to the securitizing of supply chains – 'security' is a keyword (in Williams' sense) indicating juridical treaties that reflect a pause, a momentary consolidation, in class and imperial wars. As we shall see, whether security can be achieved through planning or through other forms of regulation is an expression of different class projects and has important implications for the power of certain institutions over others.

8. Bourdieu captures the overall ethos that results from the relation of 'freedom' to the reigning in of value back to capital:

> Workers may contribute to their own exploitation through the very effort they make to appropriate their work, which *binds* them to it through the freedoms – often minute and almost always 'functional' – that are left to them … This is especially true when the dispositions that Marx calls 'vocational prejudices' … find the conditions for their actualization in certain characteristics of the work itself, such as competition in the occupational space for example … It follows that, in many work situations, the *margin of freedom* left to the worker … is a central stake; it introduces the risk of non-work or even sabotage, going slow etc.; but it opens the possibility of investment in work or self-exploitation … It is on this principle that modern management theory, while taking care to keep control of the instruments of profit, leaves workers the freedom to organize their own work, thus helping to increase their well-being but also to displace their interest from the external profit of labour (the wage) to intrinsic profit. (Bourdieu 2000: 203–4. Italics in original)

9. I speak in terms of a form of capital. Ben Fine speaks in terms of a process, but his description fits what I am talking about quite well:

> In the case of financialization, I will understand it as a process by which the various forms of capital in exchange (including financial and others assets and markets) have not only expanded in extent and diversity but become increasingly articulated with one another. And, in particular, interest-bearing capital has increasingly appropriated activities that were previously the preserve of other forms of productive and commercial capital (or not capital at all, as in unproductive labour engaged in economic and social reproduction). *Consequently, economic activity in general has become subject to the logic and imperative of interest-bearing capital.* (Fine 2010b: 98–99)

10. In the so-called 'developing' world, programmes were likewise aimed at the population as a whole, but largely in reverse terms. The absence of commodified relations and a thoroughgoing market in the 'Traditional Sector' were seen to be an impediment to the development of a properly capitalist economy. For this, programmes were introduced for the purposes of various kinds of goals, most obviously to ease the transition from the so-called traditional sector into the modern sector; but where this seemed an excessively

long-term or even insuperable goal, it was to enact a kind of trusteeship of that population (Li 2009). Spaces too could be 'protected', in which populations could be reproduced to provide cheap labour for the so-called 'Modern Sector' (Wolpe 1975; Meillasoux 1975. See also Li 2009).

11. Neoliberalism is used to refer to a wide array of phenomena. Sometimes it is used to refer to a particular kind of capitalism, sometimes to a particular kind of governance, and sometimes to a form of 'rationality' – though the archaic term ideology is usually avoided.

12. It will become clear below why I place 'local' in quotes. It implies a geographical difference where, obviously, in reference to populations and sectors we are speaking of other kinds of difference. See below.

13. 'Whatever be the proportion of surplus-value which the industrial capitalist retains for himself, or yields up to others, he is the one who, in the first instance, appropriates it' (Marx 1976: 710).

14. Marx was neither a functionalist nor a rational choice theorist: he did not argue (as some have claimed) either that the enclosure movement caused the industrial revolution (which would have entailed a gap of at least a century or so); nor did he claim that there was a devious conspiracy between modernizing landlords and labour-starved brewery and textile-factory owners to produce a mass of labour. Instead he referred to a conjuncture of conditions and the legislation that smoothed the process.

15. '[N]ecessary labour appears as superfluous, because the superfluous is … necessary only to the extent that it is the condition for the realization of capital' (Marx 1973: 609).

16. 'If a definite amount of labour capacity is given, the relation of *necessary* labour needed by capital must necessarily continuously decline; i.e. part of these capacities must become superfluous, since a portion of them suffices to perform the quantity of surplus labour for which the whole amount was required previously' (Marx 1973: 609). Marx explicitly notes that this abstract division of labour into its necessary and its surplus components could actually become a distinction among people, making some necessary and others surplus.

17. One recent author has taken these two insights – dispossession from means of subsistence (primitive accumulation) and expulsion from the labour market (industrial reserve army) – to focus especially on this third point, suggesting that it is now *the* site of capitalism's fundamental contradiction, replacing that between capital and (wage) labour. Kalyan Sanyal (2007) argues that global competition has been so acute that the second process (increases in the extraction of relative surplus value) is no longer the primary logic of accumulation. Instead the principal means for securing surplus value is, once more, the 'primary' one of dispossession. In so far as surplus populations now arise less from this productivity cycle than from a return to raw dispossession to enhance accumulation, so the way people now subjected to 'external coercive laws' put together a livelihood becomes a permanent feature of society. The problem for Item 3 then is that the maintenance of these populations cannot be left to the society as a whole, or its parts. The permanence of dispossession overwhelms any possible cyclical process whereby a 'floating population' might be re-absorbed sectorally, geographically (through migration) or in another wave of industrial expansion.

18. It is not that differences of culture, sexuality and gender were not socially recognized; it was that the principles of welfare-state citizenship were embedded in a kind of liberal republicanism that pre-empted them and reduced their social and political purchase.

19. I acknowledge that this is a controversial issue, partly having to do with the definition of a service (much of the increase in 'services' for example, could be put down to the disaggregation of departments within manufacturing firms). But, generally speaking – and its very attraction in terms of resolving unemployment – the service industry is labour intensive, making the generation of relative surplus value low if not non-existent.

The resort to the extraction of surplus through absolute means is one reason why the industry is, almost by definition, the emblem of sweated labour.

20. Hobsbawm (1984) notes that the huge expansion of factories in mid-nineteenth-century England was accompanied by a multiplication of these kinds of petty trades. Fordism had made them appear to disappear. But now the extent to which monopoly and competitive industrial capitalism depended on the non-commodified sphere for social reproduction and on the intricately commodified sphere for a vast array of supplies and services became increasingly obvious. Already by the late 1960s, southern European countries like Italy and Spain were estimating that as much as a third of real GDP was produced (and untaxed) in the 'informal sector'. A decade later discussions of 'black', 'submerged' 'off-the-books' and 'informal' economies were creating a publishing boom in Northern Europe.

21. I have noted in Smith 2011 that, in the European version, provisioning (social security) took the form of deductions from wages through taxes and could thus be distributed across society *via the state*. Under Roosevelt, state backing for insurance and finance capital to underwrite household credit (Fanny Mae etc.) produced a quite different relationship between the populace and the capital-state combine. Very different class relations resulted.

22. The history of sovereigns taking on debt to finance their military ambitions is of course nothing new, but it is way beyond the scope of this paper to discuss how they contributed to the power of merchant capital in bygone eras.

23. 'Toleration of inflation, acceptance of public debt and deregulation of private credit were no more than temporary stopgaps for governments confronted with an apparently irrepressible conflict between the two contradictory principles of allocation under democratic capitalism: social rights [*demos*] on the one hand, and marginal productivity, as evaluated by the market [*tecnos*], on the other.' (Square brackets added)

24. Whatever its origins, decline in manufacturing investment at least in Britain and the United States generated its own cumulative distortion, thereby enhancing the extent to which the logic of finance penetrated industry. Manufacturing companies far from turning money (M) into capital investments (C) through share flotation were in fact throwing it out in gigantic quantities (as dividends and other options), thereby starving the expanded reproduction essential to competitive capital. Henwood (2010) estimates that even in the golden days of the 1990s less than 6 per cent of manufacturing capital was raised through stock market public offerings (IPOs). Meanwhile the flow from manufacturing into shares became a deluge. When I was working on Wall Street in the 1960s, industrial firms were distributing about 20 per cent of their profits to shareholders. Henwood (ibid.: 86) estimates that by 1998 they were distributing 100 per cent, and by 2007 they were actually borrowing to pay out 126 per cent. Cumulative distortion is setting in here. Seeking to keep up the value of equities so as to lower the costs of the money they needed (higher share prices making it cheaper to raise money), senior management 'tarted up' shares and bonds to make them attractive to shareholders – this at the expense of wages and amortizing machinery. They were encouraged the more so to do this as increasing amounts of their incomes derived from participation in equity. For useful ethnographic insights on these kinds of shifts, see Ho 2009, and Ouroussoff 2010, 2012.

25. The flip side of sovereign debt in recent years has been Sovereign Wealth Funds. What do you do if the basis of your wealth, say oil, would be better left in the ground to appreciate in price than sold on today, and yet you need cash? What do you do, further, if you are not especially interested in using the current income to dispense through welfare to the citizenry at large but you do want to be sure that your progeny will not suffer for your current profligacy? You take unspent income and with it you form a Sovereign Fund which, with the aid of financial agents, you invest – for example, in U.S. debt instruments.

Your commitment to the strength of the U.S. dollar is now firmly secured (see Lysandrou 2011).

26. Maurer notes a similar shift but in relation to property: 'Rights and property give way to risk and insurance' (Maurer 1999: 366).

27. The very straightforward nature of this involvement of finance capitalists in key positions of state makes it surprising that even the more progressive press in North America and Europe find it unnecessary to make much of a fuss about it. It is still more remarkable to hear scholars speaking of the decentring of power in contemporary society. To take just the most obvious financial enterprise, Goldman Sachs, it alone has provided the Secretary of the U.S. Treasury from 2006 to 2009, the head of the European Central Bank since 2011, and the Prime Minister of Italy from 2011 to 2013 among many other government positions, none of them elected. Meanwhile in China, while such a capturing of the castle was not possible, nevertheless, two veteran investment bankers remark after their intensive study, 'Goldman Sachs and Morgan Stanley made China's state-owned corporate sector what it is today' (Walter and Howie, quoted in Ho-Fung 2011).

28. For evidence for the North, see especially Henwood (1999) *Wall Street*, and Ouroussoff (2010) *Wall Street at War*. Again, while the concentration of this class project can be seen most obviously in Europe and North America, a similar process was occurring beyond. In China, where as Ho-Fung notes (2011: 140), firms 'have themselves undergone the same remodelling after the style of U.S. corporations,' in 2007 20 per cent of the profits from supposedly non-financial corporate profits came from stock trading (Walter and Howie 2011).

29. The limitations of methodological nationalism become especially apparent under these conditions. Clearly much of what I am referring to applies more directly to some settings than others, but the spatial terrain over which finance capital can and must operate mitigate against tying the structural features I am here describing to any one state. Problems of exposition are made still more challenging when we recognize that we are trying to grapple with economic, juridical, social and cultural features that are reciprocally connected in a kind of moebius strip (see also Scott 2004). It is for these reasons that this can only be a skeleton that needs to be fleshed out by empirical work across an extensive field.

30. Production capital remains the baseline upon which value (through labour) is generated. It follows then that finance capital cannot be 'pervasive', and old-fashioned labour has not disappeared (though it may have moved). Rather finance capital is dominant – in the sense that its principles condition the priorities of production capital and, as we will see, the priorities of *some* kinds of labour.

31. Hudson and Bezemer (2012: 4) note that, by 2010, U.S. 'banks used the entire $700 billion of QE2 (Quantitative Easing Phase Two) supply of Fed credit for foreign exchange arbitration'.

32. Earlier in this article I have used the term 'instruments' when referring to capital tools, rather than the more frequently used 'machines'. The expression 'financial instruments' is in common parlance. Here I use it to refer to a vast array of things from derivatives like credit default swaps (CDS), or collateralized debt obligations (CDO), to models like the Gaussian Cupola, as well as the software programmes required to generate them. Use of the word across these instances is intentional.

33. Giovanni Arrighi (1994) would point out that there is nothing new in what we are speaking of here. Rather it is a symptom of financial dominance in an economic cycle. For an early attempt to create instruments for risk management in the State, see Flandreau 2013 (I am grateful to Malcolm Blincow for pointing me to this source).

34. Much has been made of the unproductive role that derivatives play in the betterment of society. Futures trading of food crops has been an especially egregious example (Akram-Lodhi 2012). I do not dispute this, but the point I wish to emphasize is that they are

one of an array of financial instruments for regulation by the market, for the market (MacKenzie 2013). Hedging against interest rates and nothing else takes up 81 per cent of all derivatives. In 2012 Goldman Sachs used this instrument to allow them to take positions 2,295 times larger than the capital that covers them (Roberts 2012: 6).

35. They propose that this logic has three dimensions:

    Segmentation: decomposing the social and economic world into more precisely defined constituent 'elements' or 'attributes'. This is an act of imagination.

    Quantification: configuring each element as a measurable entity with attributes of risk, such that each element is in principle comparable with other elements …

    Commodification: trading each attribute of risk through securities, derivative and insurance markets' (ibid. :198)

36. Anticipating his discussions in Vol III, in Capital Vol I Marx refers to interest and rents as 'modified forms of surplus-value' (Vol I, Pt VII Intro). Note, this phrase has been left out of the 1976 Penguin edition, but is to be found on page 394 of the edition of *Capital I* in the online Marx–Engels archive.

37. Michael Hudson (2010; 2011) shows how rent-seeking in all its forms (but especially in its character as compound interest) has the kinds of effects I discuss here in terms strictly of finance capital. Other forms of capital of course rely on rent. Some of the features I discuss here also apply to the rents deriving from resource extraction. The fact that resource extraction firms frequently morph into financial firms enhances the similarities. The effects of resource extraction on the production of surplus populations has its own particular features however, as I discuss in Smith 2011.

38. As Katherine Ainger (2012) notes, speaking of Spain in the autumn of 2012: 'If talk of a financial coup d'etat sounds far fetched, consider this statement from a recent Goldman Sachs report: "The more the Spanish administration indulges domestic political interests … the more explicit conditionality is likely to be demanded" … The main problem for [Spanish prime minister] Rajoy is that what Goldman Sachs calls "indulging domestic political interests" the rest of us call "democracy".'

39. As Michel Feher notes for the notion 'human capital': 'It is precisely as a consequence of [the] desire to overcome the divide between the intimate man and the entrepreneur that one should understand the promotion of human capital – that is, the presentation of the individual as "investor in him or herself"' (Feher 2009: 33). The analogy with the firm is brought out further by Feher (ibid.: 34), who notes that 'while labour power is the property of the free labourer, neoliberal subjects do not exactly own their human capital; they invest in it' – the parallel with shares in a joint stock company is patent and, lest we still resist the association with finance capital, Feher continues, 'the relationship between the neoliberal subject and his or her human capital should be called *speculative*, in every sense of the word' (ibid. Italics his). I am grateful to Drew Gilbert and Andrea Muehlbach for pointing me to Feher's reflections.

40. Porcaro speaks of a:

    passage from an 'inclusive capitalism', which redistributed the crumbs of its own profits (even if by now only in the precarious form of an insane consumer debt), to a 'zero-sum capitalism' in which profits are secured either by further wage compression or (and increasingly) by the plunder of resources formerly distributed to workers through the social state. One cannot insist too much on the existence and importance of this shift which completely changes the scenario during which the activist generations … grew up, formed their own convictions and defined their own interests and values. (Porcaro 2012: 89)

41. For many the Spanish Civil War after the bombing of Guernica was seen as evidence of the weakness of mass mobilization faced with the advanced technologies of military violence.
42. In this chapter I have discussed a state form that arises from the dominance of finance capital, but obviously other state forms as evident in China or Saudi Arabia separate the provision of social security from the demands of the demos through a parliamentary system.
43. One site where we see this is in the forms of resistance expressed by the victims (supposedly the 'beneficiaries') of micro-credit schemes, i.e. the furthest extensions of finance capital to the edge between the exploitable and the residuum. Collective refusals to repay, needless to say first characterized as crimes and signs of 'deficiency', have played a key role in highlighting the far from altruistic ideology of banks engaged in such schemes. I am grateful to Tania Li for pointing me to this issue.
44. For the link between systemic resistance and the practice of resistance on the part of simple commodity produces, see Smith 1989. For a more recent and highly provocative view, see Sanyal 2007. See also Smith n.d.

CONCLUSION
Between Reflexivity and Engagement

_____ ℰ ⤳ _____

> Politics as such has undergone remarkable degrees of diminution. Any attempt
> to *know* the world as a whole, or to hold that it is open to rational comprehension,
> let alone the desire to change it, is to be dismissed as a contemptible attempt
> to construct 'grand narratives' and 'totalizing (totalitarian?) knowledges' ...
> Affiliations could only be shifting and multiple; to speak of a stable subject
> position was to chase the chimera of the 'myth of origins' ... Theory itself becomes
> a market place for ideas, with massive amounts of theory as usable commodity,
> guaranteeing consumers' free choice and a rapid rate of obsolescence. If one
> were to refuse this model of the late-capitalist market economy, and dared
> instead to *conclude* a conversation or to advocate strict partisanship in the
> politics of theory, one would be guilty of rationalism, empiricism, historicism
> and all sorts of other ills – the idea of historical agents and/or knowing subjects,
> for example – perpetrated by the Enlightenment.
>
> – Aijaz Ahmad, *In Theory: Classes, Nations, Literatures*

Just before his death in 2000, Bill Roseberry wrote an essay in which
he strove 'to draw attention to the process of intellectual production
itself' (2002: 61). He suggested that there are a series of sociological
factors that might be taken into account, such as the experience
outside the academy that students brought to the academy, how
this shaped their subsequent formation, and how such formation, *as
anthropologists*, affected their politics. He chose to do this by looking
at three 25-year generations in the United States since the Second
World War. The third of these generations would be the one to which
Ahmad, above, refers. Since then twenty-five years have passed. The
state of the academy, the state of politics and the role of intellectuals
in both have vastly changed, although Ahmad's assessment of the
way in which the late-capitalist market has produced theory as usable
commodity with built-in obsolescence rather than as a contribution
to praxis does seem to have led to a diminution of politics.

Some intellectuals are nervous about the extent to which they can really 'know' the world – is it to a sufficient degree that it would be responsible for them to use that knowledge for radical political ends? After all, even assuming that knowledge came packaged in the way Ahmad prefers, they could be wrong. Perhaps there is no moment at which reflection should give way to decision; there is no more unstable subject than the intellectual him or herself then. Roseberry speaks of 'academic enclosure' and this certainly both suits this intellectual positioning and also gets nicely reproduced by it. Inconclusive conversations are the business of the intellectual profession perhaps, in much the same way as art is for art's sake in another sphere. When Douzinas and Zizek (2010) can bring out a book entitled *The Idea of Communism* in which the keyword is not 'communism' but 'idea', then the enclosure of intellectuals seems to be comfortably complete. As one commentator tartly remarks, 'Nothing supplies serviceable analytic distance like the conviction that you don't have a horse in this race' (Robbins 2013).

And yet is this what we want to be doing? Is where we want to go – nowhere? Of course Left intellectuals would justifiably argue that there are many constituencies and they pull in different directions. Working and writing about one of them does allow us to break out of the enclosure and get connected, and there is no doubt that this is where ethnographers feel most confident. It is here too that the most engaged political work is being done. But we cannot assume that the way in which one constituency mobilizes, and the leverage it seeks, is necessarily useful for another as opposed to restrictive in the context of dominant hegemonic projects that select among them. This means that it is important to work at a number of levels of reality: the material world, the social world and the interpreted world to mention the most obvious. Likewise it also means continuously moving across the articulated scales of space and time. Neither of these ways of getting at the world we live in is easy to do, and the discipline or guild we happen to find ourselves in, as well as the schools of thought that dominate therein, incline us to settle for one or other combination. The majority of anthropologists for example tend to be especially attracted to the constructedness of the world as experienced at a quite intimate level. Others, attracted to the grand sweeps of the world system, pay less attention to what I have been calling praxis and are often little inclined to attend to the local texture of place.

In this book I have intentionally tried to move across these levels and scales, fully aware of the fact that this can generate a sense of frustration for the reader (as it has for me). But the enterprise itself has been something of an *essaie*, an attempt: a first run at an objective. The urgency lies in asking 'What is to be done?' The cynic may respond that this is an extraordinarily hubristic question.[1] But we are all asking ourselves every day what is to be done, even if our answer is 'Very little'. If the question was easy to answer we would not keep asking it. The urgency does not call for people whose business it is to study the social world to come up with mechanistic answers – 'We should do this', 'We are wasting our time doing that', and so on. But it may mean reformulating the way they think about problems and issues in their work. I have shaped the project of this book by thinking about what happens to the shape of our research if we design it from the beginning as an interconnected series of questions that arise as a politicized critique of current reality. Not just a critique of what it *is* but a critique of what that reality has to offer within its own terms. And not just criticism, but also thinking in terms of possible contributions to subaltern leverage: not just 'What is to be done?', but 'How is it to be done?' Thinking along these lines has led me to a kind of trinity formula, focusing on the constraints and possibilities contained in historical and prevailing conditions, on forms of popular mobilization, and on assessments of their potential leverage – what makes actions strategic.

This is a kind of politicized rewriting of three forms of attention that I have used when doing historical ethnography – or, perhaps better put, historicized ethnography. It became a conscious organizing principle for fieldwork of the long-term and annual- or bimonthly-visits kind that was the form my research took in the Bajo Segura region of Spain. As a result it was strongly reflected in the way Susana Narotzky and I wrote *Immediate Struggles* (2006), where we called this approach 'historical realism'.

In the course of doing fieldwork, aspects of the social world come to the attention of the researcher in quite random ways. For example, setting out in the morning to count the animals in a flock, we are met by a pastoralist who asks where we are going and what we are doing. She begins to tell us about flock composition and is soon relating a story about a moving experience she had on a lonely night in the highlands. Unless we are especially empirically fixated it is likely that, consciously or not, we shift the gears of our attention. We do not remain focused on a particular level of the way reality manifests itself – through the number of animals in a flock – but rather begin to listen to this account of a vivid experience and possibly even watch the body language that goes with its telling. Even if, still intent on numbers, we ask how often this person has had such experiences or how many other shepherds share similar moments, what we are recording about social reality is not on the same level as the counting of animals.

This may be an especially facile example. Any ethnographer could come up with an almost infinite catalogue of such 'switches' as they have gone about their fieldwork. In fact you do not have to be engaged in fieldwork to be doing this of course; you are doing it all the time – unless you are an especially dogmatic and narrowly focused interlocutor. And indeed the tensions and frustrations of fieldwork, combined with the problematic we have set for ourselves at the outset of our project, can produce a certain amount of tunnel vision in the professional enquirer. Yet you could say that one of the great advantages of long-term fieldwork is the vastly better way in which it overcomes the induced narrowness of the sociologist's or political scientist's questionnaire or survey by setting our access to the social reality we study within the ongoing practices we find ourselves (and our interlocutors) in.

In *Immediate Struggles* we suggest that the dimensions of the social world we address can be enhanced not just by making ourselves aware of these shifts in the order of our attention, but by consciously directing attention to different realms of the social world, even counter-intuitively shifting attention back and forth between them. While the different forms of attention may be infinite, we suggested that being aware of three of them was especially important and we called these: concrete abstractions, instituted social practices, and interpretive sensibility. At a superficial level we might say that we listen to the last, we observe the practices, and the first happens behind our backs (but it happens nonetheless). Yet by identifying these levels we become aware how thoroughly interconnected they are, each of them calling up all of our faculties all the time.

In the book we speak as follows. The concrete abstractions that condition the possibilities of social reproduction, a term Marx uses in the *Grundrisse*, we associate with Wolf's 'structural power', 'the historically specific "deployment of social labour [and] how people are drawn into the social ensemble" (Wolf 1999: 289–90), as well as to the conditions of material production (machines, technologies, etc.) and the impress of such things on the landscape in the form of roads, irrigation channels, and prisons' (Narotzky and Smith 2006: 5). As to the second, 'We add "instituted" to the normal phrase "social practices" to allude to the way practices become part of the albeit malleable frame that organizes agency' (ibid.). 'Finally, our third kind of attention to the social world alerts us to the ways people interpret their social world in the immediate practical moment of living it' (ibid.). This last includes the historically and or culturally specific ways in which people communicate or transmit their sense of the world – a notion that Raymond Williams captured with his use of the expression 'structures of feeling', as I noted in Chapter 4.

Taken together these forms of attention constitute the method I associate with 'historical realism' as well as the ways in which accounts of the social world are rendered in written historical ethnography. With the exception of Chapter 1 I have started the problematic that produced each chapter by thinking about history in one direction and praxis in the other. How has history, seen through each of the three lenses, given rise to a world with its own specific character (again seen through these lenses) which is the seed bed for the forms that collective praxis takes in the making of the future – for better or worse?

In Chapter 2, I wanted to rethink how 'place-ness' arises as a result of the different articulation of scales in capitalist social formations. It seemed to me that the work geographers have done recently influenced by Lefebvre and subsequently by Harvey and Smith, has been very innovative in respect to locality and the forms of the larger social formation, issues perpetually of concern to anthropologists. Yet it would be hard to come away from reading the work I have used by geographers on scale with a strong sense of what it would mean for praxis.[2] But that is what concerned me: how did the playing out of conflicting class forces across varying scales produce the kind of place-ness that became the lived space of the Bajo Segura? I was able to frame the way such a question would be addressed but I did not have the resources to bring it up to the moment when I began fieldwork in the late 1970s or ended it in the late 1990s. It was, then, an *essaie*.

The role of place is strikingly central to the goals and organization of politics discussed in Chapter 3. In fact it was the sharp contrast in this respect between the two sites where I had done most of my fieldwork that initially led me to think about the relative importance of determining factors internal to an ethnographic site versus factors external to that site, in a piece entitled 'Knowing their Place' (Smith 1999: 133–66). If the previous chapter tended to take the journey of enquiry from concrete abstractions through to instituted practices with little said from the perspective of interpretive sensibility, then this chapter provides us with the multiple levels at which place-ness is produced and reproduced – both consciously in the projects of actors and in emergent form out of the struggles that arose. Written as a dialogue between students of history, the chapter provides an opportunity to see how different intellectuals on the Left prioritize the lenses I have been speaking of here, and how that inflects the work they produce. But besides issues of historiographical interpretation, that chapter also raises substantive questions about politics and counter-politics to which I will return in a moment.

If there is any kind of dialogue among those discussed in the next chapter, on formal culture and practical sense in contemporary Spain, it is a failed dialogue between public intellectuals (and others) as the professional producers of 'culture' and rural people getting on with the business of making a living. Despite the quarter-century difference in time and the obvious differences in the two field sites, a common factor is a grass-roots suspicion of 'politics'. In both cases the distaste is for the kind of politics practised by professional politicians in established political parties. This is not a blanket position. While it is true to say that there is a distaste directed at a figurative space, the space of institutional politics in general (at least above and beyond the *municipio*) in the case of Peru the huasicanchinos were prepared to invest a certain amount in the populist Left party APRA as were some of my interlocutors in Spain in connection with the Spanish Socialist party (PSOE). But in both cases it was the role of negotiations that turned people off, reinforcing their prior suspicion, and evoking in many of my fieldwork colleagues a kind of shrug and an expression that amounted too, 'I told you so'.

It could be argued that in each case it was the form negotiating took that was the problem, not negotiating as a normal practice of politics. And while the specificity of each incident makes it hard to deny this (perhaps we would need more evidence), such a position misses something. In the case of Juan which ended the chapter on Spain, the tension arose because for an older generation of Socialist day-labourers, whose entire adult lives had been lived under Franco's repression, being boldly stubborn in one's unwavering opposition was what legitimated being political at all. It was a question not just of honour but of responsibility – responsibility to a quite clearly defined community of 'those like us'. These were people who throughout their lives had been screwed – I think the slang is excusable in this case – and had their antennae sharply attuned for the poverty of compromise that comes with imbalances of power.

What makes the Peruvian case strikingly different – but usefully so – is that the negotiating that evoked many people's distaste was being practised by a member of the community, Elias Tacunan. As Tacunan rose, first through regional politics and subsequently to the extent of playing a role at the national level, huasicanchinos began to worry that their own marginality would reduce the weight of their influence in the decisions he would make. Crucial here was the fact that the huasicanchinos were the most radical, and the most successful in being radical, among the various rural groups supporting Tacunan. So *any* kind of recognition or reward would look good to the latter; whereas to the huasicanchinos even the least compromised recognition at that level was a symbol of the futility of the kind of politics they had been engaged in for the past fifty years in their own locality.

The impeaching of Tacunan at a village assembly was perhaps simply a formal way of stating that he was no longer part of the community engaged in the huasicanchino struggle. Juan of course, in the Bajo Segura, was nothing like the political figure of Elias Tacunan (whose birth is celebrated in Huancayo every year to this day). But it is interesting to note that he drew back in the end from the entanglements of negotiated politics at the level of the provincial PSOE. He spoke explicitly of feeling dirty, and spoke of a path back to being a responsible person. Different though these cases might be[3] in a vast array of particulars they do share a kind of rejection of politics as it is practised in the formal institutions of democracy.

And yet in both cases the refusal does not result in a vacuum, nor does it lead to a millenarian imaginary in some space or time beyond the truck and trade of capitalism and its politics – an alternative both Bloch and Hobsbawm interpreted, as I noted in the last chapter.[4] It results in a push-back that we have to call politics, though not really in the sense that we are wont to speak of politics: what I have called 'counter-politics'. In fact something that I only really understood when I returned in Huasicancha in 2013 is that a person's assertion of being a huasicanchino includes a kind of perpetual aggravation and repudiation of the normative ordering of power and property. Simultaneous with a refusal of the present however has been a refusal to despair – at least as long as I have known them.

It would be harder to say this about many of the people that I lived and worked with in the Bajo Segura region of Spain; but even so I have sought to demonstrate that there is an important potential for counter-politics there too, which raises questions about the role of intellectuals who find themselves working both within and beyond the academy (see, for example, Narotzky 2013). In Chapter 5, I have drawn on the experiences of this kind of exposure in the two settings to explore the line between the individual agency practised in daily life and absorption in or rejection of collective agency at a larger social scale and over a longer temporal scale. In so doing, I call attention to the *possibilities* that we need to be alerted to on the threshold between a sense of frustration and anger on the one hand and the realization of agency on the other. In Chapter 4 I have shown how the potentiation of this agency, frequently alive within practical sense, is kept in check by what I have glossed as 'formal culture'. I prefer this angle of vision to the more descriptive ways of looking at subaltern 'culture' that is so tempting within the temporal and spatial constraints of ethnography, a partiality that has to do not only with my political views in general but my rather more specific views about what the intellectual's responsibility is (see also Sider 2014).

Like the earlier chapter on scales of ethnography Chapter 5 too is something of test run. I have intentionally written against the inclinations we might have in (especially presentist) ethnography and also against the distinction usually made between collective solidarity and the assertion of individual will. Instead I have skewed the lens in an attempt to force a couple of awkward issues on us. The first of these has to do with the fundamentally *social* constitution of the person. Especially in the face-to-face settings in which many of us do fieldwork, this means that the constitution of the subject is a perpetual dialogical one. So the individual/collective dialectic might be a great deal more malleable and plastic than is immediately obvious in the field setting. The second is to think through the link between the fact that both individual agency and historical praxis are about working against the given-ness of the present. Working at these two features in the metaphorical space of the *threshold* where blockages and potentialities occur[5] might allow the situated intellectual (professional, organic, and so on) to produce important insights both for popular mobilization and for effective leverage.

I hope that in these chapters that make up Part II, entitled 'Scales of History and Politics', even where the argument does not persuade, then the specificity of the historical ethnographic substance is useful for the reader. The material for these chapters comes from widely diverse places separated by decades in time and, taken together are perhaps a little remote from the pressing urgencies of our present. Yet, as I have urged from the outset, we can learn from the specificities of a history or a place. What we learn from them for political purposes might be set within the kind of angle on the present I provide in Part III, entitled 'Politics' Edge'. I use this expression in order to push us, as concerned intellectuals, to think about the possibility that the power differentials in society are now so great that most of what really matters is not seriously negotiable, and how this might have implications for the way we do our work. The name of politics is synonymous with the perpetual practice of threat and negotiation, what I call here 'the politics of negotiation'. In the previous chapter I suggest that the financially top-heavy political economy (and I argue that such a political-economy is to be found in all major social formations) works on the basis of manipulating distinctions. The business of public politics perforce has to be the business of selecting; obviously selecting beneficiaries, but also either by intention or by default selecting the unselected. This means that politics becomes nothing but a frantic arena of negotiation for selection – on the terms laid out by dominant hegemonic regimes. And then selection itself gets taken up by ordinary people in ever more discriminatory ways against so-called surplus populations so as themselves offsetting being pushed off the edge and into this residual condition.

One area where the threshold I have been speaking of is of particular political interest is where hitherto selected people who once thought they had some leverage in negotiations are increasingly discovering that it is not them who are doing the negotiating that matters, but technicians and experts calling the shots in the formal institutions of politics. For them too there is surely is a kind of politics that is happening outside the arenas where real effective negotiation occurs. A wide range of people in Greece, in Spain, in Portugal ... and on and on, are quite aware that negotiations affecting their future are going on. It is just that they are not party to the negotiations, any more than the huasicanchinos felt they were. Vis-à-vis the politics of negotiation, the kind of sentiment and actions evidenced here are a kind of counter-politics: not just a disgust with one issue or another and how it is dealt with, but feelings, expressions and actions that are about to fall off the edge of orthodox politics altogether.

The kind of politics we are talking about here are not in my view of the same kind as the negotiated politics of selective hegemony.[6] Even the most progressive of political groups who work one step at a time to gain a foothold against the Hydra of capital cannot usefully extend such strategies to those whose response to capital can only be a refusal of capital's politics. That is not to say that some relation between the two is not possible and indeed essential. But it is not likely to be a conversation resulting in agreement about the nature of politics. This raises difficult questions for engaged intellectuals. Calls for the return of the Left public intellectual are not at all misplaced in so far as their practices make appeals for more responsible conduct from their audience – over climate change, the treatment of undocumented workers, or consumer awareness vis-à-vis the sweatshops of the South. But it is quite possible that the contribution intellectuals make in the case of counter-politics will have to be of a qualitatively different kind.

The issues for properly democratic politics remain the same and yet for counter-politics there are deficits on all three fronts: a deficit in assessing the conditions of possibility in the potentially explosive immanent features of the current conjuncture; a deficit in the organization and leadership (that terrifying word!) of popular mobilization; and a deficit in actions that would be strategic: strategic in the sense that they would re-establish sufficient leverage vis-à-vis dominant blocs that they would perforce be returned to negotiation. These are hard questions but it is surely the responsibility of intellectuals to address them. And given the current balance of forces I would say they need addressing from a partisan point of view.

A now quite substantial number of progressive intellectuals have written about the distortions arising in the way their work is being done by the market capitalism to which Ahmad referred back in the 1990s. Though they do not put it this way, they and the vast majority of their readers are concerned about the way in which the agenda of the dominant blocs in the social formations where they work shapes the academic enterprise, be it research, teaching, or the demands that knowledge be 'effective' in neoliberal terms. The literature on these issues arises from positions across the political spectrum. (See, for example, Newfield 2008; Tuchman 2009; Docherty 2011.) Their anxieties are by no means confined to the Left. Indeed in many ways they are much more thoroughly felt by liberals in so far as they offend the principles of freedom as applied to thought. This work is immensely important and especially so if the authors and their audience do something to remedy the ills so identified.

But within this critical enterprise or beyond it, those on the Left can shape their own intellectual contributions precisely out of the forces that come not from the hegemony produced by capital but from the counter-currents contemporary forms of capital are producing. The point is not to suggest that identifying what these issues should be – how to mobilize, for what goals, and so on – is peculiarly the task of the intellectual who is anyway one of many kinds of actors involved in negotiated and counter-politics. The point rather is to recognize that there *is* an important role for the intellectual in undertaking reflection and critique.

There is a potential bridge between the intellectual project of critique and people's refusal of current reality expressed either through their disenchantment with the leverage they have for negotiation or through counter-politics. This means that there is a threshold that needs perpetually to be crossed; the irritant and irresolution of counter-politics shapes the intellectual's reflexivity, while the intellectual continually works back and forth across the bridge between the practices of the everyday world and the incipient criticism of different forms of revindicative practice.

The challenge then is to use the sensitivity of the interpretive tools we have at our disposal to enhance the organic possibilities of bridges between the various forms of revindication while also providing the materials for assessing the possibilities thrown up by each conjuncture from one place and moment to another. It may be that the form the university now takes makes it increasingly difficult for those working in what George Thompson, carpenter, organic intellectual and founder in 1914 of the Yorkshire 'Workers' Educational Association' (WEA) called 'the controversial subjects' to work effectively in this way (Steele 2013: 28).[7] Either the new kind of university will produce its own immanent forms of counter-institutional politics making possible truly radical intellectual practice for those who seek it; or the university may no longer be the site of the kind of effective intellectual Gramsci so committed his last years to trying to develop.

Notes

1. Though for Lenin it did bear some fruit even if the grapes turned sour in the end.
2. I refer here only to my use of geographers' insights on scale. In fact the discipline itself has produced a wide range of reflections on the politics of resistance in the current conjuncture.
3. In the terms made famous by Albert Hirschman (1970), in response to such politics the huasicanchinos chose something a little more than what he would call 'voice', while the people of the Bajo Segura chose his 'exit' option.
4. It is interesting to speculate whether at least in part this was not Hobsbawm's fascination with the huasicanchinos.
5. Potentialities for example in the implications of the individual pushing back against relevant others; blockages to a certain kind of collective politics of an individual's acceptance of selected features of the present as beyond their agency.
6. For another argument that notes distinctive arenas for different kinds of politics, see Chatterjee 2004 and 2008. For my comments on his framework, see Smith 2011.
7. By the 'controversial subjects' he meant, Economics, Social and Political History, Political Philosophy and Social History (Steele 2013). After the Second World War the WEA provided the setting for people like E.P. Thompson (no relation to George) and Raymond Williams to offer their services outside the university. For a fascinating treatment of E.P Thompson's activities at this time, see the conceptual film by Luke Fowler, *The poor stockinger, the Luddite cropper and the deluded followers of Joanna Southcott* (The Hepworth Wakefield and Wolverhampton Art Gallery, 2013).

REFERENCES

Abrams, Philip. 1982. *Historical Sociology*. Ithaca, NY: Cornell University Press.

Adorno, Theodor. 1998. *Beethoven: The Philosophy of Music*. Stanford, CA: Stanford University Press.

Agamben, Giorgio. 1998. *Homo Sacer: Sovereign Power and Bare Life*, trans D. Heller-Roazan. Stanford, CA: Stanford University Press.

Aguilar, Paloma. 1996. *Memoria y olvido de la Guerra Civil española*. Madrid: Alianza Editorial.

Ahmad, Aijaz. 1994. *In Theory: Classes, Nations, Literatures*. London: Verso.

Ainger, Katherine. 2012. 'The Spanish Public Won't Accept a Financial Coup d'Etat', *The Guardian*, 25 September.

Akram-Lodhi, Haroun. 2013. *Hungry for Change: Farmers, Food Justice and the Agrarian Question*. Toronto, ON: Brunswick/Fernwood.

Alonso, Martín. (1960) 1975. *Diccionario del Español Moderno*. Madrid: Aguilar.

Anchimanya Flores, Eduardo Daniel. 2010. *Biografía del líder comunal Elías Tácunan Cahuana y la Comunidad de Huasicancha*. Ed. Particular. Huancayo.

Anderson, Perry. 1976. *Considerations of Western Marxism*. London: New Left Books.

Appadurai, Arjun. 1996. *Modernity at Large: Cultural Dimensions of Globalization*. Minneapolis: University of Minnesota Press.

Arnold, Matthew. 1994. *Culture and Anarchy*. New Haven, CT: Yale University Press.

Aróstegui, J., and F. Godicheau (eds). 2006. *Guerra civil, mito y memoria*. Madrid: Marcial Pons.

Arrighi, Giovanni. 1994. *The Long Twentieth Century: Money, Power and the Origins of our Times*. London: Verso.

_____. 2007. *Adam Smith in Beijing: The Lineages of the Twenty-first Century*. London: Verso.

Bakhtin, M.M. 1981. *The Dialogic Imagination: Four Essays*, ed. Michael Holquist, trans. Caryl Emerson and Michael Holquist. Austin and London: University of Texas Press.

Balibar, Etienne. 1995. *The Philosophy of Marx*, trans. Chris Turner. London: Verso.

_____. 2002. *Politics and the Other Scene*. London: Verso.

Bauman, Zygmunt. 2004: *Wasted Lives: Modernity and its Outcasts*. Cambridge: Polity Press.

Beck, U. 2002. 'The Cosmopolitan Perspective: Sociology and the Second Age of Modernity', *British Journal of Sociology* 51(1): 79–105.

Benhabib, Seyla. 1986. *Critique, Norm and Utopia: A Study of the Foundations of Critical Theory*. New York: Columbia University Press.

Bertaux-Wiame, Isabelle. 1985. 'Response to Tilly', *International Journal of Oral History* 6(1): 25–31.

Bloch, Ernst. 1977. 'Nonsynchronism and the Obligation to its Dialectics', *New German Critique* 11: 22–38.

Boltanski, Luc. 2011. *On Critique: A Sociology of Emancipation*, trans G. Elliott. Cambridge: Polity Press.

Boltanski, L. and E. Chiapello. 2005. *The New Sprit of Capitalism*. London: Verso.

Bottomore, Tom, L. Harris, V.G. Kiernan and R. Miliband (eds). 1983. *A Dictionary of Marxist Thought*. London: Blackwell.

Bourdieu, Pierre. 1988. *Homo academicus* (2nd Edition). Paris: Editions du minuit.

_____. 1990a. *In Other Words*. Stanford, CA: Stanford University Press.

_____. 1990b. 'The Scholastic Point of View', *Cultural Anthropology* 5(4): 380–91.

_____. 1998. *Acts of Resistance: Against the Tyranny of the Market*. New York: New Press.

_____. 1999. *The Weight of the World: Social Suffering in Contemporary Society*. Oxford: Polity Press.

_____. 2000. *Pascalian Meditations*. Stanford, CA: Stanford University Press.

_____. 2003. 'Participant Objectivation'. *Journal of the Royal Anthropological Institute* (NS) 9: 281–94.

Braudel, Fernand. 1982. *The Wheels of Commerce*. New York: Harper & Row.

_____. 1992. *The Structure of Everyday Life* (Vol. I of *Civilization and Capitalism*). Berkeley: University of California Press.

_____. 1995. *A History of Civilizations*, trans. Richard Mayne. Harmondsworth: Penguin.

Brennan, Timothy. 2006. *Wars of Position: The Cultural Politics of Left and Right*. New York: Columbia University Press.

Brenner, Neil. 1998. 'Between Fixity and Motion: Accumulation, Territorial Organization and the Historical Geography of Spatial Scales', *Environment and Planning D: Society and Space* 16(5): 459–81.

Brenner, Robert. 1985. *The Brenner Debate*. Eds T.H.Aston and C.H.E. Philpin. Cambridge: Cambridge University Press.

Brown, Wendy. 2002. 'At the Edge', *Political Theory* 30(4): 556–76.

Bryan, Dick. 2008. 'The Inventiveness of Capital'. http://www.workersliberty.org/story/2008/07/13/marxists-capitalist-crisis-6-dick-bryan-inventiveness-capital. Accessed 13 Jan 2009.

_____. 2010. 'Financialization and the Subsumption of Labour before and after the Subprime Crisis'. Paper presented to Political Science Department, York University.

Bryan, Dick, and Michael Rafferty. 2006. *Capitalism with Derivatives: A Political Economy of Financial Derivatives, Capital and Class*. Basingstoke and New York: Palgrave Macmillan.

Butler, Judith. 2009. *Frames of War: When is Life Grievable?* London: Verso.

Cadena, Marisol de la, and Orin Starn (eds). 2007. *Indigenous Experience Today*. Oxford: Berg.

Callon, Michel, C. Méadel and V. Rabeharisoa. 2002. 'The Economy of Qualities', *Economy and Society* 31(2): 194–217.

Canfora, Luciano. 2006. *Democracy in Europe: A History of an Ideology*. Oxford: Blackwell.

Carbonella, August. 2005. 'Beyond the Limits of the Visible World: Remapping Historical Anthropology', in Don Kalb and Herman Tak (eds), *Critical Junctures: Anthropology and History beyond the Cultural Turn*. Oxford: Berghahn Books.

Carrier, James G. 2013. 'The Concept in Class', in J.G. Carrier and D. Kalb (eds), *Class in Anthropology*. Forthcoming. Cambridge: Cambridge University Press.

Castells, Manuel. 1996. *The Rise of the Network Society*. New York: John Wiley.

Castells, Manuel and Alejandro Portes. 1988. 'World Underneath: The Origins, Dynamics and Effects of the Informal Economy', in Portes, Castells and Benton (eds), *The Informal Economy: Studies in Advances and Less Developed Countries*. Baltimore, MD: Johns Hopkins University Press.

Castree, Noel. 2006. 'The Detour of Critical Theory', in N. Castree and D. Gregory (eds), *David Harvey: A Critical Reader*. Oxford: Blackwell.

Cercas, Javier. 2001. *Soldados de Salamina*. Barcelona: TusQuets. Trans. Anne McLean (2003), *Soldiers of Salamis*. London: Bloomsbury.

Cenarro, Angela. 2002. 'Memory beyond the Public Sphere: The Francoist Repression Remembered in Aragon', *History and Memory* 14(1–2): 165–228.

Chatterjee, Partha. 2004. *Politics of the Governed: Reflections on Political Politics in Most of the World*. New York: Columbia University Press.

_____. 2008. 'Democracy and Economic Transformation in India', *Economic and Political Weekly* 19 April: 53–62.

Cohn, B. 1981. 'Anthropology and History in the 1980s: Toward a Rapprochement', *Journal of Interdisciplinary History* 12: 227–52.

Colmeiro, José. 2011. 'A Nation of Ghosts? Haunting, Historical Memory and Forgetting in Post-Franco Spain' [online article] *425°F Electronic journal of literature and comparative literature* 4: 17–34. www.452f.com/pdf/numero04/.../04_452f_mono_colmeiro_indiv.pdf. Accessed 18 Jan 2012.

Cooper, Fred. 2005. *Colonialism in Question: Theory, Knowledge, History.* Berkeley: University of California Press.

Cooper, Melinda. 2010. 'Turbulent Worlds: Financial Markets and Environmental Crisis', *Theory, Culture & Society* 27(2–3): 167–90.

Crehan, Kate. 2002. *Gramsci, Culture and Anthropology.* Berkeley: University of California Press.

Darnton, Robert. 1984. *The Great Cat Massacre and Other Episodes in French Cultural History.* New York: Basic Books.

Davis, Mike. 2007. *Planet of Slums.* London: Verso.

Dean, Mitchell. 1999. *Governmentality.* New York: Sage.

Deleuze, Gilles, and Michel Foucault. 1980: 'Intellectuals and Power' in Foucault, *Language, Counter-memory, Practice: Selected Essays and Interviews.* Ithaca, NY: Cornell University Press.

Deranty, Jean-Philippe. 2003. 'Jacques Rancière's Contribution to the Ethics of Recognition', *Political Theory* 31(1): 136–56.

Diamond, Jared. 2012. *The World until Yesterday: What Can We Learn from Traditional Societies?* New York: Penguin.

Dirlik, Arif. 2001. 'Place-based Imagination: Globalism and the Politics of Place', in Roxanne Prazniak and Arif Dirlik (eds), *Places and Politics in an Age of Globalization.* Lanham, MD and Boulder, CO: Rowman & Littlefield.

Docherty, Thomas. 2011. *For the University.* New York: Bloomsbury Academic.

Donham, Donald. 1999. *History, Power, Ideology: Central Issues in Marxist Anthropology.* Berkeley: University of California Press.

Douzinas, C., and S. Zizek (eds). 2010. *The Idea of Communism.* London: Verso.

Duffield, Mark. 2007. *Development, Security and Unending War: Governing the World of Peoples.* London: Polity

Escobar, Arturo. 2008. *Territories of Difference: Place, Movements, Life, Redes.* Durham, NC: Duke University Press.

Feher, Michel, 2009. 'Self-appreciation or the Aspirations of Human Capital', *Public Culture* 21(1): 21–41.

Fernández de Mata, Ignacio. 2007. 'El surgimiento de la memoria histórica. Sentidos, malentendimientos y disputas', in Diaz y Tomé (eds), *La traditción como reclamo.* Salamanca: Consejería de cultura y turismo, Junta de Castilla y León, pp. 195–208.

Fine, Ben. 2010a. 'Neoliberalism as Financialization' in A. Saad-Filho and G. Yalman (eds): *Economic Transitions to Neoliberalism in Middle-income Countries.* London: Routledge.

_____. 2010b. 'Locating Financialization', *Historical Materialism* 18: 97–116.

Flandreau, Marc. 2013. 'The First Weapon of Mass Destruction', *Monthly Review Press* 64(9): 39–46.

Forgacs, David. 2000. 'Introduction to Part VII', in *The Gramsci Reader: Selected Writings 1916–1935,* ed. David Forgacs. New York: New York University Press.

Foucault, Michel. 2008. *The Birth of Biopolitics: Lectures at the Collège de France 1978–79,* trans. G. Burchell. Basingstoke and New York: Palgrave MacMillan.

Fraser, Nancy. 2005. 'Reframing Global Justice', *New Left Review* 36: 69–90.

Friedmann, Harriet. 1978. 'World Market, State and Family Farm: Social Basis of Household Production in the Era of Wage Labour', *Comparative Studies in Society and History* 20.

Friedman, K.E., and J. Friedman. 2008a. *Modernities, Class, and the Contradictions of Globalization: The Anthropology of Global Systems*. Lanham, MD: AltaMira Press.

_____. 2008b. *Historical Transformations: The Anthropology of Global Systems*. Lanham, MD: AltaMira Press.

Ginzberg, Carlo. 1982. *The Cheese and the Worms: The Cosmos of a Sixteenth-century Miller*. Harmondsworth: Penguin.

Goldthorpe, John H., and Keith Hope. 1974. *The Social Grading of Occupations: A New Approach and Scale*. Oxford: Clarendon Press.

Graeber, David. 2013. *The Democracy Project: History, Crisis, Hope*. New York: Spiegel & Grau.

Gramsci, Antonio. 1957. *The Modern Prince and Other Writings*, trans. Louis Marks. New York: International Publishers.

_____. 1971. *Selections from the Prison Notebooks*. Ed. and trans. by Q. Hoare and G. Nowell-Smith. New York: International Publishers.

_____. 1991. *Selections from Cultural Writings*, ed. and trans. D. Forgacs. Cambridge, MA: Harvard University Press.

_____. 2000. *The Gramsci Reader: Selected Writings 1916–1935*, ed. David Forgacs. New York: New York University Press.

Grimshaw, Anna, and Keith Hart, 1994. 'Anthropology and the Crisis of the Intellectuals', *Critique of Anthropology* 14(3): 227–62. 'Forum' response by David M. Schneider, *Critique of Anthropology* 14(4): 419–24.

Grossman, Lawrence, and Cary Nelson (eds). 1988. *Marxism and the Interpretation of Culture*. Urbana: University of Illinois Press.

Guerrero, Andrés. 2012. 'Echoes Arising from Two Cases of the Private Administration of Populations: African Immigrants in 21st Century Spain and Indians in 19th Century Ecuador', *Focaal – Journal of Historical and Global Anthropology* 63: 90–112.

Gupta, Akhil. 2010. '"Overstated" Objections?', Commentary on Smith, *Anthropologica* 52: 178–81.

Gupta, A. and J. Ferguson. 1997. *Anthropological Locations: Boundaries and Grounds of a Field Science*. Berkeley: University of California Press.

Guyer, Jane. 2007. 'Prophecy and the Near Future: Thoughts on Macroeconomic, Evangelical, and Punctuated Time', *American Ethnologist* 34(3): 409–21.

Hacking, Ian. 1982. *The Emergence of Probability*. Cambridge: Cambridge University Press.

Halbwachs, Maurice. 1980. *The Collective Memory*. New York: Harper & Row.

Haldane, A.G., and R.M. May. 2011. 'Systemic Risk in Banking Ecosystems', *Nature* 469: 351–55.

Hale, Charles R. 2006a. 'Activist Research v. Cultural Critique: Indigenous Land Rights and the Contradictions of Politically Engaged Anthropology', *Cultural Anthropology* 21(1): 96–120.

_____. 2006b. '*Más que un indio*' [More than an Indian]: *Racial Ambivalence and Neoliberal Multiculturalism in Guatemala*. Santa Fe, NM: School of American Research.

Hardt, Michael, and Antonio Negri. 2000. *Empire*. Cambridge, MA: Harvard University Press.

Harman, Chris. 2009. *Zombie Capitalism: Global Crisis and the Relevance of Marx*. Chicago: Haymarket Books.

Harvey, David. 1982. *The Limits to Capital*. Chicago: Chicago University Press.

_____. 1996. *Justice, Nature and the Geography of Difference*. Cambridge, MA, and Oxford: Blackwell.

_____. 2001. *Spaces of Capital*. Edinburgh: Edinburgh University Press.

_____. 2003. 'The "New" Imperialism: Accumulation by Dispossession', in Panitch and Leys (eds), *The New Imperial Challenge: Socialist Register 2004*. London: Merlin.

_____. 2005. *A Brief History of Neoliberalism*. Oxford: Oxford University Press.

_____. 2010. *A Companion to Marx's Capital*. London: Verso.

Henwood, Doug. 1999. *Wall Street: How it Works and for Whom*. London: Verso.

_____. 2010. 'Before and After Crisis: Wall Street Lives On', in Leo Panitch, Greg Albo and Vivek Chibber, *The Crisis this Time: Socialist Register 2011*. London: Merlin Press, pp. 83–97.

Higgins, John. 1999. *Raymond Williams: Literature, Marxism and Cultural Materialism*. London and New York: Routledge.

Hirschman, Albert. 1970. *Exit, Voice and Loyalty: Responses to Decline in Firms, Organizations and States*. Cambridge, MA: Harvard University Press.

Ho, Karen. 2009. *Liquidated: An Ethnography of Wall Street*. Durham, NC: Duke University Press.

Hobsbawm, E.J. 1959. *Primitive Rebels: Archaic Forms of Social Movements in the 19th and 20th centuries*. Boston: Beacon Press.

_____. 1969. *Bandits*. New York: Delacorte Press.

_____. 1974. 'Peasant Land Occupations', *Past and Present* 62: 120–52.

_____. (1978) 1984. *The Worlds of Labour: Further Studies in the History of Labour*. London: Weidenfeld and Nicolson.

_____. 1994. *Age of Extremes*. London: Abacus.

_____. (1994) 1997. *The Age of Empire*. London: Abacus.

_____. 2005. 'In Defence of History', *Guardian Weekly*, 15 Jan. http://www.guardian.co.uk/books/2005/jan/15/news.comment. Retrieved 8 May 2013.

Hobsbawm, E.J. and T. Ranger (eds). *The Invention of Tradition*. London: Past and Present Publications.

Ho-Fung, Hung. 2011. 'Paper-tiger finance?', *New Left Review* 72: 138–44.

Holmes, Douglas. 2000. *Integral Europe: Fast-Capitalism, Multiculturalism, Neofascism*. Princeton, NJ: Princeton University Press.

Holmes, Douglas and George Marcus. 2005. 'Cultures of Expertise and the Management of Globalization: Toward the Re-functioning of Ethnography', in A. Ong and S. Collier (eds), *Global Assemblages: Technology, Politics and Ethics as Anthropological Problems*. Oxford: Blackwell.

Hudson, Michael. 2008. 'How the Chicago Boys Wrecked the Economy', *Globalresearch.ca*. Accessed 19 Sep 2008.

_____. 2010. *The Monster: How a Gang of Predatory Lenders and Wall Street Bankers Fleeced America and Spawned a Global Crisis*. New York: Henry Holt.

_____. 2011. 'How Economic Theory Came to Ignore the Role of Debt', *Real World Economics Review* 57(6).

Hudson, Michael and Dirk Bezemer. 2012. 'Incorporating the Rentier Sectors into a Financial Model', *World Economic Review* 1: 1–12.

Ivanova, Maria N. 2011. 'Money, Housing and World Market: The Dialectic of Global Production', *Cambridge Journal of Economics* 35: 853–71.

Jameson, Fredric. 1991. *Postmodernism, or the Cultural Logic of Late Capitalism*. Durham, NC: Duke University Press.

_____. 2009. 'Representing Capital: A New Reading Hypothesis about Volume I of Marx's *Capital*'. Paper presented to 6th annual Historical Materialism Conference. MS.

Jay, Martin. 1984. *Marxism and Totality: The Adventures of a Concept from Lukács to Habermas*. Berkeley: University of California.

Jessop, Bob. 2006. 'State- and Regulation-theoretical Perspectives on the European Union and the Failure of the Lisbon Agenda', *Competition and Change* 10(2): 141–61.

_____. 2008. *State Power*. Cambridge: Polity.

Juliá, Santos. 1999. 'De "guerra contra el invasor" a "guerra fratricida"' in Juliá, Casanova et al. (eds), *Victimas de la Guerra Civil*. Madrid: Temas de Hoy.

_____ (ed.). 2006a. *Memoria de la Guerra y del franquismo*. Madrid: Taurus.

_____. 2006b. 'Memoria, historia y politica de un pasado de guerra y dictadura' in Juliá (ed.), *Memoria de la Guerra*.

Kahn, Joel. 1980. *Minangkabau Social Formations*. Cambridge: Cambridge University Press.

Kalb, Don. 1997. *Expanding Class: Power and Everyday Politics in Industrial Communities, The Netherlands, 1850–1950*. Durham, NC: Duke University Press.

_____. 2005. '"Bare legs like Ice": Recasting Class for Local/Global Inquiry', in Don Kalb and Herman Tak (eds), *Critical Junctions: Anthropology and History beyond the Cultural Turn*. Oxford: Berghahn Books.

Kalb, Don and Herman Tak. 2005. 'Critical Junctions – Recapturing Anthropology and History', in Kalb and Tak (eds), *Critical Junctions: Anthropology and History beyond the Cultural Turn*. Oxford: Berghahn Books.

Ladurie, Emmanuel Le Roy. 1978. *Montaillou: The Promised Land of Error*. New York: G. Braziller.

Lanchester, John. 2008. 'Cityphilia', *London Review of Books* 30(1): 9–12.

Lefebvre, Henri. 1970 : *La révolution urbaine*. Gallimard, Paris

_____. 1977. *De l'Etat: le mode de production étatique*, Vol. 3. Paris: Union Générale d'Editions.

_____. 1978. *De l'Etat: le mode de production étatique*, Vol. 4. Paris: Union Générale d'Editions.

_____. 2001. 'Comments on a New State Form', trans. V. Johnson and N. Brenner, *Antipode* 33(5): 769–82.

_____. 2009. *State, Space, World: Selected Essays*. Eds N. Brenner and S. Elden. Minneapolis: University of Minnesota Press.

Lem, Winnie. 1988. 'Household Production and Reproduction in Rural Languedoc: Social Relations of Petty Commodity Production in Murviel-lès-Béziers', *Journal of Peasant Studies* 15(4): 500–29.

_____. 1997. 'Restructuring Work and Identity: Perspectives on Class, Region and Gender in Southern France', in M. Keating and J. Loughlin (eds), *The Political Economy of Regionalism*. London: Frank Cass.

_____. 1998. *Cultivating Dissent: Work and Politics in Languedoc*. Binghamton: State University of New York Press.

Lenin, V.I. 1956. *The Development of Capitalism in Russia*. Moscow: Progress.

Levi-Strauss, C. 1973. *Tristes Tropiques*. Trans. J. and D. Weightman. London: Cape.

Li, Tania. 2007. *The Will to Improve: Governmentality, Development and the Practice of Politics*. Durham, NC: Duke University Press.

_____. 2009. 'To Make Live or Let Die? Rural Dispossession and the Protection of Surplus Populations', *Antipode* 41(S1): 1208–35.

Lomnitz-Adler, Claudio. 1991. 'Concepts for the Study of Regional Culture', *American Ethnologist* 18(2): 195–214.

Long, N., and B. Roberts. 1984. *Miners, Peasants and Entrepreneurs: Regional Development in the Central Highlands of Peru*. Cambridge: Cambridge University Press.

Lysandrou, Photis. 2011. 'Global Inequality as One of the Root Causes of the Financial Crisis: A Suggested Explanation', *Economy and Society* 40(3): 323–44.

MacKenzie, Donald. 2008a. 'End-of-the-World Trade', *London Review of Books* 30(9): 24–26.

_____. 2013. 'The Magic Lever', *London Review of Books* 35(9): 16–19.

Marcus, George. 1998. *Ethnography Through Thick and Thin*. Princeton: Princeton University Press.

Marshall, Alfred. 1890. *The Principle of Economics*. London: Macmillan and Co.

Marshall, T.H. (1950) 1963. 'Citizenship and Social Class' in his *Sociology at the Crossroads and Other Essays*. London: Heinemann Educational Books.

Marston, Sallie A. 2000. 'The Social Construction of Scale', *Progress in Human Geography* 24(2): 219–42.

Marston, Sallie A. and Neil Smith. 2001. 'States, Scales and Households: Limits to Scale Thinking? A Response to Brenner', *Progress in Human Geography* 25(4): 615–19.

Martínez Alier, J. 1973. *Los Huacchilleros del Peru*. Lima: Instituto de Estudios Peruanos.

Marx, Karl. 1904. *A Contribution to the Critique of Political Economy*. Chicago: Charles Kerr & Co.

_____. 1913. *The Eighteenth Brumaire of Louis Bonaparte*, trans Daniel de Leon. Chicago: Charles H. Kerr.

Marx to Annenkov. 1963. Letter of 28 Dec 1846, in *Poverty of Philosophy*. New York: International Publishers

Marx, Karl. 1967. *Economic and Philosophical Manuscripts of 1844*. Moscow: Progress.

_____. 1973. *Grundrisse: Foundations of the Critique of Political Economy* (Rough Draft), trans. Martin Nicolaus. Harmondsworth: Penguin.

_____. (1867) 1976. *Capital* Vol. I., trans. Ben Fowkes. Harmondsworth: Penguin.

Marx, Karl and Frederick Engels. 1970. *The German Ideology*. Part I, ed. C.J.Arthur. London: Lawrence & Wishart.

Maskovsky, Jeff. 2013. 'Protest Anthropology in a Moment of Global Unrest', *American Anthropologist* 115: 126–29.

Maurer, Bill. 1999. 'Forget Locke? From Proprietor to Risk-bearer in New Logics of Finance', *Public Culture* 11(2): 47–67.

Mayer, Enrique. 1991. 'Peru in Deep Trouble: Mario Vargas Llosa's "Inquest in the Andes"', *Cultural Anthropology* 6(4): 466–504.

_____. 2009. *Ugly Stories of the Peruvian Agrarian Reform*. Durham, NC: Duke University Press.

Mayne, Richard. 1995. 'Translator's Introduction', in Braudel *op cit*.

Medick, Hans. 1987. 'Missionaries in a Rowboat?' Ethnological Ways of Knowing as a Challenge to Social History', *Comparative Studies in Society and History* 29(1): 76–98.

Meillasoux, Claude. 1975. *Femmes, Greniers, Capitaux*. Paris: Maspero.

Mintz, Sidney. 1978. 'Remarks on *The People of Puerto Rico*', *Revista/Review Interamericana* 8(1): 2–16.

_____. 1986. *Sweetness and Power*. Harmondsworth: Penguin.

Mitchell, Timothy. 2002. *Rule of Experts: Egypt, Techno-politics, Modernity*. Berkeley: University of California.

Mount, Ferdinand. 2004. *Mind the Gap: The New Class Divide in Britain*. London: Short Books.

Narotzky, Susana. 2002. 'The Political Economy of Political Economy in Spanish Anthropology' in Belinda Leach and Winnie Lem (eds), *Culture, Economy, Power: Anthropology as Critique, Anthropology as Praxis*. Binghamton: State University of New York Press.

_____. 2012. 'Alternatives to Expanded Accumulation and the Anthropological Imagination: Turning Necessity into a Challenge to Capitalism?', in P. Barber, B. Leach and W. Lem (eds), *Confronting Capital: Critique and Engagement in Anthropology*. New York: Routledge.

_____. 2013. '"Being out of Place": Social Analysis, the Organic Intellectual and the Production of Class', in James G. Carrier and Don Kalb (eds), *Class in Anthropology*. Forthcoming. Cambridge: Cambridge University Press.

Narotzky, Susana and Gavin Smith. 2006. *Immediate Struggles: People, Power and Place in Rural Spain*. Berkeley: University of California Press.

New York Times. 1994. 12 Dec. 'Enrique Lister 87, Dies in Spain, Communist who Battled Franco'. Accessed 19 Jan 2012. http://www.nytimes.com/1994/12/10/obituaries/enrique-lister-87-dies-in-spain-communist-who-battled-franco.html?src=pm

Newfield, Christopher. 2008. *Unmaking the Public University*. Cambridge, MA: Harvard University Press.

Ortner, Sherry. 1995. 'Resistance and the Problem of Ethnographic Refusal', *Comparative Studies in Society and History* 3(1): 173–93.

Ouroussoff, Alexandra. 2010. *Wall Street at War: The Secret Struggle for the Global Economy*. Cambridge: Polity.

_____. 2012. *Triple A: une anthropologie dans les agencies de notation*. Paris: Eds de la MSH.

Palma, José Gabriel. 2009. 'The Revenge of the Market on the Rentiers: Why Neoliberal Reports of the End of History Turned out to be Premature', *Cambridge Journal of Economics* 33: 829–69.

Peck, Jamie, and Adam Tickell. 2002. 'Neoliberal Space', *Antipode* 34(3): 380–404.

Polanyi, Karl. 1957. *The Great Transformation: The Political and Economic Origins of our Time*. Boston: Beacon.

Polier, Nicole, and William Roseberry. 1989. 'Tristes Tropes: Post-modern Anthropologists Encounter the Other and Encounter Themselves', *Economy and Society* 18(2): 245–64.

Porcaro, Mimmo. 2012. 'Occupy Lenin', in Leo Panitch, Greg Albo and Vivek Chibber (eds), *The Question of Strategy: Socialist Register 2013*. London: Merlin Press, pp. 84–98.

Portelli, Alessandro. 1997. *The Battle of Valle Giulia: Oral History and the Art of Dialogue*. Madison: University of Wisconsin Press.

Postone, Moishe. 1996. *Time, Labor and Social Domination: A Reinterpretation of Marx's Critical Theory*. Cambridge and New York: Cambridge University Press.

———. 2006. 'History and Helplessness: Mass Mobilization and Contemporary Forms of Anticapitalism', *Public Culture* 18(1): 93–110.

———. 2012. 'Thinking the Global Crisis', *South Atlantic Quarterly* 111(2): 227–49.

Preston, Paul. 1993. *Franco: A Biography*. London: HarperCollins.

———. 2011. 'Sneak Preview: Paul Preston on the Spanish Holocaust', *The Volunteer*, 18 Sept.

———. 2012. *The Spanish Holocaust: Inquisition and Extermination in Twentieth-century Spain*. New York: W.W.Norton & Co.

Radhakrishnan, R. 1996. *Diasporic Mediations: Between Home and Location*. Minneapolis: University of Minnesota Press.

Radice, Hugo. 2010. 'Confronting the Crisis: A Class Analysis', in Leo Panitch, Greg Albo and Vivek Chibber, *The Crisis this Time: Socialist Register 2011*. London: Merlin Press, pp. 21–43.

Rancière, Jacques. 1999. *Disagreement: Politics and Philosophy*, trans. Julie Rose. Minneapolis: University of Minnesota.

———. 2004. 'Who is the Subject of the Rights of Man?', *The South Atlantic Quarterly* 103(2–3): 297–310.

Restrepo, Eduardo, and Arturo Escobar. 2005. '"Other Anthropologies and Anthropologies Otherwise": Steps to a World Anthropologies Framework', *Critique of Anthropology* 25(2): 99–129. Also *Replies and a Rejoinder* 26(4): 463–88.

Richards, Michael. 1998. *A Time of Silence: Civil War and the Culture of Repression in Franco's Spain, 1936–1945*. Cambridge: Cambridge University Press.

Riley, Dylan. 2009. 'Freedom's Triumph', *New Left Review* 56: 43–59.

Robbins, Bruce. 2013. 'Balibarism!', *n+1* 16, http://nplusonemag.com/balibarism, accessed 20 Apr 2013.

Roberts, Paul Craig. 2012. 'The Economy Comes Unglued', *Counterpunch*, 6 June. http://www.counterpunch.org/2012/06/06/ accessed 12 July 2012.

Rodrigo, Javier. 2005. *Cautivos: campos de concentración en la España franquista*. Barcelona: Crítica.

Rose, Nikolas. 2000. *Powers of Freedom: Reframing Political Thought*. Cambridge: Cambridge University Press.

———. 2007. *The Politics of Life Itself: Biomedicine, Power and Subjectivity in the Twenty-first Century*. Princeton, NJ: Princeton University Press.

Roseberry, William. 1978. 'Historical Materialism and *The People of Puerto Rico*', *Revista/Review Interamericana* 8(1): 26–36.

———. 1983. *Coffee and Capitalism in the Venezuelan Highlands*. Austin: University of Texas Press.

———. 1989. *Anthropologies and Histories: Essays in Culture, History and Political Economy*. New Brunswick, NJ: Rutgers University Press.

———. 1996. 'The Unbearable Lightness of Anthropology', *Radical History Review* 65: 5–25.

———. 1997. 'Marx and Anthropology', *Annual Review of Anthropology* 26: 25–46.

———. 2002. 'Political Economy in the United States', in Belinda Leach and Winnie Lem (eds), *Culture, Economy, Power: Anthropology as Critique, Anthropology as Praxis*. Binghamton: State University of New York Press.

Rubin, Isaak Illich. (1928) 1973. *Essays on Marx's Theory of Value*, trans. M. Samardzija and F. Perman. Montreal: Black Rose Books.

Samuel, Raphael. 1992. 'Reading the Signs II: Fact-grubbers and Mind-readers', *History Workshop Journal* 33(1): 220–51.

Sanyal, Kalyan. 2007. *Rethinking Capitalist Development: Primitive Accumulation, Governmentality and Post-colonial Capitalism*. New Delhi: Routledge.

Sassen, Saskia. 2008. *Territory, Authority, Rights: from Medieval to Global Assemblages*. Princeton: Princeton University Press.

Sayer, Derek. 1979. *Marx's Method: Ideology, Science and Critique in Capital*. Hassocks: Harvester Press.

_____. 1987. *The Violence of Abstraction: The Analytic Foundations of Historical Materialism*. Oxford: Blackwell.

Schutz, A. 1971. *Collected Papers*, Vol. I. The Hague: Nijhoff.

Scott, David. 2003. 'Culture in Political Theory', *Political Theory* 31(1): 92–115.

Scott, James. 2012. *Two Cheers for Anarchism: Six Easy Pieces on Autonomy, Dignity and Meaningful Work and Play*. Princeton, NJ: Princeton University Press.

Scott, W.R. 2004. 'Reflections on a Half-century of Organizational Sociology', *Annual Review of Sociology* 30: 1–21.

Self, Will. 2013. 'The Joy of Armchair Anthropology', *Guardian*, 31 Jan. http://www.guardian.co.uk/books/2013/jan/31/will-self-joy-anthropology. Retrieved 8 May 2013.

Sider, Gerald. 1986. *Culture and Class in Anthropology and History*. Cambridge: Cambridge University Press.

_____. 2003. *Between History and Tomorrow: Making and Breaking Everyday Life in Rural Newfoundland*. Peterborough, ON: Broadview Press (2nd revised edition of *Culture and Class in Anthropology and History: A Newfoundland Illustration*. Cambridge: Cambridge University Press, 1986).

_____. 2014. *Skin for Skin: Death and Life for Indians and Inuit*. Durham, NC: Duke University Press. [Forthcoming]

Sider, Gerald and Gavin Smith. 1997. *Between History and Histories: The Production of Silences and Commemorations*. Toronto: University of Toronto Press.

Silva, Emilio and Santiago Macías. 2003. *Las Fosas de Franco: los Republicanos que el Dictador Dejó en las Cunetas*. Madrid: Temas de Hoy.

Sinfield, Alan. 2004. *Literature, Politics and Culture in Postwar Britain*, 2nd edn. London and New York: Continuum.

Smith, Gavin. 1977. 'The Account of Don Victor', *Journal of Peasant Studies* 2(3): 123–30.

_____. 1984. 'Confederations of Households: Extended Domestic Enterprises in City and Country', in Long and Roberts (eds), *Miners, Peasants and Entrepreneurs*. Cambridge: Cambridge University Press, pp. 217–34.

_____. 1985. 'Reflections on the Social Relations of Simple Commodity Production', *Journal of Peasant Studies* 13(1).

_____. 1989. *Livelihood and Resistance: Peasants and the Politics of Land in Peru*. Berkeley: University of California Press.

_____. 1991. 'The Production of Culture in Local Rebellion', in J. O'Brien and W. Roseberry (eds), *Golden Ages, Dark Ages: Imagining the Past in Anthropology and History*. Berkeley: California University Press.

_____. 1997. 'Pandora's History', in G. Sider and G. Smith (eds), *Between History and Histories: The Making of Silences and Commemorations*. Toronto: Toronto University Press.

_____. 1999. *Confronting the Present: Towards a Politically Engaged Anthropology*. Oxford: Berg.

_____. 2004a. 'Hegemony: Critical Interpretations in Anthropology and Beyond', *Focaal: Journal of European Anthropology* 43.

_____. 2004b. 'The Silent Transition: Memory and Current Politics in Spain'. Paper presented at *Council of European Studies Conference*, Chicago, 11–14 Mar.

_____. 2006: 'Hegemony', in David Nugent and Joan Vincent (eds), *The Blackwell Companion to the Anthropology of Politics*. Oxford: Blackwell.

_____. 2009. 'Formal Culture, Practical Sense and the Structures of Fear in Spain', *Anthropologica* 51(2): 279–88.

_____. 2010a. 'Hegemonía y superpoblación: límites conceptualizes en la antropología de movimientos politicos', pp. 175–96, in Victor Bretón (ed.), *Saturno devora a sus hijos: miradas críticas sobre el desarrollo y sus promesas*. Quito: Icaria.

_____. 2010b. 'The State (or Overstated)' and 'Response', *Anthropologica* 52: 165–87.

_____. 2011: 'Selective Hegemony and Beyond, Populations with "No Productive Function": A Framework for Enquiry' and 'Response', *Identities: Global Studies in Culture and Power* 18(1).

_____. n/d. '"I demand the value of my own labour as a commodity but my heartbeat derives its value from a more intimate calculus": From *morti di fame* to *sonversivo*'. Paper presented to the Wenner Gren Conference 'Crisis, Value and Hope: Rethinking the Economy', 14–20 Sept 2012, Sintra, Portugal. Available at http://utoronto.academia.edu/GavinSmith.

Smith, Neil. 1984. *Uneven Development: Nature, Capital and the Production of Space*. Oxford: Blackwell.

_____. 2010. 'The Revolutionary Imperative', *Antipode* 41(S1): 50–65.

Smith, N. and W. Dennis. 1987. 'The Structuring of Geographical Scale: Coalescence and Fragmentation of the Northern Core Region', *Economic Geography* 63: 160–82.

Smith, Neil and Cindi Katz. 1993. 'Grounding Metaphor: Towards a Spatialized Politics', in M. Keith and S. Pile (eds), *Place and the Politics of Identity*. London: Routledge, p. 67–85.

Sparke, Matthew. 2006. *In the Space of Theory: Postfoundational Geographies of the Nation-state*. Minneapolis: University of Minnesota Press.

Starn, Orin. 1991. 'Missing the Revolution: Anthropologists and the War in Peru', *Cultural Anthropology* 6(1): 63–91.

Steele, Tom. 2013. 'E.P.Thompson, the WEA and Radical Workers' Education in Yorkshire'. In Catalogue for exhibition, *The poor stockinger, the Luddite cropper and the deluded followers of Joanna Southcott*. Luke Fowler. The Hepworth Wakefield and Wolverhampton Art Gallery, 11–38.

Steward, Julian (ed.). 1956. *The People of Puerto Rico: A Study in Social Anthropology*. Urbana: University of Illinois Press.

Streeck, Wolfgang. 2011. 'The Crises of Democratic Capitalism', *New Left Review* 71: 5–29.

_____. 2012. 'How to Study Contemporary Capitalism?', *Archives of European Sociology* LIII(1): 1–28.

Swyngedouw, Erik. 1999. 'Modernity and Hybridity: Nature, Regeneracionismo, and the Production of the Spanish Waterscape, 1890–1930', *Annals of the Association of American Geographers* 89(3): 443–65.

Terkel, S., and R. Grele. 1985. *Envelopes of Sound: The Art of Oral History*. Chicago: Precedent.

Thomas, Peter D. 2009. *The Gramscian Moment: Philosophy, Hegemony and Marxism*. Leiden: Brill.

Thompson, Edward P. (1963) 1968. *The Making of the English Working Class*. Harmondsworth: Penguin.

_____. 1978. 'Eighteenth-century English Society: Class Struggle without Class?', *Social History* 3(2): 133–65.

Tilly, Louise. 1985. 'People's History and Social Science', *International Journal of Oral History* 6(1): 5–18.

Timpanaro, Sebastiano. [1970] 1975. *On Materialism*, trans L. Garner. London: Verso.

Torres López, Juan. 2013. 'Dictadura en Europa', *nuevatribuna.es*, 1 March. http://www.nuevatribuna.es/opinion/juan-torres-lopez/dictadura-en-europa/2013030110394608 9071.html. Accessed 6 Mar 2013.

Tortella, Gabriel. 2000. *The Development of Modern Spain: An Economic History of the Nineteenth and Twentieth Centuries*. Cambridge, MA: Harvard University Press.

Toscano, Alberto. 2010. *Fanaticism: On the Uses of an Idea*. London: Verso.

Trouillot, Michel-Rolph. 1997. *Silencing the Past: Power and the Production of History*. Boston, MA: Beacon Press.

_____. 2003. *Global Transformations: Anthropology and the Modern World*. New York: Palgrave Macmillan.

Tuchman, Gaye. 2009. *Wannabe U: Inside the Corporate University*. Chicago: Chicago University Press.

Turner, Terence. 2008. 'Marxian Value Theory: An Anthropological Perspective', *Anthropological Theory* 8(1): 43–56.

Turner, Victor. 1969. *The Ritual Process: Structure and Anti-structure*. Chicago: Aldine.

Vargas Llosa, Mario. 1983. 'Inquest in the Andes', *New York Times Magazine*, 31 July.

Vilar, Pierre. 1977. *Spain: A Brief History*, 2nd edn, trans. Brian Tate. Elmsford, NY: Pergamon Press [Original: *Histoire de l'Espagne* (1947). Series: Que sais-je? Paris: Presses universitaires de France].

Vincent, Joan. 1990. *Anthropology and Politics: Visions, Traditions and Trends*. Tucson: University of Arizona Press.

Walter, Carl, and Fraser Howie. 2011. *Red Capitalism: The Fragile Financial Foundation of China's Extraordinary Rise*. Singapore: Wiley & Sons.

Wang Hui. 2006. 'Depoliticized Politics from East to West', *New Left Review* 41: 29–45.

Weber, Eugen. 1976. *Peasants into Frenchmen : The Modernization of Rural France, 1870–1914*. Stanford, CA: Stanford University Press.

Williams, Raymond. 1973. *The Country and the City*. London: Hogarth.

_____. 1977. *Marxism and Literature*. Oxford: Blackwell.

_____. 1979. *Politics and Letters*. London: New Left Books.

_____. 1989a. *The Politics of Modernism*. London: Verso.

_____. 1989b. *What I Came to Say*. London: Hutchinson Radius.

Wimmer, A. and N. Glick Schiller. 2002. 'Methodological Nationalism and Beyond: Nation-State Building, Migration and the Social Sciences', *Global Networks* 2(4): 301–34.

Wolf, Eric. 1956. 'Aspects of Group Relations in a Complex Society: Mexico', *American Anthropologist* 58: 1065–78.

_____. 1957. 'Closed Corporate Peasant Communties in Mesoamerica and Central Java', *Southwestern Journal of Anthropology* 13: 1–18.

_____. 1969a. *Peasant Wars of the Twentieth Century*. New York: Harper & Row.

_____. [1969b] 1987. 'On Peasant Rebellions', *International Social Science Journal* 21. [Reprinted in T. Shannin (ed.), *Peasants and Peasant Societies*. 2nd edition. 1987]. Oxford: Blackwell, pp. 366–76.

_____. 1978. 'Remarks on *The People of Puerto Rico*', *Revista/Review Interamericana* 8(1): 17–25.

_____. 1982. *Europe and the People without History*. Berkeley: University of California Press.

_____. [1986] 2001. 'The Vicissitudes of the Closed Corporate Peasant Community', in Wolf, *Pathways of Power*. Berkeley: University of California Press.

Wolpe, Harold. 1975. 'The Theory of Internal Colonialism: The South African Case', in I. Oxaal, T. Barnett and D. Booth (eds.), *Beyond the Sociology of Development*. London: Routledge and Kegan Paul.

Zizek, Slavoj. 1999. *The Ticklish Subject*. London: Verso

_____. 2011. *Living in the End of Times*. London: Verso.

INDEX

www.ingramcontent.com/pod-product-compliance
Lightning Source LLC
Chambersburg PA
CBHW072104040426
42334CB00042B/2313